Vaishnava Women of India

Vaishnava Women of India

Original in Bengali
by
Dr Uma Bandopadhyay

Radhakrishna Goswami

KALPAZ

First Published, 2019

Published by

Kalpaz Publications
C-30, Satyawati Nagar,
Delhi – 110052
Ph.: 011-47034999, 9811692060
www.kalpazpublications.com
E-mail: kalpaz@hotmail.com

Printed at: G. Print Process, Delhi

Cataloging in Publication Data--DK
Courtesy: D.K. Agencies (P) Ltd. <docinfo@dkagencies.com>

Gosvāmī, Rādhu, author.
Vaishnava Women of India / Mr Radhakrishna Goswami.
pages cm
ISBN 9789353240783

1. Vaishnavites--India--Biography. 2. Hindu women--India--Biography. I. Title.

LCC BL1284.59.G67 2019 | DDC 294.5512092254 23

Dadicated with Respect

to

PROF. DR KANANBIHARI GOSWAMI

— Radhu

Contents

Aknowledgements ... 11
Introduction ... 13

1. Goda Devi (Devotee of Sri Ranganathji) ... 15

(9th Century AD)

2. First Tribhuban-Maha Devi (A Devotee Wife of a King) ... 23

(10th Century AD)

3. Kantimoti Devi (Mother of Ramanuja) ... 25

(11th Century AD)

4. Bama Devi (Mother of Poet Joydev) ... 29

(12th Century AD)

5. Padmabati Devi (Wife of Poet Joydev) ... 31
6. Vedabati Devi (Mother of Bosudeva or Madhwacharya) ... 35
7. Rami Rajakini (Devotion Partner of Chandidas) ... 37

(13th Century AD)

8. Chintamoni (The lady who showed the Path to Billwamongal) ... 40
9. Bhagyabatidevi The Old Grand Mother of Uddharan Dutta ... 43

(14th Century AD)

10. Mother of Upendra Old grandmother of Sri Chaitanyadeva ... 44
11. Rama Devi (Grandmother of Sri Roop and Sanatan) ... 45
12. Lachhima Devi (Wife of Raja Shiba Singha) ... 46

(15th Century AD)

13. Abhoya Devi (Grand mother of Lochandas) ... 48
14. Amita Devi Sakhi of Vishnupriya Devi ... 49
15. Indumati Basu (Mother of Kavi Gunaraj Khan) ... 50
16. Illamagaru (Mother of Ballavacharya) ... 52

17. Kamalakumari (A Devotee of Sri Chaitanyadeva of the South) 55
18. Kamala Devi (Wife of Lakshminath Lahiri) 56
19. Kamala Devi (Mother of Suryadas Sarkhel) 58
20. Kamalabati or Shova Devi (Grand Mother of Sri Cahaitanyadeva) 60
21. Kanchanadevi (A Woman Mad for Lord Sri Krishna) 63
22. Kalindidevi (Mother of Dhananjay Pundit) 65
23. Kripamoyee (Mother of Balarama) 67
24. Khersuti (Grandmother of Shankardeva of Assam) 68
25. Gangadevi (Mother of Pundarik Vidyanidhi) 70
26. Goyeedevi (Mother of Narahari Sarkar) 71
27. Gouridevi (Mother of Haridas Thakur) 73
28. Chandrakala (Wife of Raja Pratap Rudra) 75
29. Chitralekha (Sakhi of Lakshmipriya) 79
30. Jangali (Jungali) Dasi (Maid Servant of Sita Devi wife of Adwait Prabhu) 82
31. Jai Durga Devi (Foster-mother of Madhabacharya) 84
32. Janhabi Devi (Mother of Pundit Kashinath or Kashiswar) 86
33. Tara Devi (Mother of Haribangsha) 88
34. Tukka Devi (Daughter of Raja Pratap Rudra) 90
35. Damayanti Devi (Sister of Raghava Pundit) 92
36. Dukhini Devi (Wife of Jagadish Pundit) 95
37. Nandini Dasi (Disciple of Sita Devi) 98
38. Wife of Narasingha Nadial
39. Lava or Nava Devi (Mother of Adwaita Acharya) 101
40. Narayani (Nurse-Mother of Sri Gouranga Mahaprabhu) 104
41. The Widow Mother of a Certain Blessed Boy 106
42. Padmamoni Devi (Mother of Ishan Nagar) 107
43. Padmabati Devi (Mother of Sri Nityanandaprabhu) 109
44. Padmabati Devi (Mother of Raja Pratap Rudra) 112
45. Wife of Baninath (Baninath was the brother of Sri Gadadhar Pundit) 114
46. Vijaya Devi (The Grandmother of Vishnupriya Devi) 116
47. Bidhumukhi Devi (Aunt of Vishnupriya Devi) 117
48. Bimala Devi (Wife of Gouridas Pundit) 119
49. Biswas Devi (A Woman Writer) 121

50. Vishnupriya Devi (The Second Wife of Sri Gouranga Mahaprabhu) . 123
51. Bhadrabati Devi (The Mother of Sri Uddharan Dutta) 132
52. Bhadrabati Devi (The Wife of Sri Suryadas Pundit) 134
53. Bhagirathi Devi (The Mother of Sri Basudeva Sarbabhoum) 137
54. Mahamaya (The Wife of Sri Uddharan Dutta) 139
55. Maha Laxmi Devi (The Mother-in-law of Ganga Maa) 141
56. Madhabi Devi (The Sister of Shikhi Mahiti) 142
57. Manika Milkmaid (A Pious Woman) 148
58. Malini Devi (Wife of Sri Sribaas) 150
59. Malini Devi (Wife of AbhiramThakur) 152
60. Mother of Mukunda 154
61. Menaka Devi (The Mother-in-Law of Sri Adwaitaprabhu) 156
62. Ratnabati Devi (The Wife of Pundarik Vidyanidhi) 158
63. Ratnabati Devi (The Mother of Gadadhara Pundit) 160
64. Laksha Hira (Blessed by Thakur Haridas) 163
65. Laxmipriya Devi (The First Wife of Sri Gouranga Mahaprabhu) 170
66. Sachi Devi (The Mother of Sri Gouranga Mahaprabhu) 179
67. Sashikala Devi (The Sakhi of Chandrakala, wife of Raja Pratap Rudra) 185
68. Wife of Sibananda Sen 188
69. Shri Devi (The another Wife of Sri Adwaita Acharya) 191
70. Mother-in-law of Sri Sribaas 194
71. Shashti or Shati Devi (Daughter of Sri Sarbabhoum) 196
72. Sadanandi Devi (Mother of Sri Lochandas) 198
73. Sarbajaya Devi (Aunt of Sri Chaitanyadeva) 200
74. Sarbani Devi (Nearer Lady of Sachimaa of Sri Chaitanyadeva) 202
75. Sita Devi (Wife of Sri Adwaita Acharya –for whom he was called as Sitanath) 204
76. Sita Devi (The Mother of Sri Raghunath Shiromani) 211
77. Sita Devi (The Mother of Sri Lokenath Goswami) 214
78. Sunila Devi (The Old Grandmother of Sri Ramai Goswami) 216
79. Sulochana Devi (The wife of Preceptor of Mishra Family) 218
80. The Mother of Swarup Damodar 220
81. Haripriya Devi (The wife of Dhananjay) 222

(16th Century AD)

82. Indumukhi Devi (Wife of Srila Byasacharya) 224
83 Kanakpriyya Devi (Daughter of Srila Byasacharya) 225
84. Krishnapriya Devi (Second Daughter of Sri Nibas Acharya) 226
85. Ishwari Devi (The First Wife of Sri Nibas Acharya) 228
86. Gourangapriya Devi (The Second Wife of Sri Nibas Acharya) 230
87. Kanchanlatika Devi (The Youngest Daughter of Sri Nibas Acharya) ... 232
88. Chandramukhi Devi (The Daughter-in-law of Sri Nibas Acharya)..... 233
89. Indurekha (The Sakhi of Chandrakala Devi) 234
90. Kadambamala (The Daughter-in-law of Birchandra) 236
91. Ganga Devi (The Daughter of Sri Nityananda- Basudhamaa)............ 237
92. Kanaklata-Aai Chaturbhuja (The Grand Daughter-in-law of Sri Shankardeva) 240
93. Kanaklatika Devi (Narottam Shakha) 242
94. Kanchana Devi (The wife of Lochandas) 243
95. Mother of Kanhaiya (Vraja) 245
96. Krishnadassi (The Wife of Haribansa) 247
97. Gourangadasi (The Second Wife of Shyamanandaprabhu) 248
98. Hemlata Thakurani (The Eldest Daughter of Sri Nivas Acharya) 251

(19th Century AD)

99. Putlibai (Mother of Mahatma Gandhi) 253
100. Meera Bai (A Lady who Loved Sri Krishna and Sang for Him) 255
101. A Fortunate Lady of Odisha 260
102. Narayani Devi (The Mother of Poet Sri Vrindabandas) 261
103&104. Satya Bai & Lakshmi Bai 263

(18th Century AD)

105. Annapurna Devi (The Mother of Harichand Thakur) 267
106. Swarnamoyee Devi Thakurani (The Mother of Bijoykrishna Goswami) 269

(16th Century AD)

107&108. Basudha Devi & Janhaba Devi (The wives of Sri Nityananda Prabhu) 273
Index 285

Aknowledgements

The writers acknowledges the debt of Smt. Dr. Uma Bandopadhyay, the original writer of "Bharater Vaishnanva Naari" in Bangali.

The writer also acknowledges the debt of his wife Smt. Bhumika Goswami whose constant company and giving inspiration in doing the mammoth work of translation and editing at late mights also.

The writer is bound to acknowledge the debt of Sri Amit Garg who gave support and assurances in publishing the Book.

The writer also feels indebtedness to the proof- readers and other members of the staffs in the production department.

Although the writer referred the books and the names of the authors at the end of each article also acknowledges the debts of them.

Introduction

From the historic stages women have been tortured, raped, sold and affected with other social and domestic violences. They were considered as weaker section than masculine world of muscles. But the great personalities like Goutam Buddha, Jesus Christ, Sri Chaitanyadeva, Yaban Haridas, Raja Rammohan Roy, Ishwar Chandra Vidyasagar, Sri Ramkrishna, Swami Vivekananda and a good number ideal humans of the World tried their best to wipe out and ease the sufferings and pains of the women in different ages.

Although in India in the Vedas women were equally participants in the rituals and also as composers of various hymns but gradually their importance was confined in domestic world and behind the curtains.

However, till today women are being exploited by greedy beasts in the biological shape of men.

Now let us remember the women who were not less than any male personality in the path of Sadhana in different spheres of life. We like here to cite a few women whose contributions, inspirations, sacrifices etc helped the men to work successfully in the world. We know and should admit that almost in all the successes there must was a woman. Without women or females the world cannot move a single step.

We can also remember the women who from very beginning or ultimately became Vaishnava minded.

We can now come to our subject where we at first should recollect the Arber or Alawar sect of people who used to worship Lord Vishnu or Lord Ranganatha or Venkateswar.At the last Sl. Nos.107 & 108 we have recollected Basudha and Janhaba Devi two wives of Sri Nityanandaprabhu of 16th Century. Now let us remember with due respect to 108 of them.

There, obviously, remain more thousands of women who for their deeds are yet to be remembered.

— Radhakrishna Goswami

8th Century AD

1

Goda Devi (Andal or Aandal)

(Devotee of Sri Ranganathji)

Although the actual date of birth and other particulars are hardly possible to get or determine due to non availability of any document, however, some researchers have guessed according to 'Muyayirappadi' script that Godadevi was born in 98 'Kalyabda' in 'El' i.e. Adi (Aashada) during the East Falguni Star the fourth day of 'Shukla' in Tuesday in 3005 B.C. while the other researchers determined that Godadevi was incarnated on the 25th June 776 A.D. at the 51 years of age of Saint Vishnuchitti.

In one rain washed fine morning sage like a serious and sincere devotee of Lord Vishnu, Vishnuchitti was collecting flowers for worshipping the deity of Lord Vishnu and by chance found a just-born female baby lying on the ground covered with grass and Tulsi leaves helplessly. The sage like Vishnuchitti was not only astonished but also heard a divinely voice saying from behind a Tulsi Tree – Listen, this garden of flowers and Tulsi is owned by me. Take the baby up and offer it with the flower to me."

Vishnuchittaswami took up the beautiful baby in his arms and reached home. The question of origin of the baby could not be prolonged much as one of the garlands from the deity's neck fell on the baby indicating the baby was accepted by Lord. Srimati Tulsidevi the wife of Vishnuchitta had no issue so far, so she became very glad to see the baby who was left by someone in the garden. She with Vishnuchitta started to look after the new guest at their residence.

This Vishnuchitta was known as Pediya Arber or Bhattanath Swami. He was also being considered by the devotees as one of the renowned Twelve Arbers.

He with his wife used to live at Sri Billiputtur village 50 miles (almost 80 kilometers) away from Madura. He was a sincere devotee of Lord Vishnu as lying on the leaves of banyan tree as established in the village. Regularly he used to worship God with Tulsi leaves and garlands of different flowers plucked from the garden sincerely nourished by him. The whole of the days generally passed with taking care of the garden, worshipping, thoughts of Lord's name and His appearance and also the Lilas.[1]

He was a devotee with parental devotion towards God. He and his wife Srimati Tulsi Devi also used to serve Lord Vishnu as mother Yashoda used to serve Sri Krishna, little Gopala as her own son.[2]

In their worshipping there were present also parental devotion, servitude, friendship and also sweetness towards God as He and Radharani are entwined in bliss.

Not only that, there were twelve Arbers who were of high souled Vaishanava Saints and who also wrote about four thousand songs and prayers that later formed a collection entitled as 'Divya Prabanadha'. This collection is also considered as authentic and regarded as the Vedas.

It is learnt that Pediya Arber or Bhattanath Swami sold out all the paternal properties and built garden adjacent to his domestic house for his Lord.[3]

Once at the Court of the King Pandya a mega conference was held and many scholars and pundits were welcomed from different parts of the country to discuss and analyze the scriptures. Pediya Arber or Bhattanath Swami or Vishnuchitta with his proficiency and talent could easily defeat all other participant scholars and the King of Pandya declared the best of all and himself garlanded him and gifted a huge amount of Gold Coins. All the money he earned spent for further development of the garden.[4]

It is also learnt that the name of wife of Vishnuchitta Srimati Tulsi Devi was Virajaya and she had no issue.[5]

It is known to us that in the Ramayana Raja Siradhwaja Janaka found child Sita at the time of cultivating on corn field, similarly Vishnuchitta at the time of digging earth in the Tulsi garden found a female baby left by someone. He took up the baby and gave his wife Srimati Tulsi Devi. Both of them brought up the child as their own daughter.

The word 'Goda' also indicates that was given by the earth. Andal means who teaches others. The names as Goda and Andal for the female baby were rightly announced by Vishnuchitta and Srimati Tulsi Devi (Virajaya).

Again, 'Go' indicates the knowledge of the Vedas and 'da' indicates who gives. Combining 'Goda' word indicates a meaning that refers to the knowledge of the Scriptures of the Sanatan Religion's the Vedas.

Someone commented that Vishnuchitta and Tulsidevi (Virajaya) also named the beautiful divine baby as 'Kanoi' that means a golden good girl. The neighbourers used to call her as Aandal as ruler or director.

Both Vishnuchitta and Tulsidevi (Virajaya) paid their attention to educate the child and thus the baby was brought up and once became a devotee of Lord Vishnu with a pure Vaishnava mentality whole-heartedly.

Vishnuchittaswami used to worship the deity of Lord lying on a banyan tree leaf in the village Sri Billiputtur.

The grownup Andal or Goda the sincere devotee of God in the village Sri Billiputtur used to find pleasure to herself to wear around the neck the garlands of flowers made by Vishnuchitta Swami almost every day before offering these to Lord's deity. She having worn the garlands used to look at the mirror for finding how she, the loved one by God would be seen. After staring at herself sometime she used to keep the garlands at the fixed place where her father Vishnuchitta Swami used to place the garlands before entering into the temple.

But one day, the truth of the incidence was revealed. That One day, Vishnuchittaswami noticed a piece of single long black hair was swinging from a garland and he thought that Goda must have worn it before for curiosity. He could easily understand that his daughter Goda's mind was filled with the emotion of being loveable to Lord Vishnu. However, the garland once used by anyone cannot be offered to Lord Vishnu. So he went to the temple without the garland left by him. His mind was ached and so at home he could not get any peace and at night he could not sleep.

Suddenly at night he woke up and found his bedroom was flooded with divine light and in the midst there Lord Ranganatha, God Vishnu was standing with divine smiles on the face. Vishnuchittaswami heard that Lord in divine voice was asking him – "Hallow, today you've not offered me the lovely garlands! Those garlands as you offer daily are my favorite ones."

Vishnuchittaswami could not speak a single word but remained speechless with the hands folded till the daylight started to come in.

He had the realization that Goda's worn garlands always become loveable by Lord, rather He prefers it much.

From then Goda was being called 'Sudikodutta Nachchier'. The meaning of the word 'who after wearing gives it to others'.

Vishnuchittaswami used to read the scriptures of the Arbers to his daughter Goda (Andal or Aandal). At the time of reading and explaining he could not resist his emotions for God and so tears would flow from his eyes incessantly.

In listening to the talks on God, Goda also could not control her eyes from shedding tears. She used to visualize the form of Ranganatha wearing the garland worn by her and offered by her father Vishnuchittaswami. Her heart would become filled with the love for Lord. With the songs on Lord she became charmed and she too sang with her sweet and melodious voice and well selected words for love of Lord.

Thus day after days the young Goda's publicity of singing with emotions for Lord Ranganatha - Lord Sri Krishna spread thousands of miles away and around. She remembered the 'Gopijana Ballava' Ranganatha – Sri Krishna all the time.

Her love was Ranganatha – Sri Krishna and so she decided to be married to only her love Ranganatha, none else. She wrote in 'Nadiar Tirumeri' that she dreamt as:–

"*Along with many gods and goddesses Sri Krishna Ranganatha is coming to marry her. There were many pitchers made of gold filled with gems have been set at different places. The place of marriage was decorated with jewels and other glittering gems ready for welcoming the bridegroom Ranganatha. In the team of bridegroom the king of gods and goddesses and others also joined their hands to celebrate the marriage. With the recitation of the Mantras of the Vedas the priests helped us in tying the sacred threads in our hands. God holding my hands roamed around the fire of Jajna. Thus our marriage was completed. We the newly wedded couple sat on the back of an elephant decorated with ornaments and a colorful procession was started.*"[6]

But it was nothing but a dream. Actually the reality of not a marriage ached Goda. Vishnuchittaswami was much anxious for the marriage of the girl Goda. Goda cautioned her parents that without her devoted deity no scope remains to get her married with other human being and if she is forced that would lead her to finish the life. At last observing the firm determination of the girl Goda Vishnuchittaswami consoled if only God desires it may become true a marriage of Goda with the deity of Lord Vishnu-Si Krishna. Once he asked his Goda - "There are 108 divine places where God is being worshipped in 108 forms. Out of these108 forms of deities of God to which form you would prefer to be married?"

Goda wanted to know the forms elaborately. Vishnuchitta Swami explained the forms of all the 108 forms but specially mentioned Ranganatha at Sri Rangam. Goda listened to her father with full attention and she was crying for Lord and finally answered – Ranganatha at Sri Rangam is God. Would He accept me?"

The marriage of a young girl with a stone-made deity is unthinkable. There is no example of marrying deity with a living human being in real lives on the earth. However, Goda memorized the 10th Skandia of Srimad Bhagawata:-[7]

"Katyani Mahamaye Maha Yoginydhishwari.
Nanda Gopa Sutang Devi Pating Me Kuru Te Namah.
Eti Mantrang Stapastyah Pujang Chakruh Kumarikah.
Ebang Masang Bratang Cheruh Kumarajah Krishnachetasah.
Bhadrakaling Samanarchubhura Eananda Sutah Patih."

—**Dr. Uma Bandopadhaya**
Editing and Translation in English
by Radhakrishna (Radhu) Goswami

She recollected Srimad Bhagawata wherein the Braja Gopis for obtaining Sri Krishna, the Nanda Suta, as their husband maintained a vow named as 'Katyani' that continue for a long month. During the month of 'Kartik' they at early in the morning used to take bath in the water of the Yamuna River and thereafter by making the statue of mother 'Katyani' as well as mother Durga worshipped her with various Puja materials. And as a result they have been honored later by Sri Krishna in the Raasalila.

Godadevi decided to meet Lord Ranganatha by imitating the Brajagopis to observe the vow in the whole Pousha month with devotion and control on themselves.

With this determination of Goda father Vishnuchittaswami was surprised and became anxious how it would be possible for Goda to travel from Sribilliputtur of South India to Northern India's Vrindaban on the bank of the Yamuna. It was almost 2100 miles lengthy of the path. But Goda Devi at last thought and consoled herself the village Sribilliputtur itself as Vrindaban.

She used to wake up very early in the morning and collect her sakhis to take bath in the nearby river and observed the vow as she desired. She used to sing Lord's name whole of the days. She herself used to compose songs on Lord Ranganatha as well as Sri Krishna. She used to greet Lord with 'Aarti' and praying accompanied with own composed songs to God.

Thus Goda Devi continued the vow in thirty days and offered as 'Anjali' one new song each day to her beloved God. The vow was called 'Tiruppaboi'.

[Tiru = Sri, the beauty; Paboi = Vow, the Comment in tongue.]

In 30 days she wrote 30 songs for her beloved Lord Sri Krishna or Lord Ranganatha. Her talent of writing songs is thus established.[8]

Goda Devi had no other option than to remember God whole of the days. She used to lie on floor and to take minimum food vegetables boiled only. Her perseverance and devotion made her so sacred that at last Lord Ranganatha was pleased to her. She observed the vow to have Lord Ranganatha as well as Sri Krishna. So she used to worship in 'Ragatmika Sadhana'. In every stage she liked to follow 'Brajagopis' as to be beloved and to love.

In order to quench the thirsts of unison with God like an entity made of flesh and blood Vishnuchittaswami, the anxious father took her to a remote place Maliron-Pillai. There was an old temple of Lord Govinda. Around the temple there was flower garden where birds sing whole day and lotus blossom in the ponds. The beauty and the solitude peaceful environment only could not satisfy her much as she desired only the meet with Lord Sri Krishna.

Her father, the anxious father Vishnuchittaswami took her to the hills of Tirupati for his daughter's pleasure and peace. That was also divine place.

But Vishnuchitta decided to take her at Srirangam where Lord Ranganathaji stays in the big temple. There all the priests and the scholar devotees welcomed them. They were given a nice shelter in a garden house. But Goda Devi was so eager that she could not misuse any moment and ran with Vishnuchitta towards the temple. She was astonished to find really the deity was in her dreams and now in vision, she saw her love, her Lord. She was overwhelmed with her divine emotions for God. She could not resist herself from becoming almost mad for her love. With her emotions and love she cried and sang one after songs for Ranganathaji. This continued for some days.[9]

It is said in another scripture that, the chief of the temple organizers dreamt that Lord Ranganathaji was advising him – "Take my palanquin decorated with nine gems and other precious materials and also the band party to bring well dressed and decorated with necessary ornaments Goda

Devi from Sribilliputtur village. I also like to marry Goda as per scriptures. Go and meet Vishnuchittasuuri."

The chief of the administration understood that for Ranganathji nothing is impossible. He easily can show any magical happening. So he with the chief with his men arranged to meet Vishnuchittasuri at Sribilliputtur village according to God's advice. On the other hand Vishnuchitta Swami also received the same message from Ranganathji and as per His wish arranged to take his daughter to Srirangam.

The King of Madura Ballavdeva, a disciple of Vishnuchittasuri also started with a long procession to accompany them.

Afterwards Goda Devi boarded in the palanquin and the procession of thousands of people started towards Srirngam. They were advised to take rest at Nichulapuri nearer to Srirangam.[10]

The main priest of the temple of Rangeswar Sri Ranganathji also received the same message from God and accordingly did the same.

In an auspicious day at an auspicious moment the priests arranged to decorate Ranganathji and on the other part Vishnuchitta Swami came forward to the deity of festival Ranganathji. After the recitation of Vaidik Mantras Vishnuchitta Swami handed over Goda Devi to Lord Sri Ranganathaji of festivity who ultimately held her hands and entered in the sanctum of the temple. Goda Devi found there in the sanctum the lying God '*Shayane Padmanava*' and slowly she started to reach the divine feet of God lying there.

Thousands of spectators in the Kalamandapa were astonished to find that Goda Devi has been mingled with Sri Ranganathaji. All became surprised and also pleased in this divine incidence. Thus Lord Sri Ranganathaji accepted Goda Devi at her sixteen.[11]

From the day Acharya of Arber Vishnuchitta Swami was being called the father-in-law of Sri Ranganathji by the Vaishnava devotees.

Acharya Arber Vishnuchitta Swamiji used to write on the various divine and sweet Lilas Lord Sri Krishna and he had the habit to explain the inner meanings to his daughter Goda. Godadevi had the belief in the episodes and so she was inspired to love Lord Sri Krishna God '*Shayane Padmanava*' as a human being from her early ages.

Later Goda Devi was included among the twelve Arbers, the prominent ancient Vaishnava Devotees of the South. She was also expert in writing of poems on divine Lilas of Lord Sri Krishna. Her divine love to Lord

Ranganathji were beautifully elaborated in 'Nachchier Tirumourhi' that received high acclaims from the readers and devotees of the future not only in Tamil language but also in other languages of India.

Goda Devi once wrote:–

Rangesha Karunasindho Matpaanigrahanang Kuru.
Twang Binanyang Na Janami Satyang Bachami Namohstute.

-Oh, Ranganathji, the ocean of mercies please accept me as your wife. I do not know other ('Na Parah'). It is the truth you know and take my Pranamah.

References

1. Aandal Arber – Divya Charitra O Rachanabali - Bengali Translation by Swami Jatindra Ramanuacharya, Editor, Sri Nrisingha Ramanujadas, Balaram Prakashani, Khardah, North 24 Parganas, 1997, Bhumika p. 2 & 3.
2. Mahiyasi Bharatiya Naari – Edited by Swami Madhabananda & Dr. Ramesh Chandra Majumder, - Bengali Translation by Dr. Satchidananda Dhar, published by Swami Mumukshananda, Udbodhan Karyalaya, 1407 BS, p. 367.
3. Bharoter Sadhika – Edited by Shankarnath Roy (Pra. Na. Bha.) published by Bamacharan Mukhopadhyay, Karuna Prakashani 1st published in 1380 BS, 12th Print 1416 BS, p. 8.
4. *Ibid*, p. 7.
5. *Ibid*, p. 8.
6. Aandal Arber – Divya Charitra O Rachanabali - Bengali Translation by Swami Jatindra Ramanuacharya, Editor, Sri Nrisingha Ramanujadas, Balaram Prakashani, Khardah, North 24 Parganas, 1997, Bhumika p. 9.
7. Srimad Bhagawata, 10/12/45.
8. Mahiyasi Bharatiya Naadi – Edited by Swami Madhabananda & Dr. Ramesh Chandra Majumder, - Bengali Translation by Dr. Satchidananda Dhar, published by Swami Mumukshananda, Udbodhan Karyalaya, 1407 BS, p. 369.
9. Bharoter Sadhika – Edited by Shankarnath Roy (Pra. Na. Bha.) published by Bamacharan Mukhopadhyay, Karuna Prakashani 1st published in 1380 BS, 12th Print 1416 BS, p. 20.
10. Aandal Arber – Divya Charitra O Rachanabali - Bengali Translation by Swami Jatindra Ramanuacharya, Editor, Sri Nrisingha Ramanujadas, Balaram Prakashani, Khardah, North 24 Parganas, 1997, Bhumika p. 6.
11. *Ibid.*

9th Century AD

2

First Tribhuban-Maha Devi

(A Devotee Wife of a King)

In ancient Odisha about 1100 years ago there lived a woman daughter of Rajamalla of Nag clan of the South India. She was married to King Lalithar of Bhoumakar clan in Utkal. She showed the courage of protesting against the culture and behaviour of her father-in-law's family.

Actually, the people of Bhoumakar clan were from Buddhists religion and on the other hand Tribhuban-Mahadevi was a sincere devotee of Lord Vishnu. King Lalithar of Bhoumakar clan and Tribhuban-Mahadevi had a son who was named as Shubhakar.[1]

Unfortunately Tribhuban-Mahadevi lost her husband and also the only son but there remained her grandson at very tender age. After the sad premature demise of Shubhakar this lady with little grandson had to rule the kingdom for several years.[2]

In ancient times there were no customs of ruling kingdoms by wives or daughters after the deaths of any monarchs but in the same heredity Tribhuban-Mahadevi and more five queens were enthroned on the chair of the King. In history we find that the Bhoumakar clan ruled the lower Odisha from the 9th century to 11th century.

It is told that the first woman who chaired the throne of kingdom Tribhuban-Mahadevi imitating one Goswamini queen liked to have the title of Goswamini. She was known with this name also. She was originally in mind a follower of Lord Vishnu i.e. Lord Sri Krishna. With the worshipping her Lord she also expertly ruled the dominion. She was sufficiently brave in ruling the kingdom. She could easily save the father-in-law's family as well as the whole country from the enemies and religious belief in tact. She had the belief that with taking the Naam of Sri Krishna anybody can protect all the evils.

References

1. Mahiyasi Bharatiya Naari – Edited by Swami Madhabananda & Dr. Ramesh Chandra Majumder, - Bengali Translation by Dr. Satchidananda Dhar, published by Swami Mumukshananda, Udbodhan Karyalaya, 1407 BS, p. 349.
2. *Ibid.*

10th Century AD

3

Kantimoti Devi

(Mother of Ramanuja)

The belief was that Brahma as well as Lord Vishnu is the cause of all the creations of the Universe and the creations including men and Brahma are not to be considered as the same lead Kantimoti Devi that influenced her son Ramanuja.

Kantimoti Devi was the first daughter of Sri Shailapurna, the main disciple of the great Vaishnava Jamun Acharya. Her name was Bhumi Peratri or Bhudevi. She was married to a sincere Brahmin Aasuri Keshabacharya in the South India. But Kantimoti Devi could not offer any child in the family. At last both the husband and the wife arranged a Vedic 'Jagna' for the intention to have a son. And they were successful that Lord Parthasarathi Sri Krishna granted a boon of taking birth of a son.

It was the 12th Chaitra of 423 BS (March of 1017AD) with 'Adra' star and 5th day of New Moon accompanied with 'cancer' time junction and on the Thursday when in the developing village Perempudur nearer to Chennai the son was born.[1]

However another reference states that in the village of Sri Paramabar or Sri Parambur in the South India she was born. And his father's name was Keshab Tripathi and mother's was Bhumi Devi.[2]

The son of Kantimoti Devi was born in the same month with the same star of Lakshmana, the third son of Raja Dasaratha of the Ramayana and so she kept the name of her son as Lakshmana or Ramanuja (Anuja of Rama).

In the childhood of Ramanuja both of his parents gave proper care of bringing up the child. Ramanuja with his wits and intelligence made the teachers surprised and became a great scholar.

Afterwards the son came to contact of Kanchipurna of Kanchi and received the spiritual learning. Then he had only aim to worship Sri Narayana. At his sixteen he also learned the Vedas and being a Vaishnava devotee he started to propagate the Vaishnavism in the South.

Kantimoti Devi and Keshabacharya tried their son to get married and after his sixteen they joyfully arranged a marriage with Jamamba (1033 AD). But unfortunately, after a month of the marriage Keshabacharya expired.

Thereafter, Kantimoti Devi, the widow mother had change her residence and arranged to settle with her son and daughter-in-law in Kanchi.

There Ramanuja started to learn more with Jadavprakash. This Jadavprakash had the belief in 'Adwaitavad' that indicates God and Creations like men are same. On the other hand Ramanuja was 'Daitavadi' what indicates God and the Creations are not the same. God has created us and we are His sevakas, we cannot be considered the same. Being challenged by disciple Ramanuja the learned teacher Jadavprakash was so angry that he conspired to kill Ramanuja in a dense forest. Somehow a hunter couple rescued him. Afterwards, teacher Jadavprakash realized his fault and called disciple Ramanuja to coach him again.[3]

Ramanuja propagated Vaishnavism when in the South people and devotees were accustomed with the worship of Lord Shiva. No doubt it was a difficult task to propagate Vaishnavism i.e. to worship Lord Vishnu in lieu of Lord Shiva. Even he was tortured by the Chole King and he had to flee to Mysore for some days.

A remarkable incidence was occurred when Jamunacharya came to have a visit of Sri Barad (who can grant a boon) Lord Vishnu in Kanchi stared at lovely face of Ramanuja and decided to give the opportunity of becoming a prominent devotee (Sadhaka) after him in Kanchi. Ramanuja's grandfather of mother's side Shailapurna was also a disciple of great Jamunacharya.

Having known the information of the quality of Ramanuja, the son of Kantimoti Devi the people of the locality had a special respect for him. During this period suddenly the princes of Kanchi was acquired by 'Brahmarakshas' but the ministers of the King despite their efforts could not cure her. At last all of them suggested the name of Ramanuja. Ramanuja just touched the princess and with his virtuous hands she got rid of 'Brahmarakshas' and became normal with good health. This incidence made him much popular in the whole of 'Chole' kingdom. It is also learnt that the King himself became vaishnavite.[4]

During the peak time of his fame unfortunately the successful mother Kantimoti Devi breathed her last. Hear say, that Kantimoti Devi received the position of her deceased husband and was placed at the feet of Kanchpurna who attained the divine grace through austere religious practices.

However, Ramanuja for sometime did not want to survive. But fortune favored him and he read the "Stotraratna' composed by Jamunacharya. He became almost mad to have 'Darshan' of Jamunacharya. Ultimately at the end of the high-souled personality he got the chance to meet his mostly expected Master.

The son of Kantimoti Devi then started to circulate the philosophy of Vaishnavism in the own place and could spread Vaishnavism in Kanchipur, Maharastra, Dwarka and many other places.

Many of the followers of Adiguru Shankaracharya also were initiated in the Vaishnavism from Ramanuja. Afterwards he visited Varanasi (Kashidham), Prayag, Hardwar and reached the Sarada Mutt of Kashmir. There he could easily defeat in the scriptural discussion the chief of the Mutt.

However, the family-life of Ramanuja could not run in well and so peacefully and smoothly as that of his parents, specially mother Kantimoti Devi.

Once, his wife Jamamba dared to insult the wife of his Preceptor Mahapurna. With this Mahapurna with his wife left their house and went to Srirangam. With high repentance Ramanuja left the family and took asceticism to Sri Kanchipurna at the temple of 'Baradaraj' and started to meditate deeply. Some days later, he attained the divine grace through austere religious meditation and known as 'Yotiraj'. The son of Kantimoti Devi Ramanuja as 'Yotiraj' became popular in the South.

He also wrote a 'Tika' on the Ramayana and explained the Sutra of the Vedanta in his own way of philosophy.

According to the editor Sri Haridas Dasji we can note that Kuresh was the disciple of the son of Kantimoti Devi Ramanuja. His son was Rampillai and Rampillai's son was Bagvijay Bhatta. The cited above Sudarshanachary or Vedavyas Acharya was son of this Bagvijay Bhatta.

According to Sri Haridas Das at the time of Sudarshana Acharya or Vedavyas Acharya the Muslim invaders once attacked the temple of Sri Ranganathji and killed at least twelve thousand Vaishnavs. But somehow the Deity of Sri Ranganathji was transferred to the temple at Tirupati.[5]

Sri Gouranga Mahaprabhu and also Sri Nityananda Prabhu visited the holy place at Tirupati temple at different times.

Along with Ramanuja we must remember and show our sincere respect to his mother Kantimoti Devi for her devotion and bringing up the rare great son.

References

1. Brihat Sri Sri Bhactamaal – Original in Hindi by Sri Navaji, Bengali Trans by Sri Laldas Babaji, edited by Sri Dilip Mukhopadhyyay and published by Benimadhab Seals Library, printed by A B C Printers, re-printed in 1416 BS (2009AD) p. 691 (Original Mode).
2. Saral Bangala Abhidhaan – Edited by Subal Chandra Mitra, published by New Bengal Press (Pvt) Ltd.).
3. *Ibid.*
4. *Ibid.*
5. Sri Sri Goudiya Vaishnava Abhidhaan – Edited by Sri Haridas Das Babaji, 2nd, 3rd, and 4th Parts, 2nd Edition, 501 Chaitanyabda, Publisher – Haribol Kutir Poraghat, Nabadwip, Printer – Radha Press, Delhi 110031, p. 1968.

11th Century AD

4

Bama Devi

(Mother of Poet Joydev)

In the 12th century one mostly talented poet was Joydev. After the great poet Kalidas such talented poet as Joydev was rare in the history.

In the district of Birbhum village Kenduli is 20 miles away to Suri on the northern bank of the Ajay River Bama Devi was married to a local Brahmin Bhojdev. This Vojdev was a poor Brahmin but had strong belief in Good.[1]

Their son Joydev was born in 1110 AD nearer to the village now ruins of another earlier great poet Villwamanagal.

Another source states that Joydev was born in 1123 AD.[2]

Although they were poor but Bama Devi and her husband Bhojdev tried their best in bringing up the son Joydev. So, Joydev simultaneously with studies learnt music and ultimately became expert in singing and playing with musical instruments.[3]

There were several days when Bama Devi after offering meals to son and husband there remained nothing to eat by the lady. She could easily conceal the fact from them. Only water she could drink.

Bama Devi used to listen the songs on Lord Sri Krishna sang by her son Joydev. It was her happiness. Her sacrifice and love to son's singing are still being remembered by many devotees. She was contended in family life as well as in spiritual world.

References

1. Sri Sri Goudiya Vaishnava Abhidhaan – Edited by Sri Haridas Das Babaji, 2nd, 3rd, and 4th Parts, 2nd Edition, 501 Chaitanyabda, Publisher – Haribol Kutir Poraghat, Nabadwip, Printer – Radha Press, Delhi 110031, p. 1968.

2. Joydev O Tar Geetagobinda - by Sri Purnenduprasad Bhattacaharya, June 1991, Pub. Sahitya Mela, 28/1 Mannapara Road, Kolkata – 700 090, Print.Mudrani, 21 Maharaja Nandakumar Road (South), Kolkata – 700 036).
3. Brihat Sri Sri Bhaktamaal – Original in Hindi by Sri Navaji, Bengali Trans by Sri Laldas Babaji, edited by Sri Dilip Mukhopadhyyay and published by Benimadhab Seals Library, printed by A B C Printers, re-printed in 1416 BS (2009AD) p.581, (Original Mode).

12th Century AD

5

Padmabati Devi

(Wife of Poet Joydev)

Originally Padmabati loved Lord Sri Krishna. Poet Joydev was much discussed poet in the 12th century. He had no intention of consuming luxurious articles and nor his wife Padmabati Devi had any hope for any luxurious goods. The both were simple in life but very proficient in singing, dancing, playing instruments of music.[1]

After the demises of the parents Bhojdev and Bama Devi poet Joydev had to sell even his house with land to meet up all the debts borrowed by his father Bhojdev. He, being free from any bondage and any pull from back started for aimless journey but Lord Jagannath sees everything and he drew the young poet with His invisible chord of the Ratha and ultimately Joydev reached Puri, the Neelachal Dham.

On the other hand, at that time a couple with their beautiful daughter who was believed born at the boon of Lord Jagannath also reached Puri to offer their Puja to Jagannath.

Afterwards Lord Jagannath ordered the couple in a dream that they should their daughter married to the newcomer poet Joydev. Then and there the couple ran to Joydev and requested him to marry their daughter Padmabati. Joydev declined the proposal for his financial inability but the couple, the parents of Padmabati did not heed their ears to the refusal of Joydev and so they left the daughter where Joydev was seated near the temple of Jagannath Swami.

At this Padmabati also told – My father according to order of Lord Jagannath has given me to you and so I cannot welcome anybody to marry. I do not want to be an adulterous woman."

Yet, poet Joydeb remained unyielding and did not take any chance for any interaction with this beautiful girl of young age. But at night while sleeping alone he had a dream of Lord Jagannath that he is saying with the voice of an order – Accept Padmabati as your wife and go back to Kenduli and engage yourself in writing on my lovely love story for the rest of life."[2]

Thus poet Joydev had to marry the almost unknown lady Padmabati as Lord Jagannath ordered him.

On return to own village at Kenduli somehow he could erect a cottage on only a portion of their land which was not sold earlier. Poet Joydev established the deity of Sri Radhamadhava and Padmabati Devi started to worship the deity with complete devotion. Poet Joydeva began to meditate, worship and write poems on Lord Sri Krishna there.

The wife of Joydev Padmabati was like a Lakshmi and remained in servicing for her husband. She also became a perfect partner of her husband's austere endeavour.

Not only that in composing poems on Lord Sri Krishna Padmabati was a living inspiration of Poet Joydeva.

Padmabati Devi was also an unparallel singer and dancer too. Her singing capacity was beyond imagination to common people. She was specialist in singing on Gandhar Raga.

Some people liked to mention that Padmabati Devi was a 'Devadasi' in the temple of Lord Sri Sri Jagannath at Puri.[3]

The remarkable and the most beautiful creation of Poet Joydev was 'Geeta Govinda'. The poet was also a court poet in Raja Lakshman Sen's court. He had based the Brahmaboibarta Purana and the Srimad Bhagawata and framed the 'Geeta Govinda'. He received the touch of Lord Sri Krishna and so he was successful in writing the 'Priye Charushiley' song. Once he was writing the 'Pada' but could not further proceed after writing "*Smaragala Khanandanang Muma Shirashi Mandalam.....*" He could not proceed further as he did not like to see his Lord having bent at the feet of Radharani. Next day thinking only, "O Lord Sri Krishna please bestow 'Kripa' on me" and went to the sweet holy river Ajoy (some liked to mention Ganga) in order to take bath in the water.

At that time Sri Krishna in the disguise of Joydeva reached his hut and wrote the words as:-

'...Dehi Padapalavamudaram'.[4]

He also took the meal produced by Padmabati and entered into the bed room to take a little mid-day nap.

Then Padmabati Devi started to take her meal at the plate of her husband poet Jayadeva as usual.

At that moment poet Joydeva in original returned and found Padmabati Devi to receive the meal which appeared to him unusual. He was perplexed. He mildly asked her how she could start to take Prasad before him unusually. Padmabati Devi was surprised to see his husband as she just a few moments earlier offered him to take Prasad after he had written a portion of his poem. She could not speak for some moments and asked to herself then who was the person in disguise of the Poet?

The poet Joydeva entered the room to find who was the person who took Prasad after completing the verse? He found there was no one but with his astonishment he found the incomplete verse has already been completed in other handwriting divinely written as 'Dehi Padapallavamudaram'.

Both the wife and the husband then started to cry loudly - 'Oh, Lord Sri Krishna, you are so kind to us". In love to Lord Sri Krishna they cried some time and ate the rest Prasad along.

Poet Joyadeva after establishing Sri Radhamadhava engaged Padmabati Devi to serve for the deity. Both of them used to feel the eternal Prema Lila of Sri Radhamadhava. In meditating the super natural eternal Lila of Lord was the source of the Geeta Govinda.[5]

The village Kenduli in the district of Birbhum in West Bengal is regarded as the place of love of Padmabati Devi and 'Padmabati-charan-Chaaran-Chakraborty' Poet Joydeva that also reminds us the divine love of Srimati Radharani and Sri Krishna.[6]

Padmabati Devi used to serve also Poet Joydeva as Lord Sri Krishna. And Lord also showered His blessings to her. Her devotion to Lord Sri Krishna and to her husband Poet Joydeva made her a great woman that should be followed by the future wives of husbands.

References

1. Sri Sri Goudiya Vaishnava Abhidhaan – Edited by Sri Haridas Das Babaji, 2nd, 3rd, and 4th Parts, 2nd Edition, 501 Chaitanyabda, Publisher – Haribol Kutir Poraghat, Nabadwip, Printer – Radha Press, Delhi 110031, p. 1244,
2. Brihat Sri Bhaktamaal – Original in Hindi by Sri Navaji, Bengali Trans by Sri Laldas Babaji, edited by Sri Dilip Mukhopadhyyay and published by Benimadhab

Seals Library, printed by A B C Printers, re-printed in 1416 BS (2009AD) p.582, (Original Mode),

3. Naari Charitabhidhan – Sankalan and Edited by Jiban Saha,
4. Sri Sri Bhaktamaal – Written by Sri Krishnadas Babaji, Edited by Upendranath Mukhopadhyay, 5th edition, Chaitanyabda 464, p.130-31,
5. Sri Sri Geeta Govindam – Edited by Pro. Sri Krishnacharan Goswami Vidyabhushan, published by Janakinath Kavyatirtha & Sons, Kolkata – 3, Printer New Madan Press, 2nd edition – 1357 BS, Joydeva Jibani),
6. Joydeva Mela, Sekaler O Ekaler– Dr. Ajitkumar Das, Pushpa Bhavan, Tikarbeta, Joydev-Kenduli, Birbhum, PIN -731 124, Poush Sankrati 1408 BS, p.251, As refd. In Sri Geet Govindam Trans and Tika by Chaitanyadas, Sadhak Kavir Mela, p.25.

6

Vedabati Devi

(Mother of Bosudeva or Madhwacharya)

It was believed that in various scriptures only Sri Vishnu is the real thing (Sat). He is with all the good qualities. This idea was publicized by the sages and one them was Bosudeva. Vedabati Devi was his mother.[1]

One of the researchers Rebecca J. Manring commented – According to Vaisnavas, all existence arises from Mahavishnu. That is the new age is produced and brought forth by Mahavisnu…."[2]

Bosudeva the son of Vedabati Devi was also afterwards known and established as Madhwacharya. He was born in 1219 AD at Belegram in the then Tular Province in the South. His father was Brahmin and Vaishnava Acharya Madhiji Bhatta and his mother was Vedabati Devi.

Vedabati Devi was a sincere devotee and a virtuous woman. Her husband Madhiji Bhatta had low income. But she was happy with her two sons and one daughter. She had no complaint against her husband or the fortune. She was contended.

But like a thunderbolt in the blue sky suddenly the two sons succumbed at a time. The couple hardly could bear the sudden shock.

After a few years the shocked couple reached the nearer Ananteswar Temple at Rajatpithpur now known as Udupi. Both of them fell at the feet of God there. They prayed to God to bless them by giving a son as descendant. They were afraid that there would none remain to perform the obsequies after their deaths. They observed all the procedures of worshipping God and ultimately one day Madhiji Bhatta could listen the divine forecast that sooner a son would be born. As a result really a son was born and he was named as Bosudeva.

From the very childhood the son of Vedabati Devi was as strong as Bhim in the Mahabharata and could work the tedious work and so she used to call her son as Bhim. The son was also talented student at the education centre (Tole) and learnt Logic, Sankhya, the Vedas and the Vedanta from the honored teacher Acharya Achyutaprakash. The son of Vedabati Devi afterwards became famous as Purnapragna in Karnataka.

This mother and her husband wanted to arrange their son for a marriage to have a grand-son. But the son was not agreeable rather he assured them a way out for becoming grand-pa and grand-ma. It was a miracle that Vedabati Devi was again pregnant and another son was born. Then Purnapragna left the family life and became the chief of the Mutt at Udipi as established by his preceptor Acharya Achyutaprakash. There he was named as Ananda Tirtha.

Vedabati Devi's another son took initiation from Purnapragna Bosudeva i.e. Ananda Tirtha and was named as Vishnu Tirtha. This son fulfilled the desire of Vedabati Devi and Madhiji Bhatta by marrying and a son was born who continued the heredity.

References

1. Brihat Sri Bhactamaal – Original in Hindi by Sri Navaji, Bengali Trans by Sri Laldas Babaji, edited by Sri Dilip Mukhopadhyyay and published by Benimadhab Seals Library, printed by A B C Printers, re-printed in 1416 BS (2009AD) p.657, (Original Mode).
2. Reconstructing Tradition, Advaita Acarya and Gaudiya Vaisnavism at the cusp of the Twentieth Century – Rebecca J. Marning, Columbia University Press, New York, Thesis Paper, Page 210.

7

Rami Rajakini

(Devotion Partner of Chandidas)

Rajakini Rami being helpless came to Nanur in the district of Birbhum. There the people arranged her job at the temple of Vishalakshi goddess in the village Nanur. Her daily works were to wash the utensils of the temple and to keep clean the premises. She also used to wash the clothes of the people of the village. Still the stone plate on which the clothes were thrown with force in order to clean properly exists.[1]

Chandidas was a son of Durgadas Bagchi who was also a priest in the temple. On his death Chandidas was also appointed as the daily priest in the temple.

The goddess Vishalakshi is another form of Durga the goddess of 'Shakti'. In the mantra of the goddess it is clearly written that she is the power of Narayana, God of the universe. And perhaps Chandidas was advised by mother Vishalakshi to worship Lord Sri Krishna of Brajalila.

Chandidas had immense poetic talent and he could easily write poetry on Lord entwined Sri Radhakrishna of Vrindaban Lila.

The poet in day to day activities somehow got attracted to Rajakini Rami who was also known as Ramatara or Rammoni. She became a partner devotee of Chandidas. She also naturally was the main inspiration to the poet.

Poet Chandidas once wrote:–

Rajakini Roop Kishori Swarup
Kamagandha Nahi Taay.

It clearly states that the beautiful young girl like Radharni of Brajalila had no senses of human sex.

The natural love of Poet Chandidas to Rami Rajakini has also been confirmed by the poet in 'Rajaki Sangati, Chandidas Geeti (Pada No. 641).[2]

Rami Rajakini or Ramamoni Rajakini was also one of the women poets of older times. She was contemporary to Chandidas. The stanzas written by Ramamoni Rajakini prove that she was also a talented poet who wrote on the subject of Mathur:-

"Kotha Jaao Ohe Pranabadhu Mor, Daasire Upeksha Kori.
Na Dekhiya Mukh Phate Mor Book, Dhairaj Dharte Nari.
Balykaal Hote E-Deha Sanpinu, Mone Aan Nahi Jani.
Ki Dosh Payiya Mathura Jaaibe, Bolohe Se Katha Shuni".[3]

The few lines state that Sri Krishna is setting for Mathura and Srimati Radharani is asking the Love, where he was going by leaving her behind? Her heart aches as it was bursting, she could not tolerate the separation. She has given herself to him and never thought otherwise. For what fault he would leave her she wants to know.[4]

In the book 'Chandidas' in the 'Chaturdash Padaboli' some information about the poet were received. It is true some ill reputations spread in the villages at Nanur and adjacent villages. Even brother Nakul of Chandidas tried to convince him about his deep relation with Rami.

On this issue the villagers and other Brahmin people wanted to expel Chandidas from the Society for his defamation. Nakul Bagchi was a respectable Brahmin in the village. He had wisdom, money and social influence. With all these and the sweet behave could control the upsurge in the society.

Once Chandidas was requested to sing in the court of Nawab of Goud and he sang accordingly. The Begum of Nawab from behind the curtain acclaimed Chandidas and she became attracted to the poet. She disclosed her mental situation to Nawab who could not tolerate this and in reaction arranged to kill the poet.

The poet Chandidas was tied on an elephant's back and beaten repeatedly with the whippings till his death. Having witnessed the inhuman torture the Begum fainted and her fainting continued for ever.

Rami saw the incidence but in mind praised to Begum for her attraction to the poet. In great sorrow, however, Rami lamented by saying – *Banshuli Devi advised you to love me alone but tried to win the mind of others, why....why?'*

There remains another opinion about the death of poet Chandidas that at the time of singing Kirtan the whole auditorium was ruined on the poet and breathed his last under the debris. It is also hearsay that the auditorium was ruined as it fired by canon by the Nawab.

The love story of Rami Rajakini and poet Chandidas would be remembered for ever in the world.

References

1. Sri Sri Goudiya Vaishnava Abhidhaan – Edited by Sri Haridas Das Babaji, 2nd, 3rd, and 4th Parts, 2nd Edition, 501 Chaitanyabda, Publisher – Haribol Kutir Poraghat, Nabadwip, Printer – Radha Press, Delhi 110031, p. 1606.
2. *Ibid.*, p. 1226.
3. Stanzas from writing by Ramamoni Rajakini.
4. Sri Goudiya Vaishnava Abhidhaan – Edited by Sri Haridas Das Babaji, 2nd, 3rd, and 4th Parts, 2nd Edition, 501 Chaitanyabda, Publisher – Haribol Kutir Poraghat, Nabadwip, Printer – Radha Press, Delhi 110031, p. 1606.

13th Century AD

8

Chintamoni

(The lady who showed the Path to Billwamongal)

Chintamoni was a worker in the profession of prostitution but she was eager for Lord Sri Krishna. She emancipated a whore monger.

In the South at the western bank of the river Krishnabenwa there lived a Brahmin scholar Kavindra Billwamongal by name. On the other side in the eastern bank of the river there lived the prostitutes.

Unfortunately, this Billwamongal did not prefer to maintain the rituals of Brahmin culture rather he was addicted to women and had a deep relation with Chintamoni who was engaged in the profession of prostitution. His attraction was so deep that he did not bother the heavy rains but remained with Chintamoni. Even one day on the dark night of the day of his father Damodar's 'Shradh' started to pass the river in order to meet Chintamoni. Billwamongal in the stormy night used a dead body floating in furious river reached the door of Chintamoni. But the door was closed as in rained heavily and no customer could dare to come outside to reach her. Billwamongal found a snake hanging on the wall and he took the help of its long tail to cross a drain and fell there. He was ultimately fainted.

The maid servants somehow found and took him to Chintamoni. Chintamoni nursed Billwamongal and he was cured. She was an expert in singing and playing musical instruments. She was also surprised to note the eagerness of Billwamongal.

Chintamoni then spoke to Billwamongal – I see your strong eagerness to meet me in the terrible night with all these barriers. If, these eagerness you could have for Lord Sri Krishna you would be blessed by Him."

She again said to him – Alas, I am a sinner who robbed the riches and the minds of people till date. Now I have decided to leave everything and to worship only God Sri Krishna.' Afterwards she started to sing songs on Raasalila of Sri Krishna.[1]

On listening the song of Raasalila and the precious advice from Chintamoni Billwamongal was mentally prepared to leave the worldly things and connections and decided to worship Lord Sri RadhaKrishna only.

According to the scripture Brihat Sri Sri Bhaktamaal, Chintamoni and Billwamongal were known to each other for a long time so, Billwamongal did not want to disturb Chintamoni and climbed the wall with a help of a snake's long tail considering that a rope hanging from the wall. To see him in wet dresses due to uncommon rains and the hanging snake Chintamoni was surprised and also aggrieved. After a while she ran to her worshipped deity of Lord Sri Krishna. She put the deity before Billwamongal and started to speak – Oh, your mind, see I am a prostitute but your eagerness has made me mad but if this eagerness was for Sri Hari you could have seen Him. I cannot look at your eyes full of desire of enjoying human flesh. Please you leave this place and let me repent myself."

Then Billwamongal took up the deity with his hands and received a consciousness and he begged the deity to her and he bowed his head to Chintamoni. After the sunrise without leaving a single moment he ran outside the brothel. He did not return to his residence. Billwamongal showed due respect to her as Preceptor and also a Teacher for lessons of actual love to God Sri Krishna.[2]

He reached the nearer Ashram of Somgiri, a noted Vaishnava Yogi and was initiated from him. After serving to the Preceptor Somgiri for some days he with his eagerness went to Vrindaban. Here he received the 'Mantraraj' of Sri Madangopala. On the whole way to Vrindaban by remembering Lord Sri Krishna Billwamongal in natural mood was expressing the glory of Sri Krishna in an under tone. These poems were collected and were incorporated in the 'Sri Sri Krishnakarnamrita' scripture. His utterings in delirium on way to Mathura-Vrindaban were the sources have been affirmed by Sri Krishnadas Kaviraj in the 'Tika' of 'Saranga-Rangada' also.

Billwamongal wrote the books like (i) Sri Krishnabalacharitra, (ii) Govinda Strotam, (iii) Balakrishnacrirhakavyam, (iv) Krishna Stotram, (v) Govinda Damodar Stotrang, (vi) Vishnu Stuti (Adyar Mss 68 1) and (vii) Sumangal Stotrang.[3]

Billwamongal was of a pure heart man. However when Billwamongal became apparently purified was given a name as 'Lila Shuka' by his Preceptor.

The time of Billwamongal and Chintamoni was of 9th century AD. Some liked to say it was in 11th century AD as per Winternitz. Another 3rd source as Journal of the Andhra History Research Society III stated it was in 1250–1350 AD.

We can also feel that the power of Mantra of Lord Sri Krishna helped the prostitute Chintamoni to develop herself to the extent of higher meditation to have the divine touch and enabled her to speak to Billwamongal who in future became a great poet in writing on Lord Sri Krishna.

"Karnamrita Soma Bastu Nahi Tribhubaney.
Jaha Haoite Hoy Shuddha Krishnaprem Jnane.
Soundarya, Maadhurya, Krishnalilar Abadhi.
Sei Janey Ye Karnamrita Parhe Nirabadhi."[4]

During the tour in the South our beloved Sri Chaitanya Mahaprabhu collected this book and brought it in Vidyanagar then to Gambhira and thereafter this book was available in Goud Bengal. Sri Chaitanya Mahaprabhu also used to read it regularly at Gambhira.

Here I like to state that being a prostitute Chintamoni could make Billwamongal a pure Sadhaka of Lord Sri Krishna and a Poet of eminence. She made him a true Man. The role of Chintamoni in the society is also praiseworthy. We should salute her.

References

1. Sri Sri Goudiya Vaishnava Abhidhaan – Edited by Sri Haridas Das Babaji, 2nd, 3rd, and 4th Parts, 2nd Edition, 501 Chaitanyabda, Publisher – Haribol Kutir Poraghat, Nabadwip, Printer – Radha Press, Delhi 110031, p. 1460 and 1469.
2. Brihat Sri Sri Bhaktamaal – Original in Hindi by Sri Navaji, Bengali Trans. by Sri Laldas Babaji, edited by Sri Dilip Mukhopadhyyay and published by Benimadhab Seals Library, printed by A B C Printers, re-printed in 1416 BS (2009AD) p. 638, (Original Mode).
3. Sri Sri Goudiya Vaishnava Abhidhaan – Edited by Sri Haridas Das Babaji, 2nd, 3rd, and 4th Parts, 2nd Edition, 501 Chaitanyabda, Publisher – Haribol Kutir Poraghat, Nabadwip, Printer – Radha Press, Delhi 110031, p. 1460.
4. Sri Sri Chaitanya Charitamrita –by Sri Krishnadas Kaviraj, Ed. Sri Sri Madbhakti Sri Roop Bhagawata Maharaj, President Gaudiya Mission (Rgd.) and Pub. By Tridandi Bhikshu Sri Bhakti Gunakar Goswami, Printe by Radha Press, Gandhinagar Delhi – 110 031, 6th Ed.Pub. in 1990 AD (1396 BS), Madhya Lila, 9th Paricched, Shloka – 307-308.

9

Bhagyabatidevi

The Old Grand Mother of Uddharan Dutta

Originally from Ayodhya Bhabesh Dutta came to Subarna Village for trading. This Subarna Village is now called as Adi Saptagram. Bhabesh Dutta married Bhagyabati, sister of Kanjilal Dhar of the village. We may note that the son of Kanjilal Dhar Umapati Dhar was one of the members of the court of Raja Lakshman Sen. His fellow members were poet Joydeva and Gobardhan Acharya.

On the other side a son of Bhabesh Dutta and Bhagyabati Devi was born and was named as Krishna Dutta who became also a scholar. The son of Krishna Dutta was known as Srikar and Srikar's son was Uddharan Dutta who was known for friendship and rendering service to Sri Nityananda Prabhu.

Uddharan Dutta was appointed as Dewan of Noiraj, the king of Naihati or Nabahatta. He used to live towards the north Uddharanpur, perhaps the name was given to him as per his name. Bhagyabatidevi was his old grandmother and also a sincere devotee to Lord Sri Krishna and so she was considered to be a member of Vaishnava family.[1]

Reference

1. Sri Sri Goudiya Vaishnava Abhidhaan – Edited by Sri Haridas Das Babaji, 2nd, 3rd, and 4th Parts, 2nd Edition, 501 Chaitanyabda, Publisher – Haribol Kutir Poraghat, Nabadwip, Printer – Radha Press, Delhi 110031, p. 1156.

14th Century AD

10

Mother of Upendra

Old grandmother of Sri Chaitanyadeva

One Vaidik Brahmin Madhukar Mishra from the West came to settle at Sri Hatta and received some landed property that was named as Baraganga. His wife gave births of four sons and a snake. The name of the second son was Upendra. He went to secret Vrindaban nearer to the Kailash and started to worship God. On the eastern side there was flowing Ikshu River like the Yamuna in Vrindaban. There was also on the Northside a pond of nectar.

Another source stated that a Vaidik Brahmin of Batsya Muni Madhu Mishra settled at Baraganga village. The wife of Madhu Mishra gave births of four sons and one of them was Upendra. He was 'Parjanya Gopa' in Vrindaban Lila. His wife Kamalabati gave births of seven sons one of them the fifth was Jagananath Mishra whose son was Sri Chaitanyadeva.

The details of mother of Upendra were not available. However his mother was a pious and regular worshipper and for her sincerity was notable.[1]

Reference

1. Sri Goudiya Vaishnava Abhidhaan – Edited by Sri Haridas Das Babaji, 2nd, 3rd, and 4th Parts, 2nd Edition, 501 Chaitanyabda, Publisher – Haribol Kutir Poraghat, Nabadwip, Printer – Radha Press, Delhi 110031, p. 1158.

11

Rama Devi

(Grandmother of Sri Roop and Sanatan)

Rama Devi was grandmother of Roop, Sanatan and Ballav. Ramadevi was married to Padmanava a descendant of Sri Sarbajna of Bharadwaj Gotra and Brahmin so Jajurveda. They lived in the South at Vijayanagar of Karnataka State. Her father Jadujiban Tarkalankar was a Pundit in the court of Mahendra Singha of Bardhaman area.

Her husband Padmanava was a prominent scholar in the Vedas, the Upanishads, Kavya and Vyakaran (Grammar). Later he settled at Nabahatta or Naihati in Goud Bengal.

Padmanava and Rama Devi had eight daughters and five sons. The sons were Purushottam, Jagannath, Narayana, Murari and Mukunda. Mukunda was also a great scholar and so he was appointed as a Minister in the court of Pathan dynnesty in Goud Bengal.

After few years Mukunda left the capital Nabadwip and settled at Bakla. He married Rebati and they had three sons. They were Amar or Sanatan, Santosh or Roop and Ballav or Anupam. Roop Goswami and Sanatan Goswami were the main as pillars of Goudiya Vaishnava Movement initiated by Sri Chaitanyadeva. They lived in Vrindaban. Rama Devi, a completely pure and pious woman was the grandmother of them and so she is worth to be mentioned in the history of Vaishnavism.[1]

Reference

1. Sri Goudiya Vaishnava Abhidhaan – Edited by Sri Haridas Das Babaji, 2nd, 3rd, and 4th Parts, 2nd Edition, 501 Chaitanyabda, Publisher – Haribol Kutir Poraghat, Nabadwip, Printer – Radha Press, Delhi 110031, p. 1834.

12

Lachhima Devi

(Wife of Raja Shiba Singha)

Once in Bengal the readers and the devotees used to believe that the songs and poems written by Poet Vidyapati in loveable lucid language and mixed with devotion towards Lord Sri Krishna and Radha were in earlier form Bengal. Later it was discovered that the poet Vidyapati was not from Bengal nor he wrote in Bengali. He was from Mithila and wrote poems in Brajabuli as created on the basis of Maithili and Bengali old patterned language.

After the death of Deva Singha his son Shiva Singha became the King of Mithila and Vidyapati was appointed as a court poet at the court of Raja Shiva Singha.

Lachhima or Lachhimadevi was the wife of Shiva Singha.[1]

This Vidyapati was one of the notable talented poets in India like Kalidas, Vyas, Joydeva and few others.

However, suddenly after three years' of ruling Mithila he succumbed. Then his wife Lachhima or Lachhimadevi took the charge of the kingdom. In the writings of Vidyapati at several times the name of Lachhima or Lachhimadevi was also referred to in.

> *"Raja Shiva Singha Lachhimadevi Sanga.*
> *Bhanaye Vidyapati Manahu Nishanka."*[2]

Vidyapati was also inspired by Lachhimadevi as King Shiva Singha appreciated him earlier. He had a good friendly relation with King Shiva Singha and later automatically with Lachhimadevi. Her influence and also inspiration affected in the poems of Vidyapati.[3]

Vidyapati during his long life was also existed as a minister and Court Poet in the courts of Deva Singha, Shiva Singha, Rani Lachhimadevi, Rani Viswas Devi, Vairab Singha and some other King.

Vidyabati knew that tattwas of Radhakrishna were known to Lachhimadevi and King Shiva Singha. Vidyapati was one of the notable talented poets in India like Kalidas, Vyas, Joydeva and few others.

He also wrote:-

> *"Kavi Vidyapati Iha Rasa Jaane.*
> *Raja Shiva Singha Lachhima Parmane."*[4]

Rani Lachhimadevi was an educated woman having sufficient knowledge in Sanskrit. She also wrote some poems and songs. In the age when women were usually confined only in domestic world a woman like Rani Lachhimadevi had the gurts to come forward in the society and got the success. We should salute her.[5]

Shiva Singha the King of Mithila used to patronize Art, Poems and Culture. With his support and inspiration Vidyapati used to write on the eternal love of Lord Sri Krishna. The King Shiva Singha gifted a village named as 'Bisafi' to Vidyapati. The document duly inscribed on a copper sheet is still preserved in the Library of the King of Dwarbhanga. One Shivalinga worshipped by Vidyapati is also found in 'Bisafi' village on the bank of River Kamala in Jaroil Pargana under Sitamari Sub-division in the district of Dwarbhanga.[6]

References

1. Mahiyasi Bharatiya Naari – Edited by Swami Madhabananda & Dr. Ramesh Chandra Majumder, - Bengali Translation by Dr. Satchidananda Dhar, published by Swami Mumukshananda, Udbodhan Karyalaya, 1407 BS, p. 401-02.
2. Sri Sri Pada Kalpa Taru – Edited by Sri Satish Chandra Roy, 1st Part (1st & 2nd Branches), Pub. by Sri Ramkamal Sinha from Bongiya Sahitya Parishat Mandir, 1st Pub.1322 BS, Printed by Arjit Kumar, Laser Impressions, Padaboli – Vidyapati,
3. Sri Sri Goudiya Vaishnava Abhidhaan – Edited by Sri Haridas Das Babaji, 2nd, 3rd, and 4th Parts, 2nd Edition, 501 Chaitanyabda, Publisher – Haribol Kutir Poraghat, Nabadwip, Printer – Radha Press, Delhi 110031, p. 1368.
4. Sri Sri Pada Kalpa Taru – Edited by Sri Satish Chandra Roy, 1st Part (1st & 2nd Branches), Pub.by Sri Ramkamal Sinha from Bongiya Sahitya Parishat Mandir, 1st Pub.1322 BS, Printed by Arjit Kumar, Laser Impressions, p. 247.
5. Mahiyasi Bharatiya Naari – Edited by Swami Madhabananda & Dr. Ramesh Chandra Majumder, - Bengali Translation by Dr. Satchidananda Dhar, published by Swami Mumukshananda, Udbodhan Karyalaya, 1407 BS, p. 401-02.
6. Sri Sri Goudiya Vaishnava Abhidhaan – Edited by Sri Haridas Das Babaji, 2nd, 3rd, and 4th Parts, 2nd Edition, 501 Chaitanyadoba, Publisher – Haribol Kutir Poraghat, Nabadwip, Printer – Radha Press, Delhi 110031, p. 1368.

15th Century AD

13

Abhoya Devi

(Grand mother of Lochandas)

Lochandas the writer of 'Chaitanya Mongal' was a resident of Kogram just 15 miles (1.6 km =1 mile) away of Bardhaman and 5 miles north of Guskara Rly Station. Trilochandas or Lochandas was only one grandson of Abhoya Devi. She arranged his education.

Parents of Lochandas Kamalakar Das and Sadanandi were not much interested for his education rather Abhoya Devi inspired him. She used to meet Sri Narahari with taking her grandson and one day Lochandas was initiated from Sri Narahari. Thus Abhoya Devi was an important lady who arranged Lochandas and Sri Narahari meet became memorable in the Vaishnava Movement.[1]

Reference

1. Sri Nityananda Shakti Maa Janhaba – Nemaichand Goswami, Pub. By Sri Sanatan Goswami, Printer – Shyamasundar Press, 1st Pub 1389 BS, 2nd Pub 1401 BS, p. 549).

14

Amita Devi

Sakhi of Vishnupriya Devi

Amita was a 'Sakhi' of Vishnupriya Devi. Amita and Kanchan were two friends of Vishnupriya Devi, the second wife of Sri Gouranga Mahaprabhu.

> "Joya Joya Sri Kanchana Amitadi .
> Kripa Kara Kripamoya Muin Bara Dukhi".

Again,

> "...Kelikala Sukushala Sukhada Sakhinang.
> *Vishnupriya Bijayatang Jagatang Joyasri"*[1]

In order to make her strong and bear it with tolerance the separation from Sri Gouranga Mahaprabhu they tried to ease to her all along. Amita and Kanchana were like co-partners in fighting the adverse situation. So, they specially Amita the constant companion were praiseworthy and remained memorable.

Reference

1. Gambhiraya Sri Vishnupriya Devi – Composed and published by Sripad Haridas Goswami of Do Gachhiya, a descendant of Nityananda, 1340 BS, Gourabda 447, p. 35 and 32.

15

Indumati Basu

(Mother of Kavi Gunaraj Khan)

In the 16th century Kavi Maladhar Basu or Gunaraj Khan was a prominent Vaishnava Poet. His mother was Indumati Basu. She was married to Bhagirath Basu, the thirteenth later generation of Dasarath Basu of Kulingram who was brought from Kanauj to Goud Bengal by Adisura. The father-in-law was Jajneshwar Basu who was from a very influential Basu family in village Kulingram. Their village was protected by a fort.[1]

Kavi Maladhar Basu son of Indumati Basu for his excellent writings received the title 'Gunaraj Khan' from Sultan of Goud Bengal Hussein Shah.

From 1395 Shaka (1473 AD) to 1402 Shaka (1480 AD) Kavi Maladhar Basu engaged himself in writing the book 'Sri Krishnavijaya'. Once Sri Gouranga Mahaprabhu had read this book and was pleased. As in Sri Sri Chaitanyacharitamrita-

"Gunaraj Khan Koila 'Sri Krishnavijaya'.
Taha Ek Vakya Tnar Aachhe Premamoya.
'Nandanandan Krishna Mor Prannath'.
Ei Vakye Bikaunu Tnar Bangsher Haath".[2]

The father-in-law's house of Indumati Devi at the Locality at Kulingram was named as Chaitanyapur Pat. There still remain a heap of older bricks and ruins in the locality just at the South of the house of Late Bholanath Basu. It was named as 'Sri Basu Ramanander Vita'. There were also found some ditches that indicate there were fort and the ditches were around it.

Some temples like 'Shibani Maata', 'Sri Sri Jagannath', 'Sri Raghunath', 'Sri Sri Madan Gopal', 'Sri Sri Gopeswar Shiva' and the place of Bhajan of Sri Haridas Thakur also found here.

The name of Maladhar Basu was Lakshminath Basu who was known as 'Satyaraj Khan' and his son's name was Ramananda Basu.

All Vaishnavas still remember 'Kulingram' for Sri Haridas Thakur, Sri Satyaraj Basu, Sri Ramananda Basu, Sri Shankar, Sri Vidyanada and Sri Baninath Basu.[3]

And we also remember Srimati Indumati Devi when anybody reminds us Kulingram.

References

1. Sri Sri Goudiya Vaishnava Abhidhaan – Edited by Sri Haridas Das Babaji, 2nd, 3rd, and 4th Parts, 2nd Edition, 501 Chaitanyadoba, Publisher – Haribol Kutir Poraghat, Nabadwip, Printer – Radha Press, Delhi 110031, p. 1202 & 1313.
2. Sri Sri Chaitanyacharitamrita – by Sri Krishnadas Kaviraj, Ed. By President & Acharya Sri Madbhakti Sri Roop Maharaj, Published from Gaudiya Mission Tridandi Vikshu Sri Bhakti Gunakar Goswami, Radha Press, Gandhinagar, Delhi 110 031, Published in 1396 BS (1990AD), Madhya Lila, 15th Chap. Shloka 99-100.
3. Sri Sri Goudiya Vaishnava Abhidhaan – Edited by Sri Haridas Das Babaji, 2nd, 3rd, and 4th Parts, 2nd Edition, 501 Chaitanyabda, Publisher – Haribol Kutir Poraghat, Nabadwip, Printer – Radha Press, Delhi 110031, p. 1314 & 1845.

16

Illamagaru

(Mother of Ballavacharya)

Sri Gouranga Mahaprabhu once visited Arail village off Tribeni-Prayag near Varanasi at the invitation of Ballavacharya. Later Ballavacharya came to Puri to meet Sri Gouranga Mahaprabhu. He wrote a poem praising Sri Chaitanyadeva. He also desired to read his narrative 'Tika' to Sri Mahaprabhu. It has no conformity with the 'Tika' of Sri Dhar. So Sri Chaitanyadeva was much offended and ultimately he was initiated from Sri Gadadhar Pundit in Radhakrishna yugal mantra. Earlier he was initiated in Bal Gopal mantra and so his disciples were called Ballavacharya Sampradaya.

Ballavacharya or Ballav Bhatta was born in the Boishakh in 1479 AD. Fearing Muslim invasion in Kashi (Varanasi) Lakshman Bhatta with his wife tried to flee towards Andhra Pradesh. He was passing through the dense forest in Champaran district. Then his wife was pregnant and in the forest she was compelled to give birth of a son who was named later as Ballavacharya or Ballav Bhatta.[1]

The mother of Ballavacharya was Illamagaru. She was born in Vijayanagar in the family of Raj Purohit. Her father Susharma was also in the profession of a priest. So she became a devotee of Lord Sri Krishna. She was married to Lakshman Bhatta of Bharadwaj Gotra of Andhra Pradesh and her father-in-law Balaram Bhatta was also a priest. The earlier generation also wrote many books. Her grand father-in-law Ganapati Bhatta wrote against the customs of Tantrik Sadhana and wrote 'Sarba Tantra Nigraha', 'Bhakti Deep' and others in Telegu language.

Then Lakshman Bhatta used to reside in Varanasi when a rumor was spread there in 1478 AD Bahulul Lodi or his commander-in-chief would attack Varanasi to loot out the riches of the temples and so like other people

Lakshman Bhatta with his pregnant wife Illamagaru tried to flee towards the South. On the path in the dense forest of Champaran his wife could not tolerate labor-pain and was bound to give birth to a son later who was named Ballavacharya or Ballav Bhatta in 1479 AD in the month of Baisakh on Krishna Ekadasi.[2]

The son of Sri Lakshman Bhatta and Srimati Illamagaru Ballavacharya or Ballav Bhatta was Shukhdev in his earlier life it is believed.[3]

It was known that in the forest of Champaran any pregnant woman could pass only after miscarriage. The episode on Ballavacharya or Ballav Bhatta's premature birth that at the time of his birth he was seemed to be died. And the parents left the dead baby by wrapping in a piece of cloth under a tree. Afterwards they received God's advice to bring the baby back as it was alive and they did accordingly. After a few days they knew Sultan Hussein Shah defeated Lodi and peace in Varanasi was restored and they returned in Varanasi.

At his age eleven Ballavacharya or Ballav Bhatta lost his father in 1490 AD and Illamagaru decided to take shelter in Vijayanagar with her under aged children. There Ballavacharya or Ballav Bhatta was awarded 'Acharya' after establishing 'Shuddh Adwaitabad'. Ballavacharya or Ballav Bhatta travelled whole of India thrice. After marriage Ballavacharya or Ballav Bhatta settled at Arail village and after a couple of years in Vrindaban and dedicated his full time in Sadhana and writings for the next generations.[4]

Ballavacharya or Ballav Bhatta wrote 48 books in total. The remarkable are (i) Brahma Sutranuvasya, (ii) Bhagawata Tika, (iii) Sobodhani, (iv) Shudasha Grantha, (v) Mathura Mahatmya and (vi) Panchshloki.[5]

Information re Iallamagaru's death was not available. It is hearsay that in 1531 Ballavacharya or Ballav Bhatta was disappeared at the Hanuman Ghat in Kashi Dham.

The respect to husband, devotion to God and carrying the responsibilities sincerely in bringing up the children made Illamaguru a memorableVaishnava woman in the Vaishnava cult.

References

1. Sri Chaitanyadeva O Sri Gadadhar –by Sri Radhakrishna (Radhu) Goswami, 1st Pub. Jhulanyatra 1414 BS, by Smt Bhumika Goswami, Sodepur – 700 110, p. 123 – 126, Sri Gadadhar –by Sri Radhakrishna (Radhu) Goswami, 1st Pub. January 2014 AD, pub by Smt Bhumika Goswami, Sodepur – 700 110, p. 83 as refd.in Ballavacharya Ki Nij Barta printed at Vir Vijoy Press, Ahmedabad and Sampraya day Pradipe, Kankroli Vidya Bibhag Mumbai and also in Sri Chaitanya

Charitamrita Antya, Chapter 7 and also Sri Sri Goudiya Vaishnava Abhidhaan – Edited by Sri Haridas Das Babaji, 2nd, 3rd, and 4th Parts, 2nd Edition, 501 Chaitanyabda, Publisher – Haribol Kutir Poraghat, Nabadwip, Printer – Radha Press, Delhi 110031, p. 1362.

2. Bharater Vaishnava Padaboli – by Dr. Sati Ghosh, pub by Paschim Banga Rajya Pustak Parshad, Kolkata, printed by Impression, Kolkata, in 1984 AD p. 69 – 70 and also in Sri Sri Goudiya Vaishnava Abhidhaan – Edited by Sri Haridas Das Babaji, 2nd, 3rd, and 4th Parts, 2nd Edition, 501 Chaitanyabda, Publisher – Haribol Kutir Poraghat, Nabadwip, Printer – Radha Press, Delhi 110031, p. 1361.
3. Sri Chaitanyadeva O Sri Gadadhar –by Sri Radhakrishna (Radhu) Goswami, 1st Pub. Jhulanyatra 1414 BS, by Smt Bhumika Goswami, Sodepur – 700 110, p. 123 – 126, Sri Gadadhar –by Sri Radhakrishna (Radhu) Goswami, 1st Pub. January 2014 AD, pub by Smt Bhumika Goswami, Sodepur – 700 110, p. 83 as refd.in Ballavacharya Ki Nij Barta printed at Vir Vijoy Press, Ahmedabad and Samprayaday Pradipe, Kankroli Vidya Bibhag Mumbai and also in Sri Chaitanya Charitamrita Antya, Chapter 7 and also Sri Sri Goudiya Vaishnava Abhidhaan – Edited by Sri Haridas Das Babaji, 2nd, 3rd, and 4th Parts, 2nd Edition, 501 Chaitanyabda, Publisher – Haribol Kutir Poraghat, Nabadwip, Printer – Radha Press, Delhi 110031, p. 1362.
4. Bharater Vaishnava Padaboli – by Dr. Sati Ghosh, pub by Paschim Banga Rajya Pustak Parshad, Kolkata, printed by Impression, Kolkata, in 1984 AD p. 70.
5. Sri Sri Goudiya Vaishnava Abhidhaan – Edited by Sri Haridas Das Babaji, 2nd, 3rd, and 4th Parts, 2nd Edition, 501 Chaitanyabda, Publisher – Haribol Kutir Poraghat, Nabadwip, Printer – Radha Press, Delhi 110031, p. 1362.

17

Kamalakumari

(A Devotee of Sri Chaitanyadeva of the South)

During the period of South India tour Sri Chaitanyadeva had to confront with many obstacles too. But ultimately Chaitanyadeva easily could overcome all the hurdles. He could convince Buddha scholar Ramagiri and another scholar Chundiram. He also renamed Chundiram as Haridas.

Thousands of people in the South became enthusiastic to utter Harinaam and as followers of Chaitanyadeva. However, after visiting 'Akshoy Bot' and 'Bateswar Shiva' he was placed in an awkward position as two women were deployed to defame Him. Behind the curtain there was Tirtharam a moneyed person who repeatedly tried to defame Sri Chaitanyadeva. But Sri Chaitanya Mahaprabhu was firm to do the betterment of the oppressed and fallen people. So, Sri Chaitanyadeva could overcome the situation and the two women were emancipated and at last became Vaishnava. But the wife of moneyed person Tirtharam Kamalakumari was surprised to learn the activities of spreading Harinaam by Sri Chaitanyadeva. To see the precious beautiful dances in love for Sri Krishna and to listen the Harinaam by Sri Chaitanyadeva like almost all the people of the South Kamalakumari was also became a follower of Sri Chaitanyadeva and Vaishnava minded.[1]

Kamalakumari one of the followers of Sri Chaitanyadeva would be remembered for ever.

Reference

1. Sri Amiya Nemai Charita (six parts in one) –by Sri Sisir Kumar Ghosh, Pub by Shyamapada Sarkar, Letter setting by Sri Sudarshan Gatait, Type Centre, Printed by Adya Shakti Printers, 1st Kamini ed, January 2006, p 463.

18

Kamala Devi

(Wife of Lakshminath Lahiri)

Kamala Devi was the wife of Lakshminath Lahiri, son of Vaishnava Padmagarvacharya. At the time of propagating naam of Lord Sri Krishna in the eastern side Sri Gouranga Mahaprabhu met Brahmin Vaishnava at Betal village adjacent Vitadiya village nearer to the bank of the Brahmaputra. He stayed at their house for more than three days.

Both the husband and the wife Lakshminath Lahiri and Kamala Devi respectfully served Sri Gouranga Mahaprabhu sincerely and with devotion. They once begged His blessing for a son. Sri Gouranga Mahaprabhu blessed them and ultimately the couple became the parents of a son. They named the son as Roop Narayana. Later he was being called as Rupchandra.

Although Lakshminath Lahiri and Kamala Devi desired that their son one day would become a renowned scholar but Roop Narayana or Rupchandra had no interest in studying or in anything to grow up.

One day Lakshminath gave some ashes in the plate while his son was taking Lunch. Roop Narayana noticed it and leaving the dish of Lunch left the house after taking mother's silent blessings.

Later Roop Narayana reached the village Pundit Bari and for his enhanced interest in studying he became a scholar and received the titles like 'Chakraborty' and 'Acharya'. Roop Narayana was felicitated with the 'Sarswati' title also from Maharashtra.

Roop Narayan once had the opportunity to have a divine 'Darshan' of Sri Gouranga Mahaprabhu in Nabadwip. He also met Sri Sanatan and Sri Roop Goswami in Vrindaban. The two easily declared him the winner without any question. But at last Sri Jib Goswami could defeat him in debates and he gladly took the 'Padas' on his head. Ultimately he was blessed by Sri Sanatan and Sri Roop Goswami also.

Kamaladevi's profound respect to Sri Gouranga Mahaprabhu made her happy with son's success in the Vaishnava World.

Lakshminath Lahiri and Kamala Devi would be remembered by us.[1]

Reference

1. Prem Vilas – by Nityananda Das, Revised and edited by Dr. Bijon Goswami, Pub, in 1405 BS, 1999 AD, 1st Mahesh Edition, Printed at Printing Publicity, 24 Vilas, p.239.)

19

Kamala Devi

(Mother of Suryadas Sarkhel)

This Kamala Devi was wife of Sri Kangsari Mishra and mother of Suryadas Sarkhel of Shaligram. Suryadas Sarkhel was also the father of Basudha Maa and Janhaba Maa, the wives of Sri Nityananda Prabhu.

Kamala Devi the wife of Sri Kangsari Mishra had six sons. They were Damodar, Jagananath, Suryadas, Gouridas, Krishnadas (or Deen Krishnadas) and Nrisingha Chaitanya.

Kamala Devi's father-in-law's family was of Batsya Gotra and having Ghosal title. Her husband Sri Kangsari Mishra's title Mishra was probably an awarded title by a certain King. Both the husband and the wife were sincere devotees. Later Sri Kangsari Mishra with his family settled at Ambikanagar near Kalna.

Kamala Devi's all the six sons were followers of Sri Gouranga Mahaprabhu and also Sri Nityananda Prabhu. It was really a matter of praise worthy.

Kamala Devi's third son Suryadas used to work in the court of the Sultanate of Goud and so he had the opportunity of earning much money. Not only that, he was given 'Sarkhel' title fom the Yaban Administration.

The meaning of Kamala is Lakshmi. She was really a Lakshmi. Her children including grand children Balaram and Raghunath, the sons of Gouridas and also her husband Sri Kangsari Mishra could uphold the family prestige as sincere Vaishnavite in the society.[1]

Reference

1. Sri Sri Goudiya Vaishnava Abhidhaan – Edited by Sri Haridas Das Babaji, 2nd, 3rd, and 4th Parts, 2nd Edition, 501 Chaitanyabda, Publisher – Haribol Kutir

Poraghat, Nabadwip, Printer – Radha Press, Delhi 110031, ps. 1163, 1159, 1404, 1275, 1159, 1276 and Sri Sri Nityananda Shakti Maa Janhaba – Nemaichand Goswami, Pub. By Sri Sanatan Goswami, Printer – Shyamasundar Press, 1st Pub 1389 BS, 2nd Pub 1401 BS, p. 16-17).

20

Kamalabati or Shova Devi

(Grand Mother of Sri Cahaitanyadeva)

In the writing of Kavi Karnapur we can find:-

> "Mahamanyabidha Gopi Braje Jasidwariyasi.
> *Krishna Pitamohi Soiba Namnatra Kamalabati."*[1]

According to Kavi Karnapur, the lady who was an elderly glorious 'Gariyasi' named 'Gopi' in Vrindaban Lila in ealier birth now in the 'Kali Yuga' is Kamalabati as the wife of Sri Upendra Mishra i.e. grandmother of Sri Gouranga Mahaprabhu. In the district of Sylhet at Baraganga Upendra Mishra with the family used to reside.

Upendra Mishra was the eldest son of his parents. Other three brothers were Rangad, Kirtida and Kirtibaas.

Kamalabati was called as also Kalabati or Shovadevi. Kamalabati had seven sons as:-

> *"Kangsari, Paramananda, aar Jagannath.*
> *Padmanava, Sarbeshwar, Janardan, Troilokyanath".*[2]

All the seven sons were scholars but the third son of Kamalabati Jagannath Mishra was popular. Jagannath Mishra shifted the residence from Dhaka Dakshin or Baraganga to Nabadwip on the bank of of the Ganga. Before coming to Nabadwip his wife Sachidevi was pregnant and so, Kamalabati or Kalabati advised daughter-in-law Sachidevi after the birth of the son afterwards she should send the son to her at Dhaka Dakshin in Sylhet district. This son was Nemai or Gouranga or Sri Chaitanyadeva.

The glory of Sylhet district was very important as it was place of grandfather of Nemai or Gouranga or Sri Chaitanyadeva and also place of father of Sri Adwait Acharya. There 108 Sri Mahanta Sri Santadas Babaji,

Raghunandan Shiromani and many other scholars were born. Murari Gupta, Sri Baas Pundit and Chandra Sekhar Acharya were also born in the Sylhet district. Swarup Damodar had also a link with Sylhet district. Sri Bimanbehari Majumdar commented that, the people of Sylhet district have established the Goudiya Vaishnava Movement.[3]

While Sri Gouranga Mahaprabhu got the opportunity to visit East Bengal he had been to Dhaka Dakshin in Sylhet district and met the grandfather Upendra Mishra and grandmother Kamalabati Devi. Thus Sri Gouranga Mahaprabhu kept the promise of mother Sachidevi to show the grandson to Kamalabati Devi. Kamalabati Devi or Shovadevi or Kalabati Devi after receiving their grandson considered Sri Gouranga Mahaprabhu as Narayana Himself. She started to cite the mantra as:-

"Narayana Namastavyang Naptarang Mey"[4]

Sri Gouranga Mahaprabhu then exposed Himself and taught her the 'Yoga Dharma'. She was bewildered to see Lord Sri Krishna in her front and bowed her head to God.

Both Upendra Mishra and Kamalabati Devi or Shovadevi were very much pleased and Sri Gouranga Mahaprabhu stayed there for some time. Sri Gouranga Mahaprabhu also noticed that Upendra Mishra was engaged to write the Chandi and so he brought some palm leaves (much before invention of modern paper) as we find in 'Prem Vilas':-

"Upendra Mishra Chandi Likhibar Tare.
Talpata Sangraha Karila Bahutare.
Prabhu Basiyachhen Pitamahera Nikate.
Upendra Mishra Pahila Shloka Likhe Taal Pate".[5]

Upendra Mishra and Kamalabati Devi perused Sri Krishna in front of them. Still there remain a deity of Sri Krishna and also a deity of Sri Gouranga Mahaprabhu. Sri Gouranga Mahaprabhu presented them the two deities by installing at their residence at Gopalganj in Dhaka Dakshin in the district of Sylhet and advised them to worship the deities. This house is called as Thakur Bari. This place has become a pilgrimage since Mahaprabhu's arrival. As in one Sunday in the month of Chaitra Mahaprabhu reached there a fare on every Sunday in the month of Chaitra is also being observed till date.[6]

Reference

1. Sri Sri Gourganoddesh Deepika – by Kavi Karnapur, ed by Sri Ashok Kumar Bandyopadhyay, pub by Swadesh, print by Orient Press, pub in 2007, Shloka – 36.

2. Prem Vilas – by Nityananda Das, Revised and edited by Dr. Bijon Goswami, Pub, in 1405 BS, 1999 AD, 1st Mahesh Edition, Printed at Printing Publicity, 24 Vilas, p. 239.
3. SriChaitanyaChariter Upadan – by Sri Bimanbehari Majumdar, 2nd Edition, University of Calcutta, pub in 1959, p. 574.
4. Gouranger Pitribangsha Parichaya O Srihatta Lila – by Sri Pradyumna Mishra Sri Krishna Chaitanyodayaboli and by Ramaratna Dwija Sri Chaitanya Ratnaboli based, 2nd Edition, Edited by Sri Ramsaday Mishra 14th descendant of Sri Paramananda Mishra, the elder uncle of Sri Chaitanyadeva, Pub. Kishoridas Babaji, Chaitanyadoba, in 1411 BS, Print – Prankrishna Bhakti Press, p. 29-30.
5. Prem Vilas – by Nityananda Das, Revised and edited by Dr. Bijon Goswami, Pub, in 1405 BS, 1999 AD, 1st Mahesh Edition, Printed at Printing Publicity, 24 Vilas, p. 240.
6. The Souvenir – Published on the occasion of 524th Appearance of Sri Srimon Sri Krishna Chaitanya Mahaprabhu, Srihatta (Sylhet), publication in 2009 AD.

21

Kanchanadevi

(A Woman Mad for Lord Sri Krishna)

Kanchana was one of the companions who used give their company to lone Vishnupriyadevi after Sri Gouranga Mahaprabhu quitted the home and family for taking Sannyas. At that time Vishnupriyadevi used to prefer inside a room only to remember silently Sri Gouranga Mahaprabhu. She used to remember Sri Gouranga Mahaprabhu and could get his company all the time. This was her only consolation.

This Kanchana could realize the aches of heart of Vishnupriyadevi. She engaged herself to look after all the needs of Vishnupriyadevi. Kanchana was also mad for Lord Sri Krishna. She was in the shelter of Narahari Sarkar and so she was sent to Nabadwip to serve Vishnupriyadevi by Narahari Sarkar.

Kanchana Karaye Vishnupriyar Sevan.
Sarbashrestha Dasi Madhye Tahar Gaman.

And

Tare Kripa Kari Pathaila Nabadwipe.
Vishnupriyadevir Seva Karila Smipe.[1]

This Kanchana had shown freedom and courage to wake up Vishnupriyadevi while she was in deep meditation and newlywed Sri Nityanada Prabhu arrived with his wives Basudha and Janhaba at the house of Sachimaa and Vishnupriyadevi. She received the two wives cordially. She embraced them and also kissed the newly married Basudha and Janhaba. Here Kanchana had done a lot because after a long absence of husband Sri Gouranga Mahaprabhu she could get the pleasure to see newlywed Basudha and Janhaba. She had no other way to get pleasure for the last long period. Although Kanchana broke the meditation but she could bring some happiness to Vishnupriyadevi to have Basudha and Janhaba as her sisters.[2]

In the pleasant situation Vishnupriyadevi for some time forgot the sorrows of Mahaprabhu's separation and for this favorable situation caused by Kanchana is always praiseworthy.

Sri Balaramdas wrote about the 'Mad for Sri Krishna' Kanchanadevi:-

> *"Gouranga Bhabane Sada Tobo Abasthan.*
> *Tomar Prasade Pai Goura Bhagawan."*[2]

It is also our prayer to Lord Sri Chaitanyadeva our lovely Sri Gouranga Mahaprabhu.

References

1. Sri Sri Gour Bhaktamrita Lahari (1st, 2nd & 3rd Parts) – Ed. & Pub. By Sri Kishoridas Babaji, printed at Sri Prankrishna Bhakti Press, Chaitanyadoba, in 1411 BS, p. 120.
2. Sri Sri Nityananda Shakti Maa Janhaba – Nemaichand Goswami, Pub. By Sri Sanatan Goswami, Printer – Shyamasundar Press, 1st Pub 1389 BS, 2nd Pub 1401 BS, p. 116.

22

Kalindidevi

(Mother of Dhananjay Pundit)

Dhananjay Pundit was one of the twelve Gopals who took the responsibilities of spreading Harinaam under the supervision of Sri Nityananda Prabhu. Kalindidevi was the mother of Dhananjay Pundit. She used to worship Sri Radhakrishna all the time.

The husband of Kalindidevi Sripati Bandyopadhaya was a rich person in the district of Chittagong (now in Bangladesh) at Jargram. In 1484 AD (891 BS, 1404 Shaka) in the month of Chaitra Shukla Panchami Dhananjay Pundit was born.

In earlier birth in Vrindaban Lila Dhananjay Pundit was Basudam Sakha. We can recollect as under:-

"Basudeva Priya Sakh: Dhananjay Punditah".[1]

"*Basudam Naam Hobe Punditah Dhananjay".*[2]

"Jar Grame Janmabhumi Jalandite Baas
Basudam DhananjayJaniba Nirjyas".[3]

"Sanchra Panchra Karanda Shital Gram.
Dhananjay Punditer Seva Anek Bidhan"[4]

"*Pundit Dhananjaya Karila Bandana.*

Prasiddha Boiragya Jar Sansare Ghoshna.
……Bhanda Hate Kari Gela Koupin Pariya".[5]

About Dhananjay Pundit above information do not differ in the Sri Sri Goudiya Vaishnava Abhidhaan – Edited by Sri Haridas Das Babaji.

However the information in 'Sri Gouranga Madhuri' differ and states that near Bolpur at Siyan Village Dhananjay Pundit was born and father was Sri Adideva Bachaspati and mother was Srimati Dayamoyee Devi. (May be another Dhananjay Pundit).

From the very beginning in the childhood Dhananjay Pundit used to bow his head thrice a day by lying with all his body to Tulsi. His parents could sense that their son would be Sannyasi in near future. So, Kalindidevi and Sripati Bandyopadhaya arranged their son's marriage with a beautiful girl Sri Haripriya by name. Dhananjay Pundit to show his parents acted as he was enjoying the normal conjugal live. His heart was always filled with the glory of Sri Krishna. He used to think of Lord Sri Krishna. He had no attraction in family life.

Some of the people wicked and robbers having noticed his sacrifice gave in to him and became devotees of Sri Krishna.

Kalindidevi's son Dhananjay Pundit at last at the demises of Kalindidevi and Sripati Bandyopadhaya left everything behind and arrived at Nabadwip.

There he met Sri Gouranga Mahaprabhu and returned to Sanchra Panchra Karanda Shital Gram on way to Vrindaban. There signs of Dhananjay Pundit are still kept in respect in his memory at the places at Sanchra Panchra Karanda Shital Gram etc.

Reference

1. Sri Dhananjay Gopal Charit O Sri Sri Shyama Chandrodaya – Ed. & Pub. by Sri Kishoridas Babaji, printed at Sri Prankrishna Bhakti Press, Chaitanyadoba, in 1416 BS, p. 6 Source Ananta Samhita in 1411 BS, p. 120.
2. *Ibid* in Sri Sri Gour Bhaktamrita Lahari.
3. *Ibid* – Source: Sri Chaitanya Ganoddesh, Krishnadas Kaviraj)
4. *Ibid* – Source: Sri Pat Nirnoy by Sri Ramgopal Das.
5. *Ibid.*

23

Kripamoyee

(Mother of Balarama)

Kripamoyee Devi was the mother of Vaishnava Balaramdas Madhabi a follower of and blessed by Sri Nityananda Prabhu. Her husband Sriham Tarafadar was a zaminder of Kamsyatpur only 5 KMs away from Ranaghat.

Balaramdas Madhabi was born in the beginning of 15th century AD. Balaramdas Madhabi was taught Persian language from Mukhi Qutub Khan of Billwa Garh and ultimately was recommended for the chief writer in the Army of Sultan Hussein Shah of Goud. He was awarded a village named Chhutipur near Ranaghat and the title of Khan.

Balaramdas Madhabi was a quality writer too and he wrote 'Patit Pabanavatara'.

Kripamoyee Devi the mother of Vaishnava Balaramdas Madhabi deserves thanks from the Vaishnavas.[1]

Reference

1. Sri Sri Goudiya Vaishnava Abhidhaan – Edited by Sri Haridas Das Babaji, 2nd, 3rd, and 4th Parts, 2nd Edition, 501 Chaitanyabda, Publisher – Haribol Kutir Poraghat, Nabadwip, Printer – Radha Press, Delhi 110031, p. 1295).

24

Khersuti

(Grandmother of Shankardeva of Assam)

The Grandmother Khersuti of Shankardeva was known by many of Assam and also in other States. Her father-in-law's house was at Alipukhari village on the south bank of the river Brahmaputra. They were from Shiromani Bhuniya generation. They were influential and so had the facility of enjoying all comforts. The title of them was 'Bar'. One Debidas of their generation used to worship Kali and the family was as 'Shakta'. And for a long time the 'Bar's were Shaktas.

One son of Khersuti, Kusum Baro married in 1448 AD and a son of them Shankardeva was born in 1949 AD.

In Assam then there were anti-social and anti-religious functions like killing of beasts even human beings in the name of mother Shakti as sacrifice. Slaughters in the name of sacrifice to gods and goddesses were in vogue there.

Suhung Mang was an influential King of Ahom (Assam) was successful in driving out all the anti-social and anti-religious inhumane activities.

In the period of the King Mang, Shankardeva started to propagate Vaishnavism and as a result an upsurge in social and cultural atmosphere was possible.

At the Shankardeva's birth his mother suddenly succumbed and all the responsibilities of the child to bring him up were to bear by his grandmother Khersuti Devi. Her son, the father of Shankardeva was also careful to abide by the advices of mother Khersuti who was a pure heart and also devotee of Lord Sri Krishna. They were nicely an educated family too.

Shankardeva believed in 'one nation one life'. He was successful in influencing on all the people of Assam who were theistic or atheist, the leaders of the mutts or family men. Almost all kinds of men and women had much respect to him for his mission to eliminate all ills from the society and to establish unity among the people of Assam. He travelled Gaya, Puri, Kashi-Prayag, Sitakund, Brahakund, Ayodhya, Vrindaban-Mathura, Dwarka, Badarinarayana Ashram etc.

He at his father's house at Baradoba Village introduced the first 'Satra' in order to deliver rice, clothes etc to the hungry unfed people and paupers. This humane charitable work could easily attract enthusiasm to all the people.

In the 'Naamghar's located at different lonely places which were regarded as social and religious assemblage places and even the meeting places of Gram Panchayets were being used for reading, narrating and discussing on the Ramayana, the Srimadvagawata and other religious matters. Shankardeva established 'Satra' and 'Naamghar' what are still to remember.[1]

Grandmother Khersuti of Shankardeva always also deserves to be remembered.

Reference

1. **Bharater Vaishnava Padaboli** – by Dr. Sati Ghose, Publsher: Paschimbanga Rajya Pustak Parshad, July, 1984, Printer: Impression, Kolkata – 6, p. 113-124).

25

Gangadevi

(Mother of Pundarik Vidyanidhi)

Mother of Pundarik Vidyanidhi was Srimati Gangadevi. She was wife of Baneswar Brahmachari a Zaminder of Chakrashala of Chittagong district. Her son Pundarik was a sincere Vaishnava and used to become mad whenever he heard the name of Sri Krishna. He was a Barendra Brahmin.

Sri Gouranga Mahaprabhu used call him 'Premnidhi' and sometime '***Pundarik baap aamaar***'. He was the Preceptor of Gadadhar Pundit. He was also a friend of Swarup Damodar. To discuss the glory of Pundarik Vidyanidhi a separate article would be required.

Srimati Gangadevi's husband was Sri Baneswar Brahmachari, a Zaminder of Chakrashala. His name was found in the 'Touji' bearing the number 17697 in the Collectorate of Chittagong and his son's name as Pundarik was also available in the 'Touji' bearing the numbers 17781 and 26837in the same Collectorate.

The wife of Sri Pundarik Vidyanidhi was Ratnabati and the mother's name of Sri Gadadhar Pundit was also Ratnabati. The both ladies were friends as 'Ganga Sakhi'. Moreover the father of Sri Gadadhar Pundit Sri Madhab Mishra and Sri Pundarik Vidyanidhi were also friends and both of them were disciples of Sripad Madhabendra Puri.

Srimati Gangadevi would be remembered for her son Sri Pundarik Vidyanidhi's glory forever in India.[1]

Reference

1. Sri Sri Goudiya Vaishnava Abhidhaan – Edited by Sri Haridas Das Babaji, 2nd, 3rd, and 4th Parts, 2nd Edition, 501 Chaitanyabda, Publisher – Haribol Kutir Poraghat, Nabadwip, Printer – Radha Press, Delhi 110031, p. 1196, 1283, 1930).

26

Goyeedevi

(Mother of Narahari Sarkar)

Narahari Sarkar was one of the friends of Sri Gouranga Mahaprabhu. His mother was Goyeedevi and father was Sri Narayan Sarkar or Narayan Dev. Goyeedevi was also called Gouridevi. She was a woman of devotion. Sincerely she used to worship their Sri Gopinathji regularly and to look after her three sons carefully. Sri Bhaktiratnakar states:-

"Bhagyamanta Narayana Daser Nandan.
Mukunda, Madhab, Narahari – Tinjan".[1]

It has been ascertained that Goyeedevi's father was Murari Sen. Narahari was born in 1401 or 1402 Shaka (1480 AD). However, the three brothers used to prepare themselves with the Shastras in Sanskrit.

At the demise of Sri Narayan Sarkar or Naranarayan Dev Goyeedevi with the three sons changed their residence from Sri Khanda to Nabadwip and the eldest Mukunda took the responsibility of education of the two brothers there.

But Mukunda had to leave Nabadwip as he was eagerly called to work in the court of Goud. He was a physician of repute and so the then Badshah appointed him as house physician and for giving necessary advices, as and when would require. Within a short period by seeing peacock's feather felt Lord Sri Krishna who used to wear peacock's feather on his head and fainted.

On the other hand Narahari also became an expert scholar. He used to write Padaboli on Lord Sri Krishna and Lord Sri Chaitanyadeva.[2]

Sri Narahari Sarkar and Sri Gadadhar Pundit, both of them were Brahmachari, used to remain at the left of Sri Gouranga Mahaprabhu to serve at the needs immediately. Sri Narahari Sarkar preferred to fan

Sri Gouranga Mahaprabhu or Lord Sri Chaitanyadeva with the fan made of yak's tail.[3]

Goyeedevi's sons and their generations used to carry the thoughts of Lord Sri Chaitanyadeva all along. Like her they always tried to develop the women of the country in different spheres.

References

1. Sri Sri Goudiya Vaishnava Abhidhaan – Edited by Sri Haridas Das Babaji, 2nd, 3rd, and 4th Parts, 2nd Edition, 501 Chaitanyabda, Publisher – Haribol Kutir Poraghat, Nabadwip, Printer – Radha Press, Delhi 110031, p. 56, 126).
2. *Ibid*, p. 1267.
3. *Ibid*, p. 1267.

27

Gouridevi

(Mother of Haridas Thakur)

Haridas Thakur widely known as Yaban Haridas was born in the month of 'Agrahayan' in 1371 Shaka (in November-December 1449 AD) at Burhan village under Saatkshira Sub-division of Jessore (Khulna) district (now in Bangladesh). Names of his father and mother were (Dwija) Sumati Thakur and Gouri Devi respectively.

There is another opinion was that at Kalagachhi village under Burhan Pargana Yaban Haridas was born and his mother was Ujjwala Devi and father was Manohar Chakraborty.

At Burhan the sign of the residence of the parents of Yaban Haridas and his birth place is still traceable.[1]

Just at the age of six of Haridas father Sumati Thakur expired in 1455 AD. So, giving up all the hopes to look after the son and to bring him up Gouri Devi decided to accept the brutal system of burning herself at the funeral pyre of her husband's dead body.

"It is true that Sri Chaitanyadev (1486-1533) raised protest against similar village politics, tortures, oppressions, caste system etc. …." He and Raja Rammohan Roy (22nd May 1972 – 27th September 1833 AD) had "the belief that religious scriptures cannot provide such brutal inhuman rites".[2]

Gouri Devi mother of Haridas could not find any way to live with dignity and to bring up the child of six years' old burnt herself at the funeral pyre of her husband's dead body. Perhaps she depended on God to see her child in future.

As a result Haridas wandered at the doors to doors of the villagers and at last he got shelter to a kind heart Muslim person.

This person was Kari Habibullah of Hakimpur. He took all the responsibilities to look after him. Yaban Haridas being helpless and finding no doors open for him at last reached beyond the river Swarna or Salai 8-9 Kms away Halimpur and there he got shelter at the house of Khan Saheb as a son of the family. Haridas a son of Hindu Brahmin family thus was being looked after by a Muslim family. So, he was considered a Muslim or Yaban.[3]

However, from the very beginning in the childhood Haridas used to remember Lord Vishnu he learnt from his parents and in earlier life. He was initiated in Harinaam Mahamantra from Sri Adwait Prabhu. He was also loved by Sri Gouranga Mahaprabhu and other Vaishnava associates. (The divine life of Haridas would be discussed in separate article.)

Haridas was also considered as Brohma Haridas. His mother Gouri Devi should be remembered for ever.

References

1. Sri Sri Goudiya Vaishnava Abhidhaan – Edited by Sri Haridas Das Babaji, 2nd, 3rd, and 4th Parts, 2nd Edition, 501 Chaitanyabda, Publisher – Haribol Kutir Poraghat, Nabadwip, Printer – Radha Press, Delhi 110031, p. 1957.
2. Ref. Man Beyond the Time – Raja Rammohan Roy – by Radhakrishna Goswami (Radhu Goswami), Published by Raja Bhanja Chowdhury, Mainstream Publication, 1st pub in Kolkata Book Fair, 2013, p. 37).
3. Sri Sri Goudiya Vaishnava Abhidhaan – Edited by Sri Haridas Das Babaji, 2nd, 3rd, and 4th Parts, 2nd Edition, 501 Chaitanyabda, Publisher – Haribol Kutir Poraghat, Nabadwip, Printer – Radha Press, Delhi 110031, p. 1957).

28

Chandrakala

(Wife of Raja Pratap Rudra)

Srimati Chandrakaladevi the wife of Raja Pratap Rudra was also a follower of Sri Chaitanya Mahaprabhu.[1]

Raja Pratap Rudra of Odisha had four queens. They were Bhanumati, Vidyutkanti, Gouri and Chandrakala. Chandrakaladevi was the main queen and she welcomed Sri Chaitanya Mahaprabhu and Sri Nityananda Prabhu cordially. Sri Chaitanya Mahaprabhu was so pleased to see 'Bhakti' in Srimati Chandrakaladevi that He presented her the divine garland.

Jayanada commented as:-

"Rajar Shatek Stri Pradhan Chandrakala.
Gourchandra Dilo Tare Galar Divya Mala".[2]

Originally Raja Pratap Rudra of Odisha was the main Sevak of Lord Jagannath Mahaprabhu at the temple of Puri. He had attention in other religious rites and social services. But after the arrival of Sri Chaitanyadev in Puri he heard much of him from his men like Sarbabhoum Bhattacharya the King became mad and was eager to meet Sri Chaitanyadev.

On the other hand Sri Chaitanyadeva did not prefer to allow King and other men who were engaged in trade, politics etc. However, Sarbabhoum Bhattacharya assured the King that he would find a scope to arrange the meeting with Sri Chaitanyadeva. But Raja Pratap Rudra was becoming restless to meet Sri Chaitanyadeva.

We can peruse into some portion of the drama written by Sripad Haridas Goswami 'Maharaj Gajapati Pratap Rudra':-

One of the attendants Sakhi Shashikala seeing the queen dried and morose asked her what was the reason behind. Chandrakala replied to Sakhi

Shashikala that Raja Pratap Rudra is restless when he has heard about the Sannyasi named Sri Krishna Chaitanya. The King has given his mind, body and life too to Sri Krishna Chaitanya. Chandrakala knew that for the last three months the King left all the royal activities and came to Neelachal only to have a 'Darshan' of Sri Krishna Chaitanya.

Chandrakala the queen also informed her that Sri Krishna Chaitanya that Raja Pratap Rudra becomes childish in discussing the qualities, complexion and beauty of Sri Krishna Chaitanya. He cries and his body is drenched with tears in eagerness of meeting Sri Krishna Chaitanya.

Chandrakala the queen also becomes possessed in stating the condition of King Pratap Rudra. She said – *"Shuni MukheTar Apurba Sri Krishna Chaitanya Gunakatha, Aar Tnar Aparup Ruper Barnan".*[3]

On the other hand Sakhi Shashikala was fortunate that she had a scope to see Sri Krishna Chaitanya and informed Chandrakala the queen that –

"Sri Krishna Chaitanya Prabhu Advut Sannyasi.
Aparup Rup Tnar – Aparup Bhav.
Manusher Eto Rup Hoy,
Janita Na Keha".

Shashikala added –

"Darshnanande Abishranta Premdhara
Bahitechhe Nayana Yugale Tnar ...
Ajanulambita Subolita Duti Baahu
Tuli Urddhadeshe, -"

Sakhi Shashikala then expressed her feeling

"Achal Jagannath Moder
Hoye Sachal Bhabe – Jibera Uddhar Hetu
Bhramichhen Dhara Dhamey".

Chandrakala the queen knew that Sarbabhoum Bhattacharya and other associates were trying to organize the meeting of King Pratap Rudra.

The second Shakhi Indurekha also informed Chandrakala the queen that the women of Goud Bengal, especially of Nabadwip had come to Neelachal with their husbands.

Chandrakala requested her to take her to the fortunate ladies of Nabadwip. She wants to cry to them begging to allow her husband to have a 'Darshan' of Mahaprabhu Sri Chaitanyadeva.

Chandrakala also requested her to show Sri Krishna Chaitanya Mahaprabhu when He would go to Sri Sri Jagannath Temple on foot. She also wants to have a 'Darshan' of Sri Krishna Chaitanya Mahaprabhu.

She repeats:-

"Dur Hate Karajore.
Jachibo Kripa Viksha Tnar, Maharajer Tare.
Dur Hate Karibo Aatmanibedana
Tnar Ratul Charane;
Sakhi! Iha Bina Abalar Ki Aache Upaya".

Chandrakala the Queen expressed herself as a maid servant to the King Pratap Rudra. She was a sincere chaste woman.

King Pratap Rudra was a rare type of King who could give up his thrown to have 'Darshan' of Sri Krishna Chaitanya Mahaprabhu. He told her:-

"Priyatame Chandrakala!
Bolechhi Tomake Mon Khule Monobyatha Mor,
Sri Krishna Chaitanya Prabhu Darshana Tare
Mon Mor Barai Chanchal;
Pran Mor Bisham Asthir;
Dehe Mor Nahi Bol, Abasanna Chit;
Sukh Nai Bindumatra Hridayae Aamar;
Sri Krishna Chaitanya Prabhur Kripalaav
Mor Pakshe Barai Durghat".

The eagerness to meet Sri Krishna Chaitanya Mahaprabhu King Pratap Rudra had cannot be explained easily. The King became so restless that every material thing was watery in taste. He was so sad.

In the Drama King Pratap Rudra's the eagerness to meet Sri Krishna Chaitanya Mahaprabhu and also the glory of the fortunate ladies of Nabadwip and their compassion to his wife Chandrakala the Queen were expressed elaborately.

As a dignified woman Chandrakala the Queen did not bother about her rank but to seek the divne feet of Lord Sri Krishna Chaitanya Mahaprabhu for her husband King Pratap Rudra. She was a perfectly chaste wife and so our sincere respect would be to her forever.

References

1. Sri Sri Goudiya Vaishnava Abhidhaan – Edited by Sri Haridas Das Babaji, 2nd, 3rd, and 4th Parts, 2nd Edition, 501 Chaitanyabda, Publisher – Haribol Kutir Poraghat, Nabadwip, Printer – Radha Press, Delhi 110031, p.1267).

2. Sri Chaitanyamongal – by Sri Jayananda, ed.by Bimanbehari Mahumdar & Sukhomoy Mukhopadhyay, pub. by Asiatic Society, prin. by National Printing Works, Utkal Khanda, Shloka 14, p.153).
3. All othrs in) Maharaj Ganapati Pratap Rudra (Drama) –by Sripad Haridas Goswami. Pub by Sri Ramnivas Dhandariya, Aryabarta Prakashan Griha, printed by Sri Shyamasundar Goswami, Shyamsundar Press, Kolkata-5, pub on 4/6/ 1964.

29

Chitralekha

(Sakhi of Lakshmipriya)

The name of the first wife of Sri Gouranga Mahaprabhu was Lakshmipriya Devi. She had a bosom friend 'Shakhi' whose name was Chitralekha. She was a daughter of a wealthy family. She was wise and some senior to her 'Shakhi' Lakshmipriya Devi also. She used to call as 'Pundit Thakur'.

Lakshmipriya Devi used to share on various feelings with Chitralekha and vice versa. The temporary separation with the busy in studying Sri Gouranga Mahaprabhu would pain her minds. She would get peace after discussing with her Shakhi Chitralekha.

Lakshmipriya Devi used to talk generally on the glory of Sri Gouranga Mahaprabhu all the time. She used to narrate that she was fortunate to get husband like a precious gem. It was for vertues earned for the last several births.

One day Chitralekha found the pale face of and asked Lakshmipriya the reason of her discontentment. She was informed that her Pundit Thakur Sri Gouranga Mahaprabhu would go to East Bengal for a few months to earn money from teaching to students in that area. When Pundit Thakur would return Nabadwip was not scheduled.

On hearing the probability of Mahaprabhu's departure from Nabadwip to East Bengal Chitralekha also became sad and tried to convince her father to give all the wealth to Pundit Thakur so that he need not go outside Nabadwip to earn money. The precious personality Sri Gouranga Mahaprabhu should not leave behind Lakshmipriya and other thousands of people of Nabadwip. Her father assured to give all wealth to Sri Gouranga Mahaprabhu. He should see the fate of his daughter's friend Lakshmipriya Devi and the people of Nabadwip. Thus the journey towards East Bengal by Sri Gouranga Mahaprabhu leaving Lakshmipriya and others could be stopped. She tried to console Lakshmipriya Devi and told her – Please do not cry, my friend".[1]

Jayananda also confirmed the need for income by Sri Gouranga Mahaprabhu and so he wrote:-

"Artha Uparjan Bine Sansar Na Chale.
Bangadeshe Jai Aami Arthera Chhale".[2]

But Lakshmipriya Devi told – Like me an unfortunate woman has become highly fortunate that I have got the husband-wealth Nemai Pundit, I do not bother any other wealth that would be too ordinary to me."

Having heard this firmness Chitralekha with folded hands replied – To me the happiness is only to serve my Pundit Thakura. Without this my death is inevitable".

Lakshmipriya Devi consoled her Sakhi by saying – Do not worry my Shakhi, after a few days only he would return." But she herself commented at the departure of her husband's journey for unlimited time would be untolerable and she would die.

Chitralekha could understand the situation so, she said to her – Make haste Lakshmipriya, it is time for returning of Pundit Thakura. Be ready to greet him".

Lakshmipriya regained the reality and went to the room for worship. Seeing her out of her room Sachimaa indicated her to arrange to greet God as returning time of Sri Gouranga Mahaprabhu was approaching.

On that very evening Sri Gouranga, Sri Gadadhar and other associates came back as usual from the bank of the Ganga. Sri Gouranga started to greet with lamps etc. to the deity of God and offered Bhog to God. Afterwards all of them including Chitralekha Shakhi took the 'Prasad' with respect.

While Sri Gouranga Mahaprabhu travelled in East Bengal there remained back Sachimaa and Lakshmipriya Devi in Nabadwip.

Chitralekha Shakhi also remained with Lakshmipriya Devi all along. She talked with her only on Sri Gouranga Mahaprabhu. The two Sakhis exchanged their opinions to each other.

Sri Gouranga Mahaprabhu went to the river Padma and travelled on the both sides of the river. The river Padmabati also seemed to be happy to see Mahaprabhu. Sri Vrindabandas commented:-

"Padmabati Dekhi Prabhu Parama Harishe.
Se Sthane Rahilen Tnar Vagybashe".[3]

There at Panchasar in Dhaka Vikrampore he opened Education centre 'Tole'. Dhaka Vikrampore was a place of Pundits as mentioned in the book by Ananda Baruri:-

"Vidwajjananang Basascha Vikrampurjyancha Bhurima:"[4]

During this period Lakshmipriya Devi had interest in talking only on Mahaprabhu and so Shakhi Chitralekha did the same by discussing on Pundit Thakur. Chitralekha Shakhi used come to Lakshmipriya Devi almost every day. Sometime Chitralekha used to stay at the room of Mahaprabhu with Lakshmipriya Devi.

Here we can mention that in absence of Lakshmipriya Devi another person of Panchatattwa Sri Gadadhar Pundit had only the permission to stay inside the room with Sri Gouranga Mahaprabhu. He was like a shadow of Sri Gouranga Mahaprabhu. He knew only to serve Mahaprabhu for His happiness like Srimati Radharani of Vrindaban as '*Sri Krishna Sukhoika Tatparya*'.

Here we can aslo mention that Sri Gouranga Mahaprabhu sometime used to go at different places Lakshmipriya Devi generally used to go to her parents' house. But on this occasion Sri Gouranga handed over his sacred thread to Lakshmipriya and Mahaprabhu advised her not to go parents' house but to look after her mother-in-law Sachidevi and so Lakshmipriya Devi did so. Chitralekha remained with Lakshmipriya all the time. Both of them were estranged from Sri Gouranga Mahaprabhu.

Even after the sudden death of Lakshmipriya Devi Chitralekha Shakhi used come to the house of Sachidevi in order to look after her.

References

1. Sri Sri Lakshmipriya - Charit – by Sri Sripad Haridas Goswami. Pub by Sri Haridas Goswami, Bhopal, Printer – Sri Gouranga Press, 429 Gourabda, 8th Chapter p. 160 -162).
2. Sri Chaitanya Mongal – by Sri Jayananda Ed. By Bimanbehari Majumdar & Sukhamoy Mukhopadhyay, Pub by Asiatic Society, Print by National Printing Works, 1st publication 1971, Nadia Khanda, Sl. No.56, Shloka 10, p.65-66).
3. Sri Chaitanya Bhagawata – by Sri Vrindabandas, Adi Lila, 12th Chapter, Reflect Publication.
4. Digbijoy Prakash (Prachin Sangraha) – Aamar Vikrampore – by Hari Ananda Baruri, Gyan Publishers, Delhi).

30

Jangali (Jungali) Dasi

(Maid Servant of Sita Devi wife of Adwait Prabhu)

In this 21st modern century we find some people deliberately prefer to become female by changing their sex. More than a half millennium back we find such people like as Jangali, a maid servant of Sita Devi, one of the wives of Sri Adwaita Prabhu.

It was not confirmed by the officials of the then administration whether Jangali was male or female. However Sri Sukumar Sen commented Jangali was initiated from Sitadevi and was a eunuch.[1]

Jangali was disciple and also at service to Sitadevi.[2]

Sri Bimanbehari Majumdar commented – Male disciple of Sitadevi was Jangali. His original name was Jajneshwar. He was born in Hariharpur near Shantipur.

It was a question that whether Jangali was a male or female. Jungali could show the feature as female and as well as of a male. Jungali told the ruler of Goud when he approached:-

".... Jungali Bole Nari Aami, Na Hoi Purush.
Nari Jane Nari Dekhe Purushe Purush......
Sajjane Aamare Dekhe Nari Sarbakshan.
Maa Maa Boliya Kare Samvashan".[3]

The ruler after physical verification by male and female servants was so surprised and pleased to Jungali that he made a big palace for Jungali and it was called as 'Jungalitota'. It was situated near Maldaha.

About Jungali many investigations and researches have been done. Sri Sundarananda Vidybinode of 'Gaudiya' Patrika referred the name of Nandini (that also reminds us the name Jungali) when he wrote about 'Sri Nandini

Mutt' in Puri. He also accepted a reference in the matter from 'Purnia Report' (1809-10) that:-

"In the territory of Gour(d), at a place called 'Jungalitota' is the chief seat of the 'Sakhibhav Vaishnavas' who dress like girls and act as religious guides for some of the impure tribes. The order is said to have been established by Sita Thakurani, wife of Advaita; but so far as I can learn, has not spread to any distance, not any considerable number of people. The two first persons who assumed the Sakhibhav were Jungali, a Brahmin and Nandini, a kayastha. Jungali was never married and it only his pupils that remain in this district, and these are all Vaishnavas who reject marriage."[4]

Jungali's one of the disciples Haripriya's name also available. This Haripriya original named Nandaram has written 'Sri Krishna Mishra Charitra'. Haripriya or Nandaram was also a person who used to serve Sita Devi.[5]

References

1. Bangala Sahityer Itihas – by Sri Sukumar Sen, 1st Part, 1st Publication 1940, 6th Edition, Published by Ananda Publishers Private Limited, Printer – Swapna Printing Works, Kolkata -9, p. 305.
2. Sri Sri Goudiya Vaishnava Abhidhaan – Edited by Sri Haridas Das Babaji, 2nd, 3rd, and 4th Parts, 2nd Edition, 501 Chaitanyabda, Publisher – Haribol Kutir Poraghat, Nabadwip, Printer – Radha Press, Delhi 110031, p. 1243.
3. Prem Vilas – by Nityananda Das, Revised and edited by Dr. Bijon Goswami, Pub, in 1405 BS, 1999 AD, 1st Mahesh Edition, Printed at Printing Publicity, 24 Vilas, p. 234.
4. Shikshetra - Sundarananda Vidyabinode of 'Gaudiya' Patrika.
5. Sri Sri Goudiya Vaishnava Abhidhaan – Edited by Sri Haridas Das Babaji, 2nd, 3rd, and 4th Parts, 2nd Edition, 501 Chaitanyabda, Publisher – Haribol Kutir Poraghat, Nabadwip, Printer – Radha Press, Delhi 110031, p. 1243, 1264).

31

Jai Durga Devi

(Foster-mother of Madhabacharya)

Madhabacharya was the husband of Srimati Ganga Devi, daughter of Sri Nityananda Prabhu.

Jai Durga Devi brought up Madhabacharya. She was one of the wives of Bhagirath, a Brahmin, Kashyap Gotra, Chatta Gaain and Rarhi branch. Her husband Bhagirath was also a good and renowned scholar. Jai Durga Devi had already two sons Sri Nath and Sri Pati.[1]

He used to live near Katowa at Nanyapur village with his family. Jai Durga Devi had a friendship 'Sai' with Mahalakshmi Devi, wife of Bishweswar Acharya. Both Bishweswar Acharya and Bhagirath Acharya were also intimate friends.

Jai Durga Devi was present at the sudden death of Mahalakshmi Devi. So, Jai Durga Devi was shocked to see 'Sai's demise. On the other hand Mahalakshmi Devi before her death expressed that responsibility of looking after her only son would be borne by Jai Durga Devi. But Mahalakshmi Devi understood that with mother's irresistible death her son like Madhab would become almost helpless. So, she requested Jai Durga to take the son and to bring him up as another son with her two sons.

Jai Durga Devi then started to bring up three sons Sri Nath, Sri Pati and Madhab carefully.[2]

We know that without proper nourishment a small plant cannot get maturity and becomes unable to give fruits. Likewise without the necessary care and nourishment no possibility, no talent can mature. Jai Durga Devi and Sri Bhagirath both were equal careful and gave equal love to the three sons to grow.

Ultimately, Madhab became a scholar in scriptures and also an expert in playing musical instruments with vocal songs.

The Vaishnava women like Jai Durga Devi believed good relation with each other and thus they tried their best to fulfill the idealism of Sri Gouranga Mahaprabhu and also of Sri Nityananda Prabhu.

The life of Jai Durga Devi may also be compared with Maa Jashoda as she brought up Balak Krishna Lord Gopal.

References

1. Sri Sri Nityananda Shakti Maa Janhaba –Sri Nemaichand Goswami, Pub. By Sri Sanatan Goswami, Printer – Shyamasundar Press, 1st Pub 1389 BS, 2nd Pub 1401 BS, p. 152).
2. *Ibid*, p. 153.

32

Janhabi Devi

(Mother of Pundit Kashinath or Kashiswar)

One of the followers of Sri Chaitanyadeva was Pundit Kashinath or Kashiswar.We find in 'Pat Paryatan':-

> *"Chatra Ballavpure Seva Anupam,*
> *Bhaktagan Je Je Chhila Kahi Tar Naam.*
> *Kashiswar, Shankaranya, SriNath Aar,*
> *Sri Rudra Pundit Adi Baas Sabakar".*[1]

Janhabi Devi was mother of Pundit Kashinath or Kashiswar. Her husband was Basudeva Bhattacharya of Brhamandanga village in Jessore District. They were generations of Kanjilal Kanu of Batsya Gotra.

Janhabi Devi had two sons and one daughter. Her elder son Mahadeva was a pious person and her youngest son Kashinath or Kashiswar was attracted from beginning to Lord Sri Chaitanyadeva. He was born in 1420 Shaka (1498 AD) and learnt much of religion and other educative subjects. Suddenly at his seventeen in 1437 Shaka (1515 AD) he went to Puri and took shelter at the feet of Sri Chaitanyadeva. Afterwards in 1454 Shaka (1532 AD) he returned home at the repeated requests of Janhabi Devi but he did not marry and remained a bachelor follower of Lord Sri Chaitanyadeva. Pundit Kashinath or Kashiswar started to worship Sri Nityananda Prabhu and Sri Gouranga Mahaprabhu at Chatra. Including Janahabi Devi all other members of the family also joined him in the village.

Janhabi Devi had the preference of worshipping God at home not by taking Sannyas. Her son Pundit Kashinath or Kashiswar could escalate the village Chatra to a famous Goudiya Vaishnava Place.

Janhabi Devi had also daughter who gave birth three sons like Ramakanta, Rudra and Lakshman. All of them were sincere followers of

Lord Sri Chaitanyadeva. Rudra Pundit was brought up at the house of Kashinath Pundit and so he became very pious.

Janhabi Devi had a grandson Murari who was son of Mahadeva, the elder son of Janhabi Devi. Kashinath Pundit had also initiated him and gave the charge of service of Lord Sri Chaitanyadeva.

Janhabi Devi expired in 1466 Shaka (1544 AD) and then her son Pundit Kashinath or Kashiswar went to Vrindaban. Afterwards he died in 1486 Shaka on the day of 'Baruni'. To keep memory of the day every year a festival is observed at Chatra Village.

References

1. Sri Sri Goudiya Vaishnava Abhidhaan – Edited by Sri Haridas Das Babaji, 2nd, 3rd, and 4th Parts, 2nd Edition, 501 Chaitanyabda, Publisher – Haribol Kutir Poraghat, Nabadwip, Printer – Radha Press, Delhi 110031, p. 1350, Source: Pat Paryatan).
2. *Ibid*, p. 1192.

33

Tara Devi

(Mother of Haribangsha)

Taradevi was the mother of Haribangsha who founded the Radhaballavi Section. Her husband was Vyas Mishra. Tara Devi's husband worked at Badagram near Mathura under the 'Badshah' of Delhi.

Tara Devi used to abide by the rules and other rituals of religion. Above all her heart was contended with the love of Lord Sri Krishna.[1]

Haribangsha was the son of Tara Devi and Vyas Mishra. He was born in 'Shukla Ekadashi' in the month of 'Baisakh'. At the age of eleven Haribangsha married Srimati Krishnadasi and Srimati Manoharadasi, the daughters of 'Dwija' Anantaram of Chattathabol village (at that time polygamy was not illegal).

Haribangsha was highly qualified scholar with more other qualities. He was one of the disciples of Sri Gopal Bhatta, one of the Six Goswami of Vrindaban.

Once Haribangsha took betel leaf 'Prasad' of Srimati Radharani and keeping it in the mouth he went to his preceptor for some reason. His preceptor Sri Gopal Bhatta rebuked him by saying " I have already warned you not to chew betel leaf on the 'Ekadsi', you have done the same?

"Sarba PaapTomare je Karila Grahan,
Pundit Hoiya Koile Ajnar Langhan.
Ei Aparadhe Tomay Karilo Barjan."[2]

Haribangsha knew to take 'Prasad' anytime is admissible. Having well aware the day was of 'Ekadasi' he did not receive any other item from the 'Bhog Thali' he took betal leaf 'Prasad' from Srimati Radharani's 'Bhog'.

He humbly replied to preceptor – it was Srimati Radharani's 'Prasad' so I could not avoid:-

"Taba Padpadme Aami Koinu Aparadh,
Langhite Narilo Sri Radha 'Prasad'."[3]

Haribangsha knew that the advice of Preceptor should always to abide and if the Preceptor scolds a disciple, the disciple should not leave the company in any manner. Rather he should stay nearer to have his mercy and granting apologies.

Haribangsha had some disciples like Narabaahan, Nabal, Chhabile, Gaaha, Naahar, Subitan and others.

Haribangsha was also a man of literature. Two of his notable writings were 'Chowrasiji' and 'Maharani'.[4]

Our respect to his mother Taradevi who gave birth to such devotee Haribangsha should be remembered ever.

References

1. Sri Sri Goudiya Vaishnava Abhidhaan – Edited by Sri Haridas Das Babaji, 2nd, 3rd, and 4th Parts, 2nd Edition, 501 Chaitanyabda, Publisher – Haribol Kutir Poraghat, Nabadwip, Printer – Radha Press, Delhi 110031, p. 1418,
2. Prem Vilas – by Nityananda Das, Revised and edited by Dr. Bijon Goswami, Pub, in 1405 BS, 1999 AD, 1st Mahesh Edition, Printed at Printing Publicity, 24 Vilas, p.162)
3. *Ibid.*
4. Sri Sri Goudiya Vaishnava Abhidhaan – Edited by Sri Haridas Das Babaji, 2nd, 3rd, and 4th Parts, 2nd Edition, 501 Chaitanyabda, Publisher – Haribol Kutir Poraghat, Nabadwip, Printer – Radha Press, Delhi 110031, p. 1418).

34

Tukka Devi

(Daughter of Raja Pratap Rudra)

During the stayal of Sri Chaitanyadeva we have heard the nobleness of Raja Pratap Rudra in different ways. The king of Odisha Raja Pratap Rudra reigned 1496/1497 – 1540 AD. His daughter was Tukka whose other names were Jagammohini and Annapurna as in Chaitanya Karcha.

Tukka Devi's mother was Gouri Devi was throne queen of Raja Pratap Rudra.[1]

The History of Odisha states that on 23rd June in 1515 AD Raja Sri Krishnadev Rao the King of Vijayanagar attacked Kondabiru state where Birbhadra, a son of Raja Pratap Rudra was ruling. Raja Sri Krishnadev Rao could acquire some portion of Odisha and arrest Birbhadra.

Raja Pratap Rudra then proposed for a treaty to Raja Sri Krishnadev Rao the King of Vijayanagar in order to free his son. Ultimately it was settled in a peculiar way. According to the Treaty settled King of Odisha Raja Pratap Rudra was bound to get his daughter Tukka or Jagammohini married to King, Sri Krishnadeva Rao the King of Vijayanagar and a big portion of land on the South side of the river Krishna as dowry.[2]

In conjugal life Tukka could not be happy. She was tortured by husband King Sri Krishnadeva Rao. But her heart was very soft. Her feeling was deep. So one day she left the palace and started to live in a lonely place at Kadamba.[3]

She used to write 'Shlokas' and made a collection of 'Slokas' titled Tukka Panchakam. Her one of the poems is available in 'Abhidhabritti-matrika' edited by Mukul Bhatta.[4]

References

1. Sri Chaitanyer Antardhan Rahasya (1st & 2nd Parts in one binding) – Sri Yudhisthir Jana (Maliburo), Pub by Shyamsundar Sahu, Moina Prakashani, 1st Pub 1985 AD, Ornamentation – Devkumar Bhattacharya, printer – New Rajlakshmi Printers, p.301,
2. Sri Sri Goudiya Vaishnava Abhidhaan – Edited by Sri Haridas Das Babaji, 2nd, 3rd, and 4th Parts, 2nd Edition, 501 Chaitanyabda, Publisher – Haribol Kutir Poraghat, Nabadwip, Printer – Radha Press, Delhi 110031, p.1242,
3. Ref. *Ibid.*
4. Sri Chaitanyer Antardhan Rahasya (1st & 2nd Parts in one binding) – Sri Yudhisthir Jana (Maliburo), Pub by Shyamsundar Sahu, Moina Prakashani, 1st Pub 1985 AD, Ornamentation – Devkumar Bhattacharya, printer – New Rajlakshmi Printers, p. 301.

35

Damayanti Devi

(Sister of Raghava Pundit)

Dayamanti Devi was a widow sister of Sri Raghab Pundit of Panihati. Both the brother and the sister were followers of Sri Gouranga Mahaprabhu. She used to prepare dried food for Sri Gouranga Mahaprabhu so that while staying away in Neelachal and maintaining the life of Sannyasi can have tastes of different items.

Kavi Karnapur stated that she was Gunamala in her earlier life in Brajalila.[1]

"Gunamala Braje Jasiddmayanti Tu Tatswasya."

Throughout the whole year Dayamanti Devi used to prepare the food which would not be rotten or decomposed. She used to let those prepared materials dry up.

The materials as we find in Sri Chaitanya Charitamrita usually were pickles of mangoes mixed with mustard and salt, of mangoes and ginger, lemon ginger, dried mangoes, dried mangoes mixed with mustard and salt, pieces of mangoes, condensed milk made sweets, tasty sweets with camphor powder, round shaped nadu, moya, of fried rice fried in ghee, nadu of coconut pastes, dried sweets made in coconut pastes and above all she used to send a few pitchers full of well filtered water of the Ganga.[2]

She used to let those prepared materials dry up.

According to Sri Chaitanya Charitamrita:-

"Aamra Kashundi, Aada Kashundi, Jhal Kashundi, nam,
Nembu Aada Aamrakoli Bibidha Bidhan. ..."[3]

According to Sri Chaitanya Charitamrita:-

> "Aamra Kashundi, Aada Kashundi, Jhal Kashundi, nam,
> Nembu Aada Aamrakoli Bibidha Bidhan. ..."[4]

Again

> *"Dhaniya Mouharir Tndul Guda Kariya,*
> *Nadu Bandhiyachhe Chini-Pak Kariya."*[5]

Dayamanti Devi of Panihati was very much conscious about the tastes of the food and also health of Mahaprabhu. She thought if Mahaprabhu would become ill who would see him at Gambhira and who would give him proper diet? For His good health she used to make dried paste of bitter vegetables (*Sukuta*) also.

All these things prepared in a whole year were given in specific pots and were poured in bigger pot or bundles with other materials separately. These were called Raghaber Jhali. The responsibilities to protect and to hand over Govinda at service of Mahaprabhu of these Jhalis were given to Sri Makardhwaj Kar of Sukhchar. These Jhalis were carried by three porters and with them Sri Makardhwaj Kar of Sukhchar and Sri Raghab Pundit of Panihati, bother of Dayamanti Devi used to accompany. Sometime Sri Nityananda Prabhu also accompanied the 'Jhalis' from Panihati to Gambhira in Puri.[6]

Like other devotees Dayamanti Devi wished to imagine the face of Mahaprabhu always pleased, satisfied and happy. It is every devotee's desire to see Sri Krishna Chaitanya Mahaprabhu fully satisfied. Dayamanti Devi is still highly praised for her dedication and so Krishnadas Kaviraj eulogized as:-

> *"...Prabhur Bhogsamagri je Kre Baramasi.*
> *Se Sob Samagri Jata Jhalite Bhariya.*
> *Raghab Laiya Jaan Gupata Kariya."*[7]

It is hearsay that, there were at least one hundred items in the Raghab's Jhalis made by Dayamanti Devi. Not only food items, but also other requisite articles to live like teeth-washing materials including sticks of 'Neem' (Margosa) and of other needs for any person for living were sent in the Jhalis. Sri Dayamanti Devi would consider Sri Krishna Chaitanya Mahaprabhu as a beloved man and Lord Sri Krishna at the same time. Her sincerety hardly can be measured in today's outlook.

References

1. Sri Sri Gour Ganoddesh Deepika – by Sri Kavi Karnapur, Edited by Sri Ashoke Kumar Bandyopadhaya, publisher- Sadeh, Printer- Orient Press, Pub in 2007 AD, Shloka -167).
2. Panihatir Danda Mahotsav – Dr Uma Bandopadhyay, Edited by Jaharlal Bandyopadhaya, Published by Esha Mukhopadhyaya, 1st edition in Baisakh 1410 BS, N.B.Publicity, Sodepur, p. 39).
3. Sri Sri Chaitanya Charitamrita– Sri Krishnadas Kaviraj, Edited by Sri Sri Madbhakti Sri Roop Maharaj, Published from Gaudiya Mission (Rgd.) by Tridandi Bhikshu Sri Bhakti Gunakar Goswami, Printer –
4. Sri Sri Chaitanya Charitamrita– Sri Krishnadas Kaviraj, Edited by Sri Sri Madbhakti Sri Roop Maharaj, Published from Gaudiya Mission (Rgd.) by Tridandi Bhikshu Sri Bhakti Gunakar Goswami).
5. *Ibid*, p. 1040.
6. Sri Sri Nityananda Shakti Maa Janhaba – Sri Nemaichand Goswami, Pub. By Sri Sanatan Goswami, Printer – Shyamasundar Press, 1st Pub 1389 BS, 2nd Pub 1401 BS, p. 50).
7. Sri Sri Chaitanya Charitamrita– Sri Krishnadas Kaviraj, Edited by Sri Sri Madbhakti Sri Roop Maharaj, Published from Gaudiya Mission (Rgd.) by Tridandi Bhikshu Sri Bhakti Gunakar Goswami, Printer – Radha Press, Gandhinagar, Delhi – 110 031, 6th Edition, Published in 1990, Adi Lila, 10th Chapter, Shloka 24-25, p. 198.

36

Dukhini Devi

(Wife of Jagadish Pundit)

In Sri Sri Gour Ganoddesha Deepika written by Kavi Karnapur we find:-

> *" Aasid Braje Chandra Haso Nttakorasakobidah,*
> *Sohayang Nrittabinodi Sri Jagadishakhya Punditah. "*[1]

In Brajalila Rasanja Nartak Chandrahas became Sri Jagadish Pundit and so he did similar activity in this life as Nartaka Binodini.

In real life the wife of Sri Jagadish Pundit was Dukhini. Her name would be remembered by all the Vaishnavas in future also.

Her husband Sri Jagadish Pundit was one of the followers of Sri Nityananda Prabhu. He was born at Goghat (now in Bangladesh). He was also born on the day of 'Vim Ekadashi'. His father was Kamalakshya Bipra and mother was Bhagyabati Devi. From the childhood he was interested in Sri Krishna and within a short period completed necessary education with Vidyanidhi Bhatta. His Sripat was at Jashora near Chakdah and established Sri Sri Jagannath there. He used to please Sri Krishna with his songs and dances and also Sri Gouranga Mahaprabhu.He also accompanied Sri Nityananda Prabhu to come back Panihati from Neelachal. He was a brilliant participant in the Samkirtan lead by Mahaprabhu.[2]

Dukhini's father Tapan Bipra had the belief that God would decide the marriage of his daughter. In the same way Kamalakshya was also keeping the belief that marriage of his son would be decided not by him but by God. Accidentally both the unfamiliar fathers met together and the marriage was settled after verifying the stars positions etc.

Ultimately Sri Jagadish Pundit and Dukhini were married and they started to live in the family of Kamalakshya and Bhagyabati Devi.[3]

After a few days, both the parents of Jagadish Pundit Kamalakshya and Bhagyabati Devi expired.Sri Jagadish Pundit with his brother Mahesh and wife Dukhini came to Nabadwip to settle nearer to the house where Sri Gouranga Mahaprabhu was born. Like the parents of Gadadhar Pundit they also preferred to look after Nemai as their own son.

On one occasion Sri Gouranga Mahaprabhu and Sri Nityananda Prabhu visited their house. Dukhini started to prepare Mahaprabhu's preferred 'Payas' (sweet rice-porridge) and thinking of Mahaprabhu deeply in heart then somehow her hand was burnt. She did not care for it though ignited her hand.

On the other hand during the discussion on Sri Krishna's love with Sri Jagadish Pundit Sri Gouranga Mahaprabhu felt some ignition sensation on his hand.

Knowing it Sri Jagadish Pundit wanted to ease but Mahaprabhu advised him to enquire at his kitchen where Dukhini was cooking 'Payas' and her hand was actually burnt. Sri Gouranga Mahaprabhu felt Dukhini Devi as mother for her glorious devotion that could be followed by the Bhaktas. He was much respectful to her and her husband Sri Jagadish Pundit.

Hearing the news of Mahaprabhu's taking Sannyas Sri Jagadish Pundit also decided to leave Nabadwip and to serve Sri Sri Jagannatha anywhere. Then he went to Puri and became busy with worshipping Sri Sri Jagannath Mahaprabhu. With the permission of Sri Sri Jagannath Mahaprabhu through main 'Purohit' he received the deity left aside 'Boikuntha Koili' at the north of the temple. He tied the deity on his back and returned Jashorah near Chakdah and set the deity of Sri Sri Jagannath Mahaprabhu there. In the temple the deities of Sri Gouranga Mahaprabhu and Sri Sri Jagannath Mahaprabhu still exist.[4]

Ananda Das, the 5th lower generation of disciple of Sri Jagadish Pundit wrote:-

"Dhanya Mor Prabhu Jagadish Gunamani,
Dhanya Dukhi Thakurani Bhuban Pabani."[5]

Details of Dukhini can be had in 'Sri Jagadish Charit' Book published in 1737 Shaka (1815 AD).

In the Vaishnava Literature Dukhini is an immortal character. We bow our heads to her in folded hands.

References

1. Sri Sri Gour Ganoddeh Deepika – by Sri Kavi Karnapur, Edited by Sri Ashoke Kumar Bandyopadhaya, publisher- Sadeh, Printer- Orient Press, Pub in 2007 AD, Shloka -143, p. 27).
2. Sri Jagadish Charitra Vijaya – Sri Ananda Das and Sri Sri Gourbhaktaamrita Lahari Ed & Pub by Sri, Kishoridas Babaji, Printer – Sri Prankrishna Bhakti Press, p. in Editorial & 4th Part 2nd Pub 1418 BS, p. 108).
3. Sri Sri Goudiya Vaishnava Abhidhaan – Edited by Sri Haridas Das Babaji, 2nd, 3rd, and 4th Parts, 2nd Edition, 501 Chaitanyabda, Publisher – Haribol Kutir Poraghat, Nabadwip, Printer – Radha Press, Delhi 110031, p. 1256).
4. Sri Jagadish Charitra Vijaya – Sri Ananda Das & Pub by Sri, Kishoridas Babaji, Printer – Sri Prankrishna Bhakti Press, in Editorial).
5. *Ibid.*

37

Nandini Dasi

(Disciple of Sita Devi)

Nandini was a disciple of Srimati Sitadevi, wife of Sri Adwait Acharya. She was a eunuch. Probably the sex of the eunuch was changed to be a woman.[1]

In earlier life in Brajalila Nandini was Jaya and Jungali was Vijaya:-

" Nandini Jungali Jeya Jaya Cha Vijaya Kramat".[2]

Respected scholar Bimanbehari Majumdar commented that, Srimati Sitadevi, wife of Sri Adwait Acharya had a male disciple named Nandaram. He used to decorate himself as woman posing as 'Shakhi' of Braja Vrindaban. It is hearsay that at regular intervals the signs of menstruation were observed in Nanadarama.[3]

In different books we find the earlier name of Nandini was Nandaram. Nandini was in the branch of Adwait Acharya. She was also a servant or maid servant of Srimati Sitadevi. Some wanted to say that Nandini was a daughter of Adwait Acharya. The Bhaktamal also confirmed that Nandini was constant company of Sitadevi. It is also known that Nandaram was a son of Kshatriya of Hariharpur near Shantipur. Later he became disciple of Sitadevi and tried to become woman and took the name as Nandini and dressed accordingly. The Mohantas of Nandini's Gadi also remain as women as Shakhi of Brajalila.[4]

Nandini used to worship Gopinath daily. One of the researchers Rebecca J. Manring commented:-

"Sita assigns Nandini the respective meditation role of Vira (Radha's girl-friend) to use in these meditation visualization. Note on practices and sends her life in the forest."

Further she recorded both on Jangali and Nandini as under:-

"These two (Jangali and Nandini) are among the first Sakhi bhava practioners. As the name implies, Sakhi bhavas adopt the mood and manners of Radha's girl-friends and often take the statement that Krishna is the only male in Vraja to its extreme conclusion. Many Gaudiyas observe the perhaps related practice of munjari sadhana, visualizing themselves as members of the inner circle of Radha's and Krishna's very young female companions (the manjari, or "unopened flower buds," that is, young adolescent women), waiting on the divine couple during their erotic encounters. The Sakhi bhavas, however, carry the imagery far beyond mere visualization, actually dressing and behaving as women throughout their lives, and same, apparently, even sacrifice their physical maleness to do so."[5]

Some people liked to say Nandini was not a woman but used to pose herself as woman and named as Nandini.[6]

At last Nandini settled in Puri and there is mutt in the name of 'Nandini Math'.[7]

References

1. Bangala Sahityer Itihas – by Sri Sukumar Sen, 1st Part, 1st Publication 1940, 6th Edition, Published by Ananda Publishers Private Limited, Printer – Swapna Printing Works, Kolkata -9, p. 305.
2. Sri Sri Gour Ganoddesh Deepika – by Sri Kavi Karnapur, Edited by Sri Ashoke Kumar Bandyopadhaya, publisher- Sadeh, Printer- Orient Press, Pub in 2007 AD, Shloka – 89).
3. Sri Chaitanya Chariter Upadan – Sri Bimanbehari Majumdar, published by Kolkata University in 1959 AD, 2nd edition, p. 459).
4. (Sri Sri Goudiya Vaishnava Abhidhaan – Edited by Sri Haridas Das Babaji, 2nd, 3rd, and 4th Parts, 2nd Edition, 501 Chaitanyabda, Publisher – Haribol Kutir Poraghat, Nabadwip, Printer – Radha Press, Delhi 110031, p. 1254).
5. Reconstructing Tradition Advaita Acarya and Gaudiya Vaisnavism at the cusp of the Twenttieth Century - Rebecca J. Manring, Columbia University Press, New York, Thesis Paper, Page – 205).
6. Chaitanya Charchar Pansho Bachhar – by Debasis Bandyopadhyay, p.96)
7. Sri Sri Goudiya Vaishnava Abhidhaan – Edited by Sri Haridas Das Babaji, 2nd, 3rd, and 4th Parts, 2nd Edition, 501 Chaitanyabda, Publisher – Haribol Kutir Poraghat, Nabadwip, Printer – Radha Press, Delhi 110031, p. 1264).

38

Wife of Narasingha Nadial

Narasingha Nadial of Shantipur was a poor Brahmin. For his poverty the Brahmin society did not show due respect to him. One day he was invited by a Brahmin but he failed to join there and arrived late so he found all other invited Brahmins have already started to eat the meal of the feast. General rule was to wait for the invited and then to start. Other well-to-do Brahmins rather taunted him. With this insulting he returned home and told his wife. She consoled and inspired him to find some way of income.

With some efforts ultimately Raja Ganesh of Srihatta (Sylhet) called him and having known the intellect of Nadial appointed as the minister in the court.

All the poverty problems thus were solved. In the background the inspiration of his wife was the most important.

Reference

Prem Vilas – by Nityananda Das, Revised and edited by Dr. Bijon Goswami, Pub, in 1405 BS, 1999 AD, 1st Mahesh Edition, Printed at Printing Publicity, 24 Vilas, p. 271).

39

Lava or Nava Devi

(Mother of Adwaita Acharya)

Lava Devi was the mother of Sri Adwait Acharya. We know well that Sri Adwait Acharya was one of the Panchatattwa and he was called ‘Nada’ and ‘Gour Aana Adwait’.

Name of father of Lava Devi was Mahananda Bipra who was one of the generations of Nrisingha Nadial of Nabagram. Name of husband of Lava Devi was Kuber Acharya who lived at Laurgram in the district of Srihatta (Sylhet).

The pedigree of Kuber Acharya was: Narayan Bhatta of Shandilya Gotra, Chaturvedi, Adi Baraha – Boiteneya – Subuddhi – Bibudhesh – Guha – Gangadhar – Suhaas – Shakuni – Aakashbani (Aakai) – Narayan Panchatapa – Agnihotri – Prithwidhar – Kulapati – Sharav Acharya – Matta Ojha (Matanga Ojha) – Jimmani (Jaimoni) – Vaskar Vaidantik from who Barendra Branch starts – Sayan Acharya – Aaro Ojha- Aaruni – Yadunath Pundit – Sri Pati – Kulapati – Ishaan – Bibhakar – Prabhakar – Narasingha Nadial – (Seven sons as Kandarpa, Saranga, Vidyadhar, Mahadeva, Narayan, Purandar and Gangadhar) – Vidyadhar’s son Chhakari – Kuber and Nilambar.

Kuber’s son was Sri Adwaita Acharya.[1]

Lava Devi gave birth to six sons and one daughter – Sri Kanta, Lakshmikanta, Hariharananda, Sadashib, Kushaldas and Kirtichandra.[2]

The name of the daughter is not known as she expired after birth.[3]

However, Lava Devi’s six sons being adult went to pilgrimage but unfortunately four sons died outside and two sons retuned home. On this incidence Nava or Lava Devi was too much shocked. These two sons as advised by their father Kuber married and entered into family life.

The researcher Rebecca J. Manring commented:-

"Four of the boys became renunciates and left home, while the others married and moved elsewhere to raise their families. Eventually Kubera and Labha, missing their children, moved to Shantipur to live out the rest of their days in prayer beside the River Ganga."[4]

Their father Kuber Acharya coming to Shantipur engaged himself in worshipping Lord Narayana. After a few months Lava Devi was again pregnant. In the meantime, Raja Divya Singha of Laud cordially called Kuber Acharya and made him as a minister in the court. He then returned to their original place Laud of Sylhet and their seventh son the youngest was born who was named as Kamalakshya. This Kamalakshya was known to us and also to the whole world as Adwait Acharya.

On this context the researcher Rebecca J. Manring commented:-

"One day while Kubera was worshipping at the river, a beautiful woman suddenly appeared before him.

He recognized her as Lakshmi, consort of Mahavishnu. She instructed him to take his wife and return home to Navagram, where her own husband would soon become their son. Kubera was not sure whether this meeting had actually occurred or simply been a dream, but he went home and told his wife the whole story. Shortly thereafter Labha did indeed conceive, and as she approached the time for delivery the couple returned to Navagram. Their son was born in the winter, on the seventh day of the moon of Markara,....the whole world was performing appropriate rituals and shouting 'Hare Krishna".[5]

Adwaita Acharya was born in 1355 Shaka (1433 AD) on the Shukla Saptami of Magha at Navagram in the Laur Pargana in the district of Srihatta (Sylhet). After a few days the child surprisingly used to take meals after offering to Lord Sri Krishna and would cry if until anybody uttered 'Hare Krishna".

Also on this context the researcher Rebecca J. Manring commented:-

"Already he (Labha's son) had marked himself as a devotee of Sri Krsna, long before Vaushnavism had gained any sort of foothold in the region".[6]

Adwait Acharya the youngest son of Lava or Nava Devi and Kuber was more than fifty two years' senior to Sri Gouranga Mahaprabhu. He was considered as an Avatara of Lord Vishnu. It is believed that Adwait prabhu was an Avatara of Mahavishnu and Sadashiva.[7]

Lava or Nava Devi was highly fortunate lady as people would call her the mother of Adwaita Acharya.

References

1. Sri Sri Adwaita Mongal – Sri Haricharandas, Pub by Kishoridas Babaji, 1st Edition, 1408 BS, Printed by Sri Sri Prankrishna Bhakti Press, Editorial, p. 3).
2. Sri Sri Goudiya Vaishnava Abhidhaan – Edited by Sri Haridas Das Babaji, 2nd, 3rd, and 4th Parts, 2nd Edition, 501 Chaitanyabda, Publisher – Haribol Kutir Poraghat, Nabadwip, Printer – Radha Press, Delhi 110031, p. 1176).
3. Prem Vilas – by Nityananda Das, Revised and edited by Dr. Bijon Goswami, Pub, in 1405 BS, 1999 AD, 1st Mahesh Edition, Printed at Printing Publicity, 24 Vilas, p. 225).
4. Reconstructing Tradition Advaita Acarya and Gaudiya Vaisnavism at the cusp of the Twenttieth Century - Rebecca J. Manring, Columbia University Press, New York, Thesis Paper, Page – 48).
5. *Ibid*, p. 48-49.
6. *Ibid.*
7. Sri Adwaita Vilas – Collected by Sri Bireswar Pramanik, Srimadacharya Prabhur Charitakshyan, 1st Part, Adi & Madhyakanda, Printed by Sannyal & Co. Published in 1821 Shakabda, Adi Kanda, p. 15).

40

Narayani

(Nurse-Mother of Sri Gouranga Mahaprabhu)

We can quote Jayananda as:-

"Chaitanya Gossainer Dhatri Mata Narayani"

It indicates that at the time of divine birth of Sri Gouranga Mahaprabhu Narayani as Nurse-Mother was present at the lying in room of Sachimaa. She also used to visit little Nemai regularly. Her presence in the house would make happy everyone. Before the birth of Nemai Shachimaa looked a nice lady and so people in the surroundings and also Narayani liked to say that there might have been a divine baby in the ovary of Shachimaa.

Narayani was really a fortunate lady as she was present at the time of the birth of Nemai people and vaishnavas gathered at the house and she had the scope of seeing the vaishnavas.

Sri Jayananda wrote as:-

"Sutika Mandire Nara-Nari Lakhe Lakhe.
Dwi-Bhuja Sada-Bhuja Cahturbhujamoy Dekhe."[1]

According to Jayananda's comment this Narayani also had the opportunity to have 'Darshan' of the child two-handed, four-handed and also six-handed.

At the time of the rituals of wearing the sacred thread 'Dhaimata' Narayani was also present. She also offered alms to Nemai as the Brahamachari when he aksed as saying – Bhabati Bhikshang Dehi Mata:" to her.

She used to be pleased to listen to the Samkirtan Movement lead by Sri Gouranga Mahaprabhu.

Narayani also shared the shock and sorrow of Shachimata while Sri Gouranga Mahaprabhu's first wife Lakshmipriya died of a snake bite.

She witnessed all the advancement of the Movement of Samkirtan lead by Sri Gouranga Mahaprabhu in Nabadwip.

The nurse mother of Sri Gouranga, Narayani would be remembered by the Vaishnavas in the country.

Reference

1. Sri Chaitanya Mongal – Sri Jayananda Ed by Bimanbehari Majumdar & Sukhamoy Mukhopadhaya, Asiatic Society, Pub in 1971, Printer – National Printing Works, Nadia 7, Shloka 7, P.17.

41

The Widow Mother of a Certain Blessed Boy

In Puri a beautiful boy used to come to Sri Chaitanya Mahaprabhu and Mahaprabhu also used to give him some time to the boy. Both Mahaprabhu and the boy loved each other.

But the boy was so little that without company he could not meet Mahaprabhu and so his mother a young lady but widow used to accompany him every day. She only stood at outside the door and after her son's meeting used to return.

However, Swarup Damodar who used to look after different aspects of Lord Sri Chaitanyadeva could not take the matter as easy.

Keeping in mind Mahaprbhu's fame and prestige he advised Mahaprabhu not to indulge the innocent boy to meet regularly. The little boy and his widow mother did no wrong.

But only the fault was the mother was widow, young aged and beautiful in looking. Swarop Damodar had the fear if anybody takes the subject for scandaling and defaming Him.[1]

The Widow mother also deserves due respect from us.

Reference

1. Sri Chaitanya Mongal – Sri Jayananda Ed by Bimanbehari Majumdar & Sukhamoy Mukhopadhaya, Asiatic Society, Pub in 1971, Printer – National Printing Works, Nadia 7, Shloka 7, p. 17).

42

Padmamoni Devi

(Mother of Ishan Nagar)

The person who used to perform domestic activities at the house of Sri Gouranga Mahaprabhu was Ishan. We find him for sometime also at the house of Sri Adwaita Acharaya.

The husband of Padmasmoni Devi was Padmanava Chakraborty who lived at Nabagram under Laud Pargana under Sunamganja of Sri Hatta District (Sylhet, now in Bangladesh). Srimati Padmamoni Devi and Sri Padmanava Chakraborty had a son who was known as Ishan Nagar and was born in 1414 Shaka (1492 AD).[1]

Padmamoni Devi lost her husband while Ishan was only of five years' old. They were almost pauper. At that time she had to sell all her belongings to meet up the costs of husband's funeral etc.

Afterwards she wandered from door to doors to have means to earn in order to maintain her family with her only child. She prayed to Lord Shiva once and He made her remember the name of Sri Adwaita Acharaya of the same village Nabagram. Sri Adwaita Acharaya was then known by people in the whole Bengal. He was not only a great scholar but also was a kind hearted and benevolent in nature. So, holding hands of son little Ishan she accompanied the pilgrimages of bathing in the Ganga and reached the house of Sri Adwaita Acharaya at Shantipur.[2]

Widow Padmamoni Devi with her only little son Ishan got shelter at the house of Sri Adwaita Acharaya at Shantipur. Thus Ishan Nagar was brought up by Sri Adwaita Acharaya with reasonable care and love. At the same time Achyutananda was also learning from the renowned scholar father Sri Adwaita Acharaya.

Ishan Nagar in his matured stage started to write his boyhood incidences as he could remember. Once he wrote:-

More Painya Sita Devi Sneha Prakashila.
Aapan Tanaya Sama Poshan Karila."[3]

The mother and son Ishan both were inititated from Sri Adwaita Acharaya. Ishan Nagar was at any kind of service with Sri Adwaita Acharaya during the lifetime.

His mother Padmamoni Devi was a Vaishnava as inspired by Sri Adwaita Acharaya and Sri Gouranga Mahaprabhu. She was so brave that she had the courage of coming miles after miles from Srihatta to Shantipur to meet Sri Adwaita Acharaya. With son she also liked Sri Gouranga Mahaprabhu more than their lives.

References

1. Sri Sri Goudiya Vaishnava Abhidhaan – Edited by Sri Haridas Das Babaji, 2nd, 3rd, and 4th Parts, 2nd Edition, 501 Chaitanyabda, Publisher – Haribol Kutir Poraghat, Nabadwip, Printer – Radha Press, Delhi 110031, p.1267).
2. Sri Sri Adwaita Prakash – by Ishan Nagar, Collected Edited and Printed by Kishoridas Babaji, Sri Sri Prankrishna Bhakti Press, (Halisahar, Chaitanya Doba) Published in 1406 BS, Editorial P. 19, Source: Introduction of Sri Achyuta Charan Chowdhury Tattanidhi).
3. *Ibid.*

43

Padmabati Devi

(Mother of Sri Nityanandaprabhu)

She Padmabati Devi who with an ache in heart showed little hesitation to leave her of only twelve years' old Nityananda to a mendicant forever. Such a woman as may be an example of Vaishnava Movement as her optimum sacrifice. She was wife of Hadai Pundit at Ekchakra village in the district of Birbhum. The place is also known as Birchandrapur.

The name of the son Padmabati Devi originally was Kuber or Sri Nityananda. Her father was a king at Moureswar as Mukut Narayana Roy and she was married to Sri Mukunda Ojha or known as Hadai Ojha with Sandilya Gotra living at Ekchakra village in the district of Birbhum. Her husband Mukunda Ojha or Hadai Ojha was also called as Hadai Baduri. Baduri is a short form of Banerjee or Bandyopadhyaya.[1]

Sri Nityananda was born in 1473 AD. His place of birth was at Ekchakra – Garvabaas. Now this Garvabaas has been added with the name of Ekchakra with the flavour of ancientness.[2]

Raja Mukut Narayana of Moureswar at the time of his daughter Padmabati's marriage with Mukunda or Hadai Pundit, son of Nakari Baduri spontaneously dug a pond in the name of Padmabati as Nakari Baduri demanded nothing as dowry. Raja Mukut Narayana donated this pond to Hadai Pundit himself. Afterwards Sri Nityananda used to play water in that pond.[3]

Padmabati Devi and Mukunda Ojha or known as Hadai Ojha had seven sons: Nityananda, Krishnananda, Sarbananda, Brhamananda, Purnananda, Premananda and Bishuddhananda. Sri Nityananda was born in shukla Trayaodashi of Magha in 1395 Shaka (1473 AD) on Tuesday.[4]

The unparallel with beauty and qualities Kuber or Nityananda achieved the 'Naya Churamoni' title before his twelfth year and he was given also the sacred thread. He became a famous Pundit. He had a desire to see the outer world and to know the people. Hadai Ojha knew his intention so he and Padmabati Devi remained cautious about their son Kuber. They did not leave him alone anywhere. During different spheres of activities for livelihood Hadai Ojha used to take him and all the time looked at him.

While Sri Nityananda grown up at his only twelve years, Padmabati Devi and Hadai Ojha wanted to arrange a marriage for him. At that time suddenly an unknown mendicant arrived at their house. He was given shelter at the house for a night as per extant rules of the time. The parents of Nityananda deputed him to perform the duties of hospitality on behalf of the house.

The Mendicant was pleased with the hospitality offered to him. In addition to their hospitality the Mendicant was pleased to Nityananda for his strong and stout health and intellect. At the time of departure he begged Nityananda for giving him company in different pilgrimages. He also assured them that he would teach and train the 12 years' boy properly. As he was old enough he needed help from a young and strong companion. He also informed them that after his demise the boy would return home again and settle in life. He again said – fulfill my desire."

On hearing this Padmabati Devi screamed at that moment. Hadai Ojha was so shocked that he could not speak for some time. He was well aware of the then customs not to dishearten any Mendicant whatever he would beg.

However the mother of Nityananda Padmabati Devi at last told her husband – what you suggest that would be final."

But she could not resist her tears for a long time. Shocked Hadai Pundit at last gave Nityananda in the hands of the certain Mendicant and burst into tears.

He and his wife Padmabati Devi could not maintain usual normal lives for a long time. Padmabati Devi had more six sons who were still then dependant to mother and Padmabati Devi had to close her mind and look after the remaining sons. People were afraid lest Hadai Pundit becomes mad for the departure of his elder son.

The glory of Padmabati Devi was stated as:-

"Tnar (Hadai Pundit) Patni Padmabati Naam Patibrata.
Parama Vaishnavi Shakti - Sei Jaganamata."[5]

Sri Nityananda was considered as 'Ananta Basudeva' and Balarama by Sri Gouranga Mahaprabhu. We should pay our respect to mother Padmabati Devi who gave birth to our beloved Sri Nityananda Prabhu.

References

1. Sri Sri Goudiya Vaishnava Abhidhaan – Edited by Sri Haridas Das Babaji, 2nd, 3rd, and 4th Parts, 2nd Edition, 501 Chaitanyabda, Publisher – Haribol Kutir Poraghat, Nabadwip, Printer – Radha Press, Delhi 110031, p.1278,
2. Brihat Bhaktamal – Sri Navaji in Hindi – Bengali Translation by Laldas Babaji – Edited by Sri Dilip Mukhopadhaya and Published by Benimadhab Sil's Library, Printer – ABC Printers, mRe-printed 1416 BS (2009 AD), P. 615, .
3. Prem Vilas – by Nityananda Das, Revised and edited by Dr. Bijon Goswami, Pub, in 1405 BS, 1999 AD, 1st Mahesh Edition, Printed at Printing Publicity, 24 Vilas, p.237,
4. Sri Sri Adwait Prakash – by Ishan Nagar, Collected Edited and Printed by Kishoridas Babaji, Sri Sri Prankrishna Bhakti Press, (Halisahar, Chaitanya Doba) Published in 1406 BS, Editorial P.57 and Sri Chaitanya Mongal – Sri Jayananda Ed by Bimanbehari Majumdar & Sukhamoy Mukhopadhaya, Asiatic Society, Pub in 1971, Printer – National Printing Works, Nadia Khanda Page.13 and also in others,
5. Sri Sri Chaitanya Bhagawata – Sri Vrindabandas, Madhya Khanda, 3rd Chapter, Shlokas 64 to 66, P. 486-87.

44

Padmabati Devi

(Mother of Raja Pratap Rudra)

Name of father Raja Pratap Rudra was Sri Purushottam Deva lower generation of Ganga. His wife was Padmabati or Rupambika Devi.

Padmabati or Rupambika Devi was daughter of Kanchi Mahraja. At the desire of Jagannath Mahaprabhu the marriage of Padmabati or Rupambika Devi was held with Sri Purushottam Deva, the King of Utkal. He could easily defeat the king of Kanchi and succeeded to marry Padmabati or Rupambika Devi. It has been stated in "Kanchi-Kaveri" poem in Odiya language that seeing the Raja Purushottam Dev was cleaning the way of Ratha Yatra with a broom made of gold decided not to hand over his daughter to a sweeper. Hearing this Raja Purushottam Dev attacked Raja of Kanchi and won the battle that was possible for the kindness of Lord Jagannathdeva.[1]

Raja Purushottam Deva was a son of Parvati Devi and Kapilendra Deva but he was not the eldest among the sons, yet he was nominated as the heir under the advice and the kindness of Lord Jagannathdeva. It made adispute and other brothers attacked the Raja while he was engaged in 'Sankirtan' but no weapon could touch him for kindness of Lord Jagannath-deva.

The husband of Padmabati or Rupambika Devi Sri Purushottam Deva, the King of Utkal both were considered as servants of Lord Jagannatha Mahaprabhu. Sri Purushottam Deva, the King of Utkal also constructed the 'Bhoga Mandapa' in the temple of Lord Jagannatha Mahaprabhu.[2]

Padmabati or Rupambika Devi was a sincere worshipper of Lord Jagannatha Mahaprabhu. For her and her husband's influence their son 'Gajapati' Raja Pratap Rudra became a devout of Lord Jagannatha Mahaprabhu.

References

1. Sri Sri Goudiya Vaishnava Abhidhaan – Edited by Sri Haridas Das Babaji, 2nd, 3rd, and 4th Parts, 2nd Edition, 501 Chaitanyabda, Publisher – Haribol Kutir Poraghat, Nabadwip, Printer – Radha Press, Delhi 110031, p.1286).
2. (*Ibid*).

45

Wife of Baninath

(Baninath was the brother of Sri Gadadhar Pundit)

We could not trace the name of the wife of Baninath but we can say that the lady was a fortunate as she gave birth to two sons like Hridayananda and Nayayananda who served for the Vaishnava Movement led by Sri Chaitanyadeva.

Baninath or Jagannath was born in the village of Beleti of the district of Chittagong (Chattragram now in Bangladesh) and Pundit Gadadhar was born in Nabadwip just after three fortnights of divine birth of Sri Gouranga Mahaprabhu (Sri Chaitanyadeva).

Their father Madhab Mishra was a friend of Pundarik Vidyanidhi. Their wives had also the same name Ratnabati Devi. So, both of them were also friends –'Gangajal'. Madhab Mishra and Pundarik Vidyanidhi were the disciples of Sripad Madhabendra Puri.

Baninath or Jagannath was married and Gadadhar Pundit remained unmarried to serve Sri Gouranga Mahaprabhu (Sri Chaitanyadeva) for the whole life and stayed till the last day their disaapearances in the 'Gundicha' temple.

The elder son of Baninath or Jagannath Sri Nayananda settled at Bharatpur near Kandi of Murshidabad district. He made 'Gour Padabali' in lucid language and he was a remarkable writer in Vaishnava Literature. One of his writings was 'Sri Sri Gouragadadharastaka'.

The younger brother was Hridayananda who in future was called 'Hridaya Chaitanya'. Sri Gadadhar Pundit trained the two brothers personally in Vaishnava scriptures and also initiated them. Once seeing sincerety like Mahaprabhu and brought up properly by Sri Gadadhar Pundit Sri Gouridas Pundit of Kalna in the district of Bardhaman begged

Hridayananda for serving 'Sri Sri Gour-Netai' deities at his house. In future, Sri Shyamananda Prabhu was one of the disciples of Hridayananda-'Hridaya Chaitanya'.

In 'Shakha Nirnoy':-

> *"Bhakta Sanghattang Bhaktakhyang Bhaktabrindena Rajitam.*
> *Brhmacharinimirhe Tang Baninatha-Mahasayam."*[1]

Again,

> *"Bande Sri Nayanandaya Mishrah Premsudharnabam.*
> *Gadadharasya Gourasya Premratnoik Bhajanam."*[2]

About Hridayananda-'Hridaya Chaitanya' we find:-

> *"Bande sri hridayanandang magnang premarase sada.*
> *Mahabhava – chamatkar – gourabhava – kalebaram."*[3]

Their grandmother's Sripat was at Beleti Village. Nayananda had Sripat at Bharatpur. The generation still continues at Bharatpur.

We could not trace the name of the wife of Baninath but we should pay our respect to her for the sons who were much more important in the Vaishnava Movement led by Sri Gouranga Mahaprabhu (Sri Chaitanyadeva). She deserved thanks a lot.

References

1. Sri Sri Goudiya Vaishnava Abhidhaan – Edited by Sri Haridas Das Babaji, 2nd, 3rd, and 4th Parts, 2nd Edition, 501 Chaitanyabda, Publisher – Haribol Kutir Poraghat, Nabadwip, Printer – Radha Press, Delhi 110031, p. 1363, Source; Shakha Nirnoy, 17).
2. *Ibid*, p.1265-66, Source; Shakha Nirnoy, 17).
3. *Ibid*, p.1265-66, Source; Shakha Nirnoy – Pitambaradas Shloka-58).

46

Vijaya Devi

(The Grandmother of Vishnupriya Devi)

The Grandmother of Vishnupriya Devi was Vijaya Devi. She was the wife of Durgadas Mishra of Nabadwip.[1]

Durgadas Mishra was a Vedic Brahmin. His wife Vijaya Devi gave birth of two sons named as Sri Sanatan and Sri Kalidas. Her eldest son Sri Sanatan was married to Mahamaya Devi. Her only daughter was Vishnupriya Devi who became the 2nd wife of Sri Gouranga Mahaprabhu.

Sri Kalidas, another name Parasar was a worshipper of Shakti Devi – Durga and Kali and so he was named as Kalidas.

Vijaya Devi was a devotee of Lord Sri Krishna and she tried immense efforts to glorify the little family life and ultimately she succeeded in every sphere. We should also remember her who indirectly gave support to the Harinaam Movement of Lord Sri Gourangadeva.

Reference

1. Sri Sri Goudiya Vaishnava Abhidhaan – Edited by Sri Haridas Das Babaji, 2nd, 3rd, and 4th Parts, 2nd Edition, 501 Chaitanyabda, Publisher – Haribol Kutir Poraghat, Nabadwip, Printer – Radha Press, Delhi 110031, p. 1366).

47

Bidhumukhi Devi

(Aunt of Vishnupriya Devi)

Bidhumukhi Devi was the wife of Sri Kalidas Mishra, the uncle of Vishnupriya Devi. They lived at Shantipur. The writer of 'Krishna Mongal' was Madhab Mishra who was son of Bidhumukhi Devi.

Sri Durgadas Mishra was her father-in-law and Sri Sanatan was her elder brother-in law. At the time of immatured death of Sri Kalidas Mishra the son Madhab was too young. So, Sri Sanatan Mishra the elder uncle brought up Madhab with care and thus he became one of the renowned scholars in that time.

Bidhumukhi Devi, being a young aged widow was enthusiastic when the marriage of Vishnupriya Devi was going to be arranged with Sri Gouranga Mahaprabhuor, Nemai Pundit of Nabadwip. Sri Gouranga Mahaprabhu's second wife Vishnupriya Devi was some senior to the son Madhab of her aunt Bidhumukhi Devi. She explained the glory of Sri Gouranga Mahaprabhuor, Nemai Pundit of Nabadwip to Srimati Vishnupriya Devi.

Her only son became a sincere follower of Sri Gouranga Mahaprabhu (Sri Chaitanyadeva).[1]

Sri Madhab Mishra did not marry. When his mother Bidhumukhi Devi tried to tie the son in bondage by getting him married Sri Madhab Mishra went to Vrindaban.

According to the Premvilas Sri Madhab Mishra was given Sri Krishna Mantra from Sri Adwaita Acharya and later became also a renowned writer:-

"Pare Mahaber Ballavacharya Khyati.
Sove Bole Kalir Vyas Ei Mahamati."[2]

On receiving the news of mother Bidhumukhi Devi's demise Sri Madhab Mishra returned to Shantipur and accompanied Sri Achyutananda towards Kheturi to attend the Tri-deities' installation the mamoth Conference led by Janhaba Devi, the second wife of Sri Nityananda Prabhu.[3]

References

1. Prem Vilas – by Nityananda Das, Revised and edited by Dr. Bijon Goswami, Pub, in 1405 BS, 1999 AD, 1st Mahesh Edition, Printed at Printing Publicity, 19 Vilas, p.187).
2. *Ibid*,
3. *Ibid* p. 188.

48

Bimala Devi

(Wife of Gouridas Pundit)

Sri Gouridas Pundit was the fourth brother of Sri Suryadas Sarkhel, the father of Basudha Maa and Janhaba Devi.

Before marriage Sri Gouridas Pundit shifted his residence from Shaligram to Ambika Kalna with a vew to worship Lord Sri Krishna-Balarama incarnated as Sri Gour-Nityananda. He was one of the beloved followers of Sri Gour-Nityananda. His wife was Bimala Devi.[1]

Twice Sri Gouranga Mahaprabhu (Sri Chaitanyadeva) and Sri Nityananda Prabhu visited along at Kalna. At the first time Sri Gouranga Mahaprabhu after giving lesson to Sri Adwaita Acharya for his debate on 'Jnana Marg' accompanying Sri Nityananda Prabhu sailed a boat from Shantipur to Ambika Kalna. Sri Gouridas Pundit became overwhelmed to see them for their sudden visit.

Being pleased to Sri Gouridas Pundit Mahaprabhu gifted the scull and told him:-

"Ei Leha Boitha Ebe Dilam Tomare.
Bhaba Nadi Paar Karo Sakal Jibere".[2]

Both of Sri Gouranga Mahaprabhu and Sri Nityananda Prabhu returned Nabadwip with Sri Gouridas Pundit. There at the temple at the house of Sri Gouridas Pundit still are remaining the scull and the copy of the Srimad Bhagwata Geeta written by Sri Gouranga Mahaprabhu.[3]

At the second visit of Sri Gouranga Mahaprabhu (Sri Chaitanyadeva) and Sri Nityananda Prabhu along at Kalna Sri Gouridas Pundit was not present there at the house. However, later when he expressed his desire to establish the deities of Sri Gour-Nityananda at his temple Sri Gouranga

Mahaprabhu advised him to bring the tree of margosa from Nabadwip and to prepare their statues there.

We find:-

"Nabadwip Hoite Nimbabriksha Aanaibe.
Mor Bhrata Saha More Nirman Karaibe."[4]

Sri Gouranga Mahaprabhu also advised him to marry and to settle at family life and to worship the deities sincerely and he did so by marrying Bimala Devi who gave birth of two sons. The names of her sons were Balarama and Raghunathdas.[5]

Sri Gouridas Pundit was considered as Subal Sakha of earlier life in Braja Lila.[6]

After sudden death of Bimala Devi both of them were brought up by Srimati Bhadrabati Devi, the mother of Basudha and Janhaba, the wives of Sri Nityananda Prabhu.

Bimala Devi was a fortunate lady whose short time deeds also helped the Harinaam Movement.

References

1. Sri Sri Nityananda Shakti Maa Janhaba – Sri Nemaichand Goswami, Pub. By Sri Sanatan Goswami, Printer – Shyamasundar Press, 1st Pub 1389 BS, 2nd Pub 1401 BS, p.23 and Sri Sri Goudiya Vaishnava Abhidhaan – Edited by Sri Haridas Das Babaji, 2nd, 3rd, and 4th Parts, 2nd Edition, 501 Chaitanyabda, Publisher – Haribol Kutir Poraghat, Nabadwip, Printer – Radha Press, Delhi 110031, p.1369,
2. Sri Sri Bhakti Ratnakar – by Sri Narahari Chakraborty, edited by Pundit Navinkrishna Paravidyalankar, published by Srimat Sundarananda Vidyavinode, printed by Sri Anantaram Bhakti Shastri, Nadia Prakash Printing Works, pub in 1490 AD, Gaudiya 6th edition, 7th Wave, Shloka – 335, p. 352).
3. *Ibid*, p. 340 41).
4. Sri Sri Nityananda Shakti Maa Janhaba – Sri Nemaichand Goswami, Pub. By Sri Sanatan Goswami, Printer – Shyamasundar Press, 1st Pub 1389 BS, 2nd Pub 1401 BS, 2nd Chapter, p. 20).
5. Sri Sri Goudiya Vaishnava Abhidhaan – Edited by Sri Haridas Das Babaji, 2nd, 3rd, and 4th Parts, 2nd Edition, 501 Chaitanyabda, Publisher – Haribol Kutir Poraghat, Nabadwip, Printer – Radha Press, Delhi 110031, p. 1369).
6. Sri Sri Gour Ganoddesh Deepika – by Sri Kavi Karnapur, Edited by Sri Ashoke Kumar Bandyopadhaya, publisher- Sadeh, Printer- Orient Press, Pub in 2007 A D,

49

Biswas Devi

(A Woman Writer)

During the 15th century a woman writer of 'Ganga Bakyabaoli' the learned Biswas Devi was born.

She was the wife of Padma Singha a brother and inheritance of Divya Singha the King of Mithila. She was the eldest queen of Padma Singha. Her capability in different types of work of quality and her refined taste made her popular to all in her time.[1]

Biswas Devi also participated in the royal activities on behalf of the King Padma Singha even at his presence.[2]

She wrote a collection on the procedure of worshipping the Ganga 'Ganga Bakyabaoli'and at her request poet Vidyapati the 'Rajpundit' in the court of Raja Divya Singha and also Raja Padma Singha has modified the book by including some authentic reasonable references. He was a renowned poet in the court. 'Padaboli', 'Shaiba Sarbaswasar' and 'Durgabhakti Tarangini' were written by him. In 'Shaiba Sarbaswasar' Vidyabati has mentioned the name of Biswas Devi as self-taught, expert administrator, a sincere wife, devotee and a noble lady.[3]

Biswas Devi was a quality woman in the 15th century and so she deserves respectful mention by us.

References

1. Sri Sri Goudiya Vaishnava Abhidhaan – Edited by Sri Haridas Das Babaji, 2nd, 3rd, and 4th Parts, 2nd Edition, 501 Chaitanyabda, Publisher – Haribol Kutir Poraghat, Nabadwip, Printer – Radha Press, Delhi 110031, p.1371 and Mahiyasi Bharatiya Naari – Edited by Swami Madhabananda & Dr. Ramesh Chandra Majumder, - Bengali Translation by Dr. Satchidananda Dhar, published by Swami Mumukshananda, Udbodhan Karyalaya, 1407 BS, p. 449,

2. Mahiyasi Bharatiya Naari – Edited by Swami Madhabananda & Dr. Ramesh Chandra Majumder, - Bengali Translation by Dr. Satchidananda Dhar, published by Swami Mumukshananda, Udbodhan Karyalaya, 1407 BS, p. 449,
3. *Ibid.*

50

Vishnupriya Devi

(The Second Wife of Sri Gouranga Mahaprabhu)

The writers, readers and the people men or women whoever thinks of Vishnupriya Devi, the second wife of Sri Gouranga Mahaprabhu (Sri Chaitanyadeva) still to day feel sorrow because before the fulfillment of life she was left at home.

Vishnupriya Devi was the 'Bhu Shakti', the energy of the earth and Satyabhama in her earlier life at Dwarka.[1]

We May quote from Sri Sri Gour Ganoddesh Deepika:-

"Sri Sanatana Mishrohayang Pura Satrajito Nripah.
Vishnupriya Jaganmata Jatvrikanya Swarupini".[2]

It clarifies that in the earlier birth King Satrajit has been named Sri Sanatan in the present Kaliyuga and his daughter was Vishnupriya Devi as 'Bhu Shakti', the energy of the earth. Her mother was Mahamaya Devi.[3]

Vishnupriya Devi was born on the Panchami (5th day of the bright fortnight) of Magha probably in 1494-95 AD. Sri Durgadas Mishra was the grandfather of Vishnupriya Devi. He had two sons Sri Sanatan Mishra and Sri Kalidas Mishra. Vishnupriya Devi was the daughter of Sri Sanatan Mishra. The name of the son Kalidas Mishra was Madhab Acharya and his son was Jadav Acharya.

Sri Sanatan Mishra was a 'Rajpundit' and was also a good-heart person who could make others as own beloved men. He knew not hypocracy. He was not a deceitful, cruel rather he was noble, simple, charitable and of a great personality. With frank and sincere nature Sri Sanatan Mishra was loveable and respectable by others in Nabadwip.

Mother of Sri Gouranga Mahaprabhu Shachimaa was much pleased to find Vishnupriya Devi as her daughter-in-law. Shachimaa would prefer

Vishnupriya Devi from the Ghat of the Ganga where both of them used to go to bathe everyday and so, she wished to marry her son Sri Gouranga Mahaprabhu with this beautiful and good habit Vishnupriya Devi. She informed her preference after a long time of Lakshmipriyadevi's sad demise to Sri Kashinath Mishra and appointed him who was also a match-maker in Nabadwip to talk and arrange the marriage of Sri Gouranga Mahaprabhu on behalf of her.[4]

As a result, all the members and closed relatives including Vishnupriya Devi agreed to the marriage proposal intimated by Sri Kashinath Mishra. At that time in the whole of Nabadwip Sri Nemai Pundit was the most acceptable prospective bridegroom. As in the Srimad Bhagawata the girls of Vrindaban who worshipped during a month Katyayani wishing Nanadasuta Sri Krishna as their prospective husband, the marriageable girls kept in mind secretly to have husband like Sri Nemai Pundit. But in Kaliyuga it was not possible to satisfy all the women by marrying by a single personality like Sri Nemai Pundit.

However the marriage of Nemai Pundit known as Sri Gouranga Mahaprabhu was scheduled with Vishnupriya Devi and the followers became much enthusiastic with the news of Nemai's second marriage.

Buddhimanta Khan has assured to bear the entire expenditure of the marriage ceremony of Nemai Pundit known as Sri Gouranga as a prince of Nabadwip. According to Sri Vrindabandas:-

"Buddhimanta Khan Bole – Shuna Shakha Bahai,
Bramaniya Sajja e-Bibahe Kichhu Nai.
E-Bibaha Punditera Karaibo Hena,
Rajkumarer Mata Loke Dekhe Jena".[5]

Buddhimanta Khan, one of the Zaminders of Nabadwip was also a rich person and a devotee friend of Sri Gouranga Mahaprabhu. But Sri Gouranga Mahaprabhu did not show any interest as he showed at the time of marrying Lakshmipriya Devi earlier. It happened only for giving the taste of satisfaction of mother Shachidevi. He also obeyed the Social customs. But the marriage was conducted with all the necessary and extant rules and rites.

At the afternoon of the day of marriage the house of Sri Sanatan Rajpundit was decorated with illuminating lights, pandals and sounds of music of different instruments.

Vrindabandas expressed the beauty of the bridegroom Sri Gouranga as he was decorated with sandal wood paste and garlanded with fragrant flowers. The bridegroom party advanced through the roads on the bank of the Ganga.

And on the other side Vishnupriya Devi was also a beautiful bride bearing with different types of ornaments, clothes and precious cosmetics. She was comparable to her only. It appeared that God has created her with His extreme Perfection and adding beauty of the Universe. Sri Sanatan Mishra in order to please Sri Vishnu gave the hands of Srimati Vishnupriya Devi to Sri Gouranga (later known as Sri Chaitanyadeva or Sri Chaitanya Mahaprabhu).

All the people who had marriageable daughters had sighs to see bridegroom as Sri Gouranga, a complete perfect beautiful in every respect e.g. figure and godlike golden complexion, learning's, wits, wisdom and above all a loveable nature that could not be compared with any of the world.

On the next afternoon of the marriage Sri Gouranga returned with newly married Vishnupriya Devi and Shachimaa welcomed them with happiness. At the time of their coming home the followers on both sides of the road congratulated them delightedly. They also wished good wishes and blessed the newly couple of Sri Gouranga with newly married Vishnupriya Devi.

All the people who were standing on the sides of the road applauded the married couple considering them as Lakshmi-Narayana.

After the marriage ceremony Sri Gouranga Mahaprabhu embraced Buddhimanta Khan and other followers with gratitude.

Shachimaa could forget the sorrow and pain of Lakshmipriya's sudden demise and gladly she received Vishnupriya Devi. And she hoped that newly married Vishnupriya Devi would bring the happiness and peace in the family of her.

After almost two years later Mahaprabhu with some followers and students and maternal uncle Sri Chandra Sekhar decided to go to Gaya after taking permission from Sachimaa to offer 'Pinda' to the deceased father and the fore fathers. Having performed the rituals Sri Gouranga visited the sign of holy feet of Lord Vishnu and became almost mad for Lord Vishnu as well as Lord Sri Krishna.

There came by chance Ishwarpuri who Sri Nemai Pundit met once in Nabadwip earlier. Sri Gouranga observing the devotion to Lord Sri Krishna of Ishwarpuri became overwhelmed and after some time he begged to get initiation and thus Ishwarpuri giving the initiation in Sri Krishna 'mantra' to Sri Gouranga became the preceptor of Sri Gouranga.

At that time Sri Gouranga Mahaprabhu was only twenty three years' old. Mahaprabhu met Ishwarpuri twice in life. Ishwarpuri then proceeded towards Vrindaban alone. Sri Gouranga had the intention to be with him for Vrindaban but could not proceed for his followers and the attraction of mother Sachidevi. He returned Nabadwip after some travelling, specially visited the birth place of Ishwarpuri at Kumarhatta.[6]

This was the last meeting of Mahaprabhu Sri Gouranga with the preceptor Ishwarpuri.[7]

However, Shachimaa and Vishnupriya Devi became anxiety free to find Mahaprabhu again in Nabadwip and they were satisfied.

Sri Gouranga Mahaprabhu was a loveable personality whom any mother or any woman or any senior personality would consider him as a man of their hearts. Not only man or woman all other creatures of the world would become calm and quiet to see him, as later we find all the beasts of Jharikhand became overwhelmed to find Mahaprabhu while singing and dancing for love of Lord Sri Krishna.

But returning from Gaya Sri Gouranga acted as a changed man who always remained in thoughts of Lord Sri Krishna. He was seen like a mad person as he could not resist himself whenever he felt Lord Sri Krishna is coming to him and also disappears. He used to shed tears from the eyes incessantly in love for Sri Krishna.

Once Sri Gouranga Mahaprabhu told his beloved friend Sri Gadadhar Pundit – Hello, Gadadhar since the boyhood you are worshipping and thinking of Lord Sri Krishna but I was engaged with debates with others. See I have lost Sri Krishna what is difficult to obtain".

The family with wife and mother Sri Gouranga was peaceful. Sachimaa could work domestic activity while Vishnupriya Devi would assist her in every work. Vishnupriya Devi remained always ready to serve her life-partner Sri Nemai or Sri Gouranga Mahaprabhu. In turn Mahaprabhu also tried to please Vishnupriya Devi showing cordiality and also love.

Vishnupriya Devi, however, used to sit lonely on bed without sleeping in order to serve tired Mahaprabhu when he would return home from the Sankirtan Movement that continued some time the whole night at Sribaas Angan.

Sri Gouranga Mahaprabhu was being considered as 'Jagatprabhu' the master of the universe or 'Mahaprabhu'. His style and movement was of rarely available, rather he was an incomparable different personality. He could not be compared with anyone in this universe.

Some of the writers like Dr. Khudiram Das commented that, Sri Gouranga Mahaprabhu did not share bed with Vishnupriya Devi.[8]

Sri Gouranga Mahaprabhu was born in order to eliminate the sorrows of all the creations of the universe. So knowing it well Vishnupriya Devi had the anxiety for him whether her husband would be confined with family ties with wife and mother. She used to discuss all these to her friend Kanchana and was afraid lest her husband Sri Gouranga Mahaprabhu would take Sannyas later.

Sachimaa always tried to share the sorrows and anxiety of daughter-in-law Vishnupriya Devi sympathetically. Her hope was to see a child of her son and daughter-in-law. On this aspect Sri Lochandas wrote:-

"Pitrihina Putra Tumi – Dila Dui Bibha,
Apatya Santati Kichhu Na Dekhilo Iha".[9]

Vishnupriya Devi could get her husband for a few hours whereas the other women would get their husband of ordinary domestic life for hours after hours. With patience Vishnupriya Devi could tolerate the absences at home of Sri Gouranga Mahaprabhu but remained for the care and services that Mahaprabhu needed. She at her teen age was a virtuous woman. She started to consider her husband as God:-

"Krishna Anabaena Shuni, Vishnupriya Mone Guni,
Swatantra Ishwar Tumi Prabhu".[10]

Sri Gouranga Mahaprabhu once declared her a Sati (chaste wife) and a Vaishnava Janani (mother of Vaishnava). Afterwards actually the lady Vishnupriya Devi was given the charge to look after all the Vaishnava people of Nabadwip.

Vishnupriya Devi was not informed about the time and day of taking Sannyas by Sri Gouranga Mahaprabhu. He just used to talk to her that everything in this world is illusion, only to worship Lord Sri Krishna is the real thing for all the creatures to which Vishnupriya Devi could not answer. She just liked to weep silently presuming her husband would leave her and even his mother.

Sri Gouranga Mahaprabhu also said to her – In this world only God is the real husband of all and all the creations are His wives".

All these verbal advices made Vishnupriya Devi understand that Sri Gouranga is a different personality, he was himself God.

After being initiated in the Sannyas Mantra when Sri Gouranga left her and his mother Vishnupriya Devi used to remain at home without facing any other man outside. She used to bathe in the Ganga with Sachimaa in the early morning otherwise she did not appear in the Sun. Only she used to hear Harinaam. She did not see anything but the picture of Sri Gouranga Mahaprabhu painted by her. She liked to worship it with extreme devotion daily. She dedicated herself to her husband Sri Gouranga Mahaprabhu only.[11]

Vishnupriya Devi used to enter into the room where the picture of Sri Gouranga Mahaprabhu painted and set by herself after the bathing for meditation of Sri Gouranga Mahaprabhu. Once Sri Nibas Acharya waited for the 'Darshan' of Vishnupriya Devi without taking any food for three days and at last she allowed Sri Nibas Acharya and some selected devotees. All of them including Sri Nibas Acharya to find the red feet of Vishnupriya Devi were fainted in respect.

Although the authentic writers like Sri Vrindabandas and Sri Krishnadas Kaviraj did not mention Sri Chaitanyadeva's visit in Nabadwip, some of the writes liked to narrate that once Sri Chaitanyadeva after 12 years of Sannyas as an extant rule visited Nabadwip and met Vishnupriya Devi at his pre-Sannyas home. He gifted Vishnupriya Devi his wood made slippers and advised to have peace in mind and to take Harinaam all the time. It is also said that Sri Chaitanyadeva reappeared to Vishnupriya Devi then with the dress not of a Sannyasi, but in informal dress.[12]

Sri Gouranga Mahaprabhu i.e. Sri Chaitanyadeva did not hesitate to give the proper knowledge of Lord Sri Krishna to Vishnupriya Devi. He also declared her as the'Vaishnava Mata'. However, Vishnupriya Devi would get affection from Sachimaa. Sachimaa also was sympathetic to her.

There lived Bangshibadan who was known as Bangshi, Bangshidas, Sri Badan, Badananda, and Pancham Prakash was engaged to care after Sachimaa and Vishnupriya Devi as advised by Sri Chaitanyadeva. He was received by Sachimaa and Vishnupriya Devi as own man. In earlier life in Brajalila he was Krishnadhar Vilasini as described in Gourganoddesh Deepika. He was also a prominent disciple of Vishnupriya Devi.

After the demise of Sachimaa Vishnupriya Devi became alone but maintained the rituals for her obsequies. After wards she left her dresses of a daughter-in-law and became a Brahmachari in dresses and action only to worship Lord Sri Gouranga Mahaprabhu.

In 1533 AD Sri Chaitanyadeva with the lifelong associate Sri Gadadhar Pundit who was engaged in worshipping Sri Sri Gopinath at Tota disappeared in the Gundicha temple. There are several hearsays about their disappearances. But Sri Chaitanya Mahaprabhu still remains immortal for

His devotion to Lord Sri Krishna and He is still being remembered by thousands of devotees, followers sincerely.

On knowing this disappearance Vishnupriya Devi became very shocked and started to worship and engaged herself in meditation in closed room where the picture was painted and set by her.

At one night she dreamt the deity of Mahaprabhu and thereafter with the help of Bangshibadan and her brother Sri Yadav Mishra arranged to build the deity by certain architecture in wood of margosa tree that was standing in the courtyard of the house. She started to worship Lord Sri Chaitanya Mahaprabhu more rigidly.

After the disappearances of Lord Sri Chaitanya Mahaprabhu with Sri Gadadhar Pundit, afterwards disappearance of Sri Nityananda Prabhu and normal demise at 125 years of age of Adwaita Prabhu the Vaishnava followers started to rely on Sri Vishnupriya Devi only for their next duties to observe. She had the rigidity of maintaining the idealisms of Lord Sri Gouranga Mahaprabhu i.e. Sri Chaitanyadeva advised.

On the other hand, Janhaba Devi, the wife of Sri Nityananda Prabhu also came up to uphold the Vaishnavism in Bengal and Sri Nityananda-Basudha's son Birchandra took the responsibility of spreading Vaishnavism in the whole of Bengal.

Although, Sri Vishnupriya Devi did not give birth of any child she was highly regarded as the Mother of Vaishnavas to all the followers of Sri Gouranga Mahaprabhu i.e. Sri Chaitanyadeva. Thus Sri Vishnupriya Devi had thousands of children in Bengal. She did not engage herself in propagating Harinaam but she was considered as the Mother spontaneously by almost all the Vaishnavas in Nabadwip.

She also was pleased to see the birth of grandson of Bangshibadan. Sri Vishnupriya Devi accompanied Sitadevi, Basudhamaa and Janhabadevi in a covered with clothes cart to see grandson of Bangshibadan who was named Ramchandra or Ramai.[13]

We may remember that this son was taken or adopted by Janhaba Devi as her own son and afterwards Ramchandra or Ramai established the cult of Baghnapara.

Sri Vishnupriya Devi once noticed a piece of smile in the lips of Sri Gouranga Mahaprabhu i.e. Sri Chaitanyadeva and understood that his husband was calling her. It was the day of birth of Sri Gouranga Mahaprabhu i.e. Sri Chaitanyadeva when she remembered her friends like Kanchana,

Chitralekha or Amita and called the Sebait Yadav Mishra. She advised to maintain the rites and continue the worshipping to Lord Gouranga Mahaprabhu in future. On the morning of the day of full moon of Phalguna or Holi she entered the temple and shut the doors for a long time.The gathered followers after waiting for a reasonable time Yadav Mishra on their request opened the doors and found Sri Vishnupriya Devi was no more in the earth. Perhaps she met Sri Gouranga Mahaprabhu i.e. Sri Chaitanyadeva in another world.

Some liked to say that Sri Vishnupriya Devi expired at her 96 years of age.

"After the demise of Sri Bishnupriya Devi her brother Jadavacharya's son Madhabacharya continued the Seva Puja (worship) according to the rules and systems introduced by Sri Bishnupriya Devi".

However the family history of the Goswami Sri Bishnupriya Debi was alive till 1573 AD what means that she expired at 80 years of age.[14]

The deities of Sri Vishnupriya Devi and Sri Lakshmipriya Devi along with Sri Gouranga Mahaprabhu (Sri Chaitanyadeva) were established by Sri Narottam Thakur at Sripat Kheturi. This was the first time when Lakshmipriya Devi's deity with Sri Gouranga Mahaprabhu i.e.Sri Chaitanya Mahaprabhu was set.[15]

Sri Haridas Das Babaji wrote that Lakshmipriya at the left and Vishnupriya at the right side of Sri Gouranga Mahaprabhu, at the extreme right Sri Vallavikanta, Sri Krishna, Sri Radhamohan and Sri Radharaman were set by Sri Narottam Thakur at Kheturi.[16]

Afterwards the deities of Vishnupriya and of Sri Gouranga Mahaprabhu were established by many of the followers in Goudiya Vaishnavism introduced by Sri Gouranga Mahaprabhu (Sri Chaitanyadeva).

Srimati Radharani without giving birth to any child she became the mother of the Universe. The writers of the scriptures have commented her as *'Bande Radha Jagatprasu'* as she was the nature and strength of Lord Sri Krishna. In the vast Universe Sri Krishna and Radha are entwined in bliss in one Soul.

Like Srimati Radharani without giving birth to any child Sri Vishnupriya Devi became mother of all the followers of Lord Gouranga Mahaprabhu.

Srimati Vishnupriya wife of Sri Gouranga Mahaprabhu was also being considered as the mother of the World who did not give birth to any children.

We should keep in mind the pathetic life of Sri Vishnupriya Devi in the eyes of ordinary people but we are to remember her sacrifice, devotion and accepting all the devotees in Goudiya Vaishnavism as the mother.

References

1. Sri Sri Goudiya Vaishnava Abhidhaan – Edited by Sri Haridas Das Babaji, 2nd, 3rd, and 4th Parts, 2nd Edition, 501 Chaitanyabda, Publisher – Haribol Kutir Poraghat, Nabadwip, Printer – Radha Press, Delhi 110031, p.1373 and Sri Sri Gadadhar Charitamrita – Edited by Sri Swarup Das Maharaj, Published by Sri Animesh, Printed by Sri Krishnanada Computer Press (Vrindaban), 1st Edition, 1998, p. 91,

2.&3. Sri Sri Gour Ganoddesh Deepika – by Sri Kavi Karnapur, Published by Ramdeva Mishra 4th Edition, Published in 1320 BS, Shloka – 47,

4. Sri Sri Chaitanya Bhagawata – Sri Vrindabandas, Adi Khanda, 15th Chapter, Shloka 40-43, P.318,

5. Sri Sri Goudiya Vaishnava Abhidhaan – Edited by Sri Haridas Das Babaji, 2nd, 3rd, and 4th Parts, 2nd Edition, 501 Chaitanyabda, Publisher – Haribol Kutir Poraghat, Nabadwip, Printer – Radha Press, Delhi 110031, p.1296 and Sri Sri Chaitanya Bhagawata – Sri Vrindabandas, Adi Khanda, 5th Chapter, Shloka 71-72, P.321,

6. Bangla Sahityer Itibritta – by Dr. Asit kumar Bandyopadhaya, Published by Kolkata Viswavidyalaya (Bangla Bibhag) in 1962 AD, p. 198,

7. Sri Sri Gour Sundara or Srikrishnachaitanya Mahaprabhur Charit – by Syamlal Goswami, Adi Lila, p. 68,

8. Jagat Prabhu Sri Gouranger Sannyas – by Dr. Uma Bandyopadhyay P. 42 "Sri Chaitanya Prasanga",

9. Sri Chaitanya Mongal – by Sri Lochandas, Madhya Khanda, Shloka 25, P.141,

10. *Ibid*, Shloka 39, p.151,

11. Sri Sri Adwita Prakash – by Ishan Nagar, Collected Edited and Printed by Kishoridas Babaji, Sri Sri Prankrishna Bhakti Press, (Halisahar, Chaitanya Doba) Published in 1406 BS, p. 21,

12. Sri Chaitanya Pradakshin – by Sri Vishnupada Panda, P.145-146, Amiya Nemai Charit - by Sri Sisir Kumar Ghosh and Vishnupriya Prannath Nadia Behari - by Sri Vishnu Prasad, Published by Sri Sukhdeva, Printed at Poramaa Press, Nadia in 1413 BS (2007) p. 51)

13. Sri Sri Gour-Vishnupriya Charita – compiled by Sri Harinarayan Das p. 68).

14. Vishnupriya Prannath Nadia Behari – by Sri Vishnuprasad, p. 35-36).

15. Sri Sri Nityananda Shakti Maa Janhaba – Sri Nemaichand Goswami, Pub. By Sri Sanatan Goswami, Printer – Shyamasundar Press, 1st Pub 1389 BS, 2nd Pub 1401 BS, p. 316).

16. Sri Sri Goudiya Vaishnava Abhidhaan – Edited by Sri Haridas Das Babaji, 2nd, 3rd, and 4th Parts, 2nd Edition, 501 Chaitanyabda, Publisher – Haribol Kutir Poraghat, Nabadwip, Printer – Radha Press, Delhi 110031, p. 1855).

51

Bhadrabati Devi

(The Mother of Sri Uddharan Dutta)

Udhdaran Dutta of Saptagram was a prominent devotee under Sri Nityananda Prabhu. In different activities he accompanied and co-operated Sri Nityananda Prabhu. His mother was Bhadrabati Devi and father was Sri Kar Dutta. Originally Udhdaran Dutta was named as Dibakar Dutta but Sri Nityananda Prabhu called him as Udhdaran Dutta. He was born in 1403 Shaka (1481 AD). Once, Sri Nityananda Prabhu travelled at every house for propagating Harinaam as advised by Sri Gouranga Mahaprabhu (Sri Chaitanyadeva).[1]

Bhadrabati Devi was a woman who used to worship God Sri Krishna with proper care and above all, with the most cleanliness. She was also a follower of Gour-Nityananda. She had affection for them.

Sri Kar Dutta was a monied man. His son also worked as Dewan under Koi king for some time and thereafter engaged himself in business at Saptagram near the river the Ganga and also earned lot of money. The parents of Sri Uddharan Dutta arranged the marriage with Mahamaya. Their son's name was Priyankar or Sri Nivas. At the age of twenty-six of Sri Uddharan Dutta his wife Mahamaya expired. From then Sri Uddharan Dutta became like a Sannyasi and started to worship and serve Sri Krishna-Balarama. To him Sri Nityananda Prabhu was as Balarama. He established the Goura-Netai deities with also Sri Gadadhar Pundit at Saptagram temple wherein the yugal Radhakrishna also are being worshipped till today.

Uddharan Dutta was one of the twelve Gopals who in earlier life was Subahu Sakha in Dwarka Lila. He always accompanied everywhere with Sri Nityananda Prabhu and sometime cooked food for him without any hesitation.[2]

He was also a benevolent to the needy people. Once he established an institution for charitable supply of food at his own expenditure. In addition he erected houses at Vedaban (Bhadraban) for the houseless persons. He and Krishnadas Hore of Baragachhi, the prince arranged the marriage of Sri Nityananda Prabhu with Basudha Maa and Janhaba Maa, the daughters of Suryadas Sarkhel of Shaligram. Udhdaran Dutta and Krishnadas Hore spent sufficient money for the wedding of Sri Nityananda Prabhu. Uddharan Dutta spent then ten thousand of Rupees and Krishnadas Hore kept his royal chest open for the expenditure.[2]

Subahu Sakha in Dwarka Sri Udhdaran Dutta, the fifth Gopal breathed his last in between 1483-1597 Shaka (1561-1575 AD). However, the devotees at Saptagram usually observe the day of his passing away in the month Poush on the 14th day of black moon every year.

Sri Bhadrabati Devi was one of the lucky women who gave birth to a son like Sri Udhdaran Dutta. We should bow our heads to her.

References

1. Sri Sri Goudiya Vaishnava Abhidhaan – Edited by Sri Haridas Das Babaji, 2nd, 3rd, and 4th Parts, 2nd Edition, 501 Chaitanyabda, Publisher – Haribol Kutir Poraghat, Nabadwip, Printer – Radha Press, Delhi 110031, p. 1299).
2. Sri Sri Nityananda Shakti Maa Janhaba – Sri Nemaichand Goswami, Pub. By Sri Sanatan Goswami, Printer – Shyamasundar Press, 1st Pub 1389 BS, 2nd Pub 1401 BS, p. 521).

52

Bhadrabati Devi

(The Wife of Sri Suryadas Pundit)

Bhadrabati Devi was the wife of Suryadas Sarkhel.

Suryadas Sarkhel was a Brahmin of Rarhi sect with Batsya Gotra and his title was Ghosal. For his expertness in royal employment he was given the title as 'Sarkhel'. His father was Sri Kangsari Mishra, perhaps the title 'Mishra' was given by any King. And his mother was Kamaladevi. Both of them were devotees of Lord Sri Krishna from the very beginning.[1]

Once at the call of his 4th brother Gouridas Pundit who in earlier life was Subal Sakha in Brajalila lived shifted his residence from Shaligram to Ambika Kalna. Suryadas who was considered Kukudmi in earlier Brajalila came to Ambika Kalna with the full family and also with the deities of Lord Lakshmi-Narayana that was worshipped at his home there. He built a separate house at Ambika Kalna nearer to the house of Gouridas.

"Subalo Ya: Priyashrethah Sa Gouridas Panditah"

And

"....*Sri Suryadasasya Mahatamanah Sute,*
Kukudmirupasya Cha Suryatejasah."[2]

Suryadas were six brothers viz. Damodar Ghosal, Jagannath Ghosal, Suryadas Pundit, Gouridas Pundit, Krishnadas Ghosal and Nrisingha Ghosal. All of them were pure heart and devotees of Lord Sri Krishna and also Sri Gouranga-Sri Nityananda.

The wife of Suryadas Pundit Bhadrabati Devi was a pious lady and she did not know to sit idle for a moment. With domestic activities she used to perform the needs for worshipping of the deities of Lakshminarayana and Netai-Gouranga sincerely.

Once, the wife of Gouridas Pundit, Srimati Bimala Devi expired leaving her two sons Balarama and Raghunath and her husband. Bhadrabati Devi the wife of Suryadas took the responsibility of worshipping at the temple and also the two sons along with her own two daughters and a son. To look after the children in the bigger family was not so easy, however she could alone manage all the responsibilities along with the arrangements for the worshipping the four deities every day. She was a hardy woman indeed.[3]

Basudha Maa and Janhaba Maa the two daughters of Suryadas Pundit and Bhadrabati Devi were born at Shaligram. Probably Basudha was born in 1429 Shaka Asada Shukla Dwitiya (2nd day of full moon of the month of Asada) on the day of Rathayatra. Janhaba Devi was born in Shukla Navami (ninth day of full moon) in the month of Baisakh in 1431 Shaka.

Bhadrabati Devi used to take cooperation from them in plucking flowers and Tulsi leaves. Sometime Basudha used to help mother in cooking also. All the three women used to sing songs of Poet Jaydeva, Vidyapati and others on Lord Sri Krishna and Srimati Radhika in joyous mood. They had also a son named Sri Chandra Sekhar who was born after Basudha and Janhaba.

With the advice of Sri Chaitanyadeva and reminding from Adwait Prabhu and also Sachimaa, mother of Sri Chaitanyadeva ultimately Sri Nityanada agreed to marry. Uddhran Dutta of Saptagram and Krishnadas Hore, a prince of Baragachhi arranged the marriage of Sri Nityananda Prabhu with the elder daughter Bausdha Maa. Both of them spent sufficient money for the wedding of Sri Nityananda Prabhu then.

Bhadrabati Devi gladly accepted the proposal of the marriage and welcomed the bridegroom. Thereafter she agreed to the wedding of Janhaba Maa with the same bridegroom Sri Nityananda Prabhu and cordially welcomed.

In earlier lives at Brajalila both Bausdha Maa and Janhaba Maa were considered as 'Ananga Manjari'.

"Sri Baruni-Rebatabangsha Sambhabe,
Tasya Priye Dwe Basudha Cha Janhabi (Janhaba)."[4]

In the house of Suryadas Pundit and Bhadrabati Devi there was an atmosphere of festival almost every day. Particularly at the entrance of Sri Nityananda Prabhu as the bridegroom of the two sisters enhanced the position to a certain height that there was no want of anything. The family was really with the ambience of Lord Sri Krishna's blessings.

So, we should bow to Sri Bhadrabati Devi and Sri Suryadas Pundit, the mother-in-law and the father-in-law respectively of Sri Nityananda Prabhu.

References

1. Sri Sri Goudiya Vaishnava Abhidhaan – Edited by Sri Haridas Das Babaji, 2nd, 3rd, and 4th Parts, 2nd Edition, 501 Chaitanyabda, Publisher – Haribol Kutir Poraghat, Nabadwip, Printer – Radha Press, Delhi 110031, p. 1299).
2. (Ref.Sri Sri Gour Ganoddesh Deepika – by Sri Kavi Karnapur, Published by Ramdeva Mishra 4th Edition, Published in 1320 BS, Shloka – 128, P.25 and Shloka 65, p.15).
3. Sri Sri Nityananda Shakti Maa Janhaba – Sri Nemaichand Goswami, Pub. By Sri Sanatan Goswami, Printer – Shyamasundar Press, 1st Pub 1389 BS, 2nd Pub 1401 BS, p.16-17).
4. Sri Sri Gour Ganoddesh Deepika – by Sri Kavi Karnapur, Edited by Sri Ashoke Kumar Bandyopadhaya, publisher- Swadesh, Printer- Orient Press, Pub in 2007 AD, Shloka -65, p. 15)

53

Bhagirathi Devi

(The Mother of Sri Basudeva Sarbabhoum)

Bhagirathi Devi was the mother of the Nationwide famous Pundit Basudeva Sarbabhoum. He was born in between 1430 to 1435 AD as a son of Maheswar (Narahari) Visharad, a renowned scholar and Bhagirathi Devi. With his scholarly activities at Nabadwip at the beginning he left Goud Bengal and he was appointed as the Rajpundit of Kalinga-Odisha by Raja Purushottam Deva and after the demise of Raja he worked as Rajpundit under Raja Pratap Rudra with great respect and money. He was an honourable and influential personality in Puri.

He had another brother named Chandidas was also scholar in Sanskrit. They were Brahmin by caste of Rarhi section. Their father Sri Maheswar (Narahari) Visharad was expert in Navya Nyaya (Logics) in Nabadwip.

Pundit Basudeva Sarbabhoum after completing the studies in Nabadwip went to Mithila for higher studies in Nyaya (Logics) under Pakshadhar Mishra. Both of father Mahswar (Narahari) Visharad and son Pundit Basudeva Sarbabhoum had emmense popularity amongst the educated personalities at that time.

Afterwards Pundit Basudeva Sarbabhoum collected new Ascetic Sri Chaitanyadeva from the temple of Lord Jagannath and took him at his residence in Puri. He tried to coach Sri Chaitanyadeva on Vedanta and found him as a rare personality like God became a devotee in Goudiya Vaishnavism. He was a sponsor of Sri Chaitanyadeva too.[1]

His mother Bhagirathi Devi was a fortunate lady for her husband Sri Maheswar (Narahari) Visharad had easy entrance in Logics, Hindu Law (Smriti) and Vedanta. For his teachings the fame of Nabadwip was enhancing day by day and so, the Scholars of Mithila, Vikrampore and other educating centres became interested about Nabadwip. He also wrote a book on Hindu Law (Smriti) at the inspiration from Sultan Barbak Shah. Sri Maheswar (Narahari) Visharad was a class mate of maternal grandfather of Sri Gouranga Mahaprabhu-Sri Chaitanyadeva.

The mother Bhagirathi Devi was also fortunate for her son Pundit Basudeva Sarbabhoum. Pundit Basudeva Sarbabhoum had profound skill of memory. He learnt Nyaya (Logics) but was forbidden to take any copy of the books from Mithila to Nabadwip. So, he memorized all the books and returned Goud Bengal. At that time the centres at Nabadwip also started to coach Nyaya (Logics).[2]

Afterwards he was awarded the title 'Sarbabhoum' with due respect from Mithila. He used to have 'Darshan' of Lord Jagannath, Balarama and Subhadra daily as a practice. He also had the opportunity to peruse the Six-Handed Sri Chaitanyadeva.

Sri Basudeva Sarbabhoum wrote many books on Nyaya (Logics) and also Vedanta. His writings 'Anuman Pariksha' and a 'Tika'on Vedanta of 'Adwaita Makaranda' were also notables. After perfoming with respect from the post of Rajpundit in 1532 AD he left Puri and settled in Varanasi.[3]

The mother Bhagirathi Devi was a successful lady who inspired husband, sons and also grandchildren in the path of education. Our respect would flow and remain to her forever.

References

1. Sri Sri Chaitanya Charitamrita– by Sri Krishnadas Kaviraj, Edited by Sri Sri Madbhakti Sri Roop Maharaj, Published from Gaudiya Mission (Rgd.) by Tridandi Bhikshu Sri Bhakti Gunakar Goswami, Printer – Radha Press, Gandhinagar, Delhi – 110 031, 6th Edition, Published in 1990, Adi Lila, 11th Chapter, Shloka 41 and Smarane Manane Sri Chaitanyadeva - by Sri Samir Chattopadhyay, published by Dilip Bose printed at Maa Sarad Offset Press, in 1415 BS, p. 76).
2. Sri Sri Goudiya Vaishnava Abhidhaan – Edited by Sri Haridas Das Babaji, 2nd, 3rd, and 4th Parts, 2nd Edition, 501 Chaitanyabda, Publisher – Haribol Kutir Poraghat, Nabadwip, Printer – Radha Press, Delhi 110031, p. 1265).
3. Sri Sri Chaitanya Charitamrita – by Sri Krishnadas Kaviraj, Edited by Sri Sri Madbhakti Sri Roop Maharaj, Published from Gaudiya Mission (Rgd.) by Tridandi Bhikshu Sri Bhakti Gunakar Goswami, Printer – Radha Press, Gandhinagar, Delhi – 110 031, 6th Edition, Published in 1990, Madhya Lila, 1st Chapter, Shloka 141).

54

Mahamaya

(The Wife of Sri Uddharan Dutta)

Mahamaya Devi was the wife of Udhdaran Dutta of Saptagram who was a prominent devotee under the shelter of Sri Nityananda Prabhu. His mother was Bhadrabati Devi and father was Sri Kara Dutta. Originally Udhdaran Dutta was named as Dibakar Dutta but Sri Nityananda Prabhu called him as Udhdaran Dutta. He was born in 1403 Shaka (1481 AD).

Once, Sri Nityananda Prabhu travelled at every house for propagating Harinaam as advised by Sri Gouranga Mahaprabhu i.e. Sri Chaitanyadeva.[1]

Mahamaya Devi was a woman who used to worship Lord Sri Krishna with proper care and above all, with the most cleanliness. Her cooking of 'Bhog' was very palatable. Her husband Udhdaran Dutta occasionally used to say that her cooking food were so nice that Lord Sri Krishna preferred much. She was like her husband also a follower of Gour-Nityananda.

Sri Kara Dutta was a monied man. His son also worked as Dewan under Koi King of Naihati for sometime and thereafter engaged himself in business at Saptagram near the river the Ganga and also earned lot of money.

The parents of Sri Uddharan Dutta arranged the marriage with Mahamaya. Their son's name was Priyankar or Sri Nivas at Saptagram in the district of Hooghly.

Uddharan Dutta was one of the twelve Gopals who in earlier life was Subahu Sakha in Dwarka Lila. He always accompanied everywhere with Sri Nityananda Prabhu and sometime cooked food for him without any hesitation.[2]

He was also a benevolent to the needy people. Once he established an institution for charitable supply of food at his own expenditure. In addition, he erected houses at Vedaban (Bhadraban) for the houseless persons.

Mahamaya Devi used to support and rather to inspire Uddharan Dutta in these and other charitable activities.

Later Uddharan Dutta and Krishnadas Hore of Baragachhi, the prince arranged the marriage of Sri Nityananda Prabhu with Basudha Maa and Janhaba Maa, the daughters of Suryadas Sarkhel of Shaligram. Udhdaran Dutta and Krishnadas Hore spent sufficient money for the wedding of Sri Nityananda Prabhu. Uddharan Dutta spent then ten thousand of Rupees and Krishnadas Hore kept his royal chest open for the expenditure.

Uddharan Dutta also used to cook for Sri Nityananda. He was considered as Subahu Sakha in Dwarka. In different activities he accompanied and co-operated Sri Nityananda Prabhu

Mahamaya Devi hailed from moneyed family and she was the aunt (father's sister) of Gouri Sen in whose name a legend is in vogue that 'Laage Taka Debe Gourisen' means whatever you spend the whole amount of your expenditure would be paid by Gouri Sen, you need not worry.[3]

At the age of twentysix of Sri Uddharan Dutta his inspiring life partner the wife Mahamaya Devi suddenly expired.

From then Sri Uddharan Dutta became like a Sannyasi and started to worship and serve Sri Krishna-Balarama. To him Sri Nityananda Prabhu was as Balarama. He established the Goura-Netai deities with also Sri Gadadhar Pundit, the combination of three Netai-Goura- Gadadhara is rare, at Saptagram temple wherein the yugal Radhakrishna also are being worshipped till today.

We should bow our heads to broad minded Mahamaya Devi without whose inspiration Sri Uddharan Dutta hardly could open the charitable institution of supplying food to unfed and arranging shelter to houseless people.

References

1. (Sri Sri Goudiya Vaishnava Abhidhaan – Edited by Sri Haridas Das Babaji, 2nd, 3rd, and 4th Parts, 2nd Edition, 501 Chaitanyabda, Publisher – Haribol Kutir Poraghat, Nabadwip, Printer – Radha Press, Delhi 110031, p. 1299).
2. Sri Sri Nityananda Shakti Maa Janhaba – Sri Nemaichand Goswami, Pub. By Sri Sanatan Goswami, Printer – Shyamasundar Press, 1st Pub 1389 BS, 2nd Pub 1401 BS, p. 521).
3. *Ibid* p. 76).

55

Maha Laxmi Devi

(The Mother-in-law of Ganga Maa)

The mother-in-law of Gangamaa, only daughter of Sri Nityananda Prabhu was Mahalakshmi Devi. The only son of Mahalakshmi Devi and Bishweswar Acharya was Sri Madhvacharya.

Jai Durga Devi brought up Sri Madhavacharya. She was one of the wives of Bhagirath, a Brahmin, Kashyap Gotra, Chatta Gaain and Rarhi branch. Her husband Bhagirath was also a good and renowned scholar. Jai Durga Devi had already two sons Sri Nath and Sri Pati.[1]

Jai Durga Devi one of the wives of Bhagirath and Mahalakshmi Devi wife of Bishweswar Acharya had friendship 'Sai'. Jai Durga Devi was present at the sudden death of Mahalakshmi Devi. So, Jai Durga Devi was shocked to see 'Sai's demise. On the other hand Mahalakshmi Devi before her death expressed that responsibility of looking after her only son would be borne by Jai Durga Devi. But Mahalakshmi Devi understood that with mother's irresistible death her son like Madhab would become almost helpless. So, she requested Jai Durga to take the son and to bring him up as another son with her two sons.

Jai Durga Devi then started to bring up three sons Sri Nath, Sri Pati and Madhab carefully.[2]

Afterwards Bishweswar Acharya left the family and became an ascetic in Varanasi despite opposition of Bhagirath. Thus Madhvacharya, son of Mahalakshmi Devi was brought up by Jai Durga Devi and later married Gnaga Devi, the only daughter of Sri Nityananda Prabhu.

References

1. Sri Sri Nityananda Shakti Maa Janhaba –Sri Nemaichand Goswami, Pub. By Sri Sanatan Goswami, Printer – Shyamasundar Press, 1st Pub 1389 BS, 2nd Pub 1401 BS, p. 152).
2. *Ibid* p.153.

56

Madhabi Devi

(The Sister of Shikhi Mahiti)

Madhabi Devi was a sister of Shikhi Mahiti. She was a Vaishnava woman from the entrance of Mahaprabhu Sri Chaitanyadeva in Puri or Neelachal. Her brothers were also followers of Sri Chaitanyadeva from very beginning. They were the writing personalities of Sri Jagannath Mahaprabhu in the temple. She was a successful woman in Vaishnavism. She was considered as one and half of the three and a half persons who were closed companies of Mahaprabhu. She was also considered as one of the persons of Srimati Radhika.

Madhabi Devi used to write 'Padas' on Sri Chaitanyadeva and Radhakrishna.

Madhabi Devi had some contribution in 'Padabali Sahitya'. With the introduction four 'Padas' in 'Padakalpataru' as numbered 075, 776, 1853 and 2239 in the Parishat Edition and had also more two 'Padas' numbring 140 and 240 appeared or published by 'Sadhana' Phalguna Issue in 1337 BS edited by Sri Jatindranath Roy. With the research by he informed us a translation from Charitra-Ratnamala in Telegu to Kenarij language these have been included. But somehow the Editor has not mentioned the above two 'Padas' However the undernoted stanza is available:-

"Shamera Goura Barana Ekadeha,
Pamara Jana Ithe Karai Sandeha,
Sourave Agora Murati Rasasara,
Paakala Bhela Joichhe Phala Sahakara,
Gopa Janama Punh Dwija Avatara?
Nigam Na Payi Niguraha Vihara,
Prakat Karala Harinaam Byakhana,

Nari Purush Mukhe Na Shuniye Aan,
Kori Gouracharana Kamala Madhupaan,
Sarasa Sangeet Madhabidas Bhana."[1]

In addition to it the drama titled 'Purushottamdeva' was also written in Sanskrit by Madhabi Devi.

They were two brothers and one sister named Shikhi Mahiti, Murari Mahiti and Madhabi Mahiti. At first Sri Chaitanyadeva was introduced with Murari Mahiti and Madhabi Mahiti. But at one night Shikhi Mahiti dreamt in sleeping that Sri Chaitanyadeva is entering in Sri Sri Jaganatha Mahaprabu temple and coming out repeatedly. He was perplexed. On the next day Sri Chaitanyadeva finding Shikhi Mahiti at the entrance gate of the temple of Sri Sri Jagannatha Mahaprabu called him by name and forwarded his hands to embrace with 'Kripa'.

Kavi Karnapur has described as:-

"Neela Shaila Tilakang Bilokayangstratra Prabishati Pratikhsanam.
Bhuya Taba Bahiretya Pahyati Praayasho Bytnutoibameba Sah."[*]

Not only that Sri Chaitanyadeva also recognized him as an elder brother of Murari Mahiti and Madhabi Mahiti. All the three were followers of Sri Chaitanyadeva in Neelachal-Puri. Madhabi Mahiti had the right to sit along the Vaishnavas in any conference. She although was the youngest to her brothers was an aged woman.

However, once Sri Bhagwan Acharya, a lame man but sincere devotee Sri Sri Jaganatha Mahaprabhu invited to feed Sri Chaitanyadeva with associates. He sent Sri Haridas (younger) to Madhabi Mahiti to bring a maund of fine rice from her stock. Chhoto (younger) Haridas met Madhabi Devi and spent some time to bring the superfine rice for Sri Chaitanyadeva and his associates.

At the time of taking 'Prasada' Sri Chaitanyadeva was astonished to find such rare special kind of superfine rice and he asked Sri Bhagawan Acharya who was the person collected rice and from where. Bhagwan replied – Your beloved Kirtaniya Haridas has brought the rice himself carrying the whole path from one of your followers Madhabi Mahiti".

* Sri Sri Gour Ganoddesh Deepika – by Sri Kavi Karnapur, Edited by Sri Ashoke Kumar Bandyopadhaya, publisher- Swadesh, Printer- Orient Press, Pub in 2007 AD, Shloka -13/100 and (Ref.Sri Chaitanya Pradakshina – by Bishnupada Panda, published by –Dey's Publishing, printed by Dey Printers, 1st Edition, 1400 BS (1993 AD), p.149)

Sri Chaitanyadeva did not speak anything but after taking Prasada advised his aide Govinda saying – Do not allow Chhoto Haridas at my place any more. He has broken the rules of a Sannyasi, as he spent much time with a woman. For him the door is closed for ever."

Many of the associates like Swarup Damodar, Sri Gadadhar Pundit and others tried their best to convince Sri Chaitanyadeva to allow Chhoto Haridas who used to sing and play Mridanga etc. at the Sankirtan. So, no one could change the decision of Chaitanyadeva. It was Chaitanya Mahaprabhu who could be hard nut person to preach that the Sannyasis never should have any contact with any woman, whoever she is.

The Goudiya Vaishnavas know that Sri Chaitanyadeva was an ocean of compassion but he did not show any kindness to Choto Haridas. Why?

Sri Chaitanyadeva did not indulge any illegiment acts of a Sannyasi who has left his previous family life. The legitimate relation between man with his own wife and woman with her own husband is only possible for family person only. Sannyasis are to maintain their strict rules not to touch even a wooden female doll decorated with dresses and ornaments. He wanted to see all Vaishnavas are adhered to the rules of society and as advised by the teachers, guru and parents in every respect of life but those who have left family life are to maintain in accordance with the strict rules of a Sannyasi. This action taken by Sri Chaitanyadeva also made effect on the lives of general people of the Country as well as the Nation as an educative measure in order to maintain lifestyle in more peaceful manner.

Chhoto Haridas some days remained on fasting and wandered here and there in Neelachal and waited for Sri Chaitanyadeva's rethinking and kripa. But, Sri Chaitanya Mahaprabhu was the personality of one word. He was so strict for Chhoto Haridas that he could leave any hope further. Although Chhoto Haridas was inevitable in the Kirtaniya Groups but Sri Chaitanyadeva knew well that there is no question of inevitability in the world of reality.

There from own Ashram in Neelachal-Puri Paramananda Puri came who was in the same rank of Sripad Ishwar Puri like the Preceptor of Sri Chaitanyadeva was. He tried to convince and in reply Sri Chaitanyadeva in very calm voice said – Better I go to Alalnath where in the temple remains Lord Janardan (Vishnu)". We should cite that earlier Sri Chaitanyadeva stayed there at the time of 'Anabasar' of Sri Sri Jagannatha Mahaprabhu. At that time no one can see Sri Sri Jagannatha Mahaprabhu. On hearing this hard and strong decision Paramananda Puri could not try to convince Sri Chaitanyadeva and returned to his Ashram.[2]

At last Chhoto Haridas left Puri and went to Allahabad-Praying, the junction of the Ganga, the Yamuna and the Saraswati rivers. Therein he finished himself.[3]

Madhabi Mahiti was a pious woman. She usually used to write 'Padas' on Sri Sri Radhakrishna and Sri Chaitanya Mahaprabhu. She with her brothers and her forefathers were Sevaka of Sri Sri Jagannath Mahaprabhu as writers on papers relating to various activities of the temple.

The critics presumed that in the 'Padakalpataru' the 'Padas' written by her in the name of Madhabi Dasi were composed by her about the Neelachal Lila of Sri Chaitanyadeva.

She wrote:-

"....Prakata Karala Harinaam Byakhan,
Nari Purush Mukhe Na shuniye Aan.
Kori Gouracharana Kamala Madhu Pan,
Sarasa Sangeet Madhabi Das Bhana."[4]

Madhabi Mahiti also wrote:-

".....Du Baahu Tuliya Beraya Nachiya,
Bhakataganera Sanga,
Neelachalabasi Mone Abhilashi
Koutuke Dekhaye Ranga.
Baje Karatala, Bole Bhali Bhalo
Aar Baje Tahe Khola.
Madhabi Das, Monete Ullasa,
Sada Bole Hari Bola."[5]

The father of Sankirtan Sri Chaitanyadeva used to become mad in the Sankirtan and to note it Madhabi Dasi also would become mad in love of Lord Sri Krishna.

Madhabi Mahiti wrote 'Padas' on Sri Chaitanya Mahaprabhu one of them was:-

"....Anandey Naachata Sngete Bhakata,
    Gour Kidhore Raja,
Phagu Ujhaali Kore Phelapheli,
    Neelachal Puri Majha.
Madhabi Das Monete Ullas
Sada Bole Haribol.[6]

Practically in the heart of Madhabi there remained Sri Chaitanya Mahaprabhu and thus it filled with the 'Phagu' in her devotion.

The Avatara of Kaliyuga Sri Chaitanya Mahaprabhu i.e. Nemai Pundit was the soul of Nabadwip. Without him the place seemed to an environment of grief-stricken. Sri Jagadananda, a disciple of Sri Gadadhar Pundit and a sincere follower of Sri Chaitanya Mahaprabhu used to visit Nabadwip once a year to give some articles and "Prasad' of Sri Sri Jagannatha Mahaprabhu. On this subject Madhabi Mahiti wrote with her expertness:-

"... ...Bhabe Pundit Roy,
Pai Ki Na Pai Shachire Dekhite
Ei Anumane Jai.

Again she wrote on Sri Krishna:-

"Parashite Rai Tanu Aapane Bhulalo
Murachhi Parhala Dhani Kora'
Shyamak Heraite Dhani Bhelo Gada Gada
Dharaki Dharaki Bohe Lor.
Upajala Ullaas, Kahai Madhabi Das
Bidagdha Madhaba Radhye.[7]

She wrote on also 'Pancha Tattwa':-

"Nityanada Sanhati Mukunda Gadadhare,
Dekhilen Gourachandra Sarbabhoum Ghare...
Dakshine Netai Bosi Bame Gadadhar,
Mililen Gorachandera Yata Anuchara."[8]

Let us try to evaluate as under:-

1. Madhabi Mahiti became a famous associate of Sri Chaitanyadeva,
2. She was like a 'Manjari' who served Sri Sri Radhakrishna in Braja Lila,
3. Madhabi Mahiti or Dasi wrote Padas from their devotion and sincerety, later in Rajasthan Mirabai engaged herself with the writing of Padas on Lord Sri Krishna,
4. In the 'Padas' the devotees and also the anti socials were referred to,
5. She was sponsored by Raja Pratap Rudra,
6. She had a good handwriting skill so, she was appointed as a writer of diaries of day to day programmes of Lord Sri Sri Jagannatha Mahaprabu,
7. In addition, to see her efficiency in work Raja Pratap Rudra sanctioned some honorium to her,

8. Madhabi Dasi would write diaries of day to day programmes of Lord Sri Sri Jagannatha Mahaprabu what were called as 'Madla Panji' by the Pandas in future,
9. Despite the want of publicity for her tolerance and efficient work she was praised by the elite people then. Moreover she established the deity of Gopinath in the village of Bentpur near the house of Bhabananda Roy,
10. She was brave lady without any kind of greediness.

Actually Madhabi Dasi was successful lady who helped the Goudiya Vaishnavism and also the status of women in the society. Let us bow our heads in memory to her.

References

1. Sri Sri Goudiya Vaishnava Abhidhaan – Edited by Sri Haridas Das Babaji, 2nd, 3rd, and 4th Parts, 2nd Edition, 501 Chaitanyabda, Publisher – Haribol Kutir Poraghat, Nabadwip, Printer – Radha Press, Delhi 110031, p. 1601).
2. Sri Sri Chaitanya Charitamrita – Sri Krishnadas Kaviraj, Edited by Sri Sri Madbhakti Sri Roop Maharaj, Published from Gaudiya Mission (Rgd.) by Tridandi Bhikshu Sri Bhakti Gunakar Goswami, Printer – Radha Press, Gandhinagar, Delhi – 110 031, 6th Edition, Published in 1990, Antya Lila 2nd Chapter, Shloka 109-132, P.928-932).
3. *Ibid* p. 932.
4. Sri Gourapada Tarangini – 13/2/38 Pada).
5. PadaKalpataru – 4/21/73 Pada.
6. *on Dol Lila (Holi)*
7. Bangiya Sahitya Patrika 1305 BS, 3rd Issue 'Stri Kavi Madhabi, p. 161-63).
8. PadaKalpataru – 4/21/23 Pada.

57

Manika Milkmaid

(A Pious Woman)

Manika who used to sell cowmilk was a resident of Anandapur village five miles (5*1.6=8 kms) away from Puri Dham at the sea-bank. She was pious and also a glorious lady.[1]

Once earlier the father of Raja Pratap Rudra, Raja Purushottamdeva's marriage was settled with the daughter of Raja of Kanchi but in the Rathayatra Festival the King of Kanchi found that the King of Odisha Purushottamdeva was sweeping the road of the Rathayatra with a Gold made broom. The King of Kanchi was not aware of the customs and so, he cancelled the proposed marriage as he did not prefer own daughter's marriage with a sweeper.

Raja Purushottamdeva then took the shelter of Lord Sri Sri Jagannatha Mahaprabhu. He got the assurance from Lord Sri Sri Jagannatha Mahaprabhu. At the time of processing towards Kanchi somehow the King of Odisha met the lady Manika who used to sell cow milk. Manika then gave a ring to the King saying that two advanced soldiers drank milk and curd from her but they did not pay the price of milk instead gave the ring and advised to show the ring to the person who was coming by the same route. They also advised her to take payment from the person who is coming next to them. To see the ring the King Purushottamdeva understood that it was a play of Lord Jagannatha and Lord Balarama whom he worshipped with their lovely sister Subhadra every day.[2]

Then he felicitated the woman Manika with royal manner. Afterwards, the King Purushottamdeva attacked Kanchi and announced the battle in between Kanchi and Odisha. As a result the King of Kanchi was defeated. Having victory in the battle Raja Purushottam Deva occupied the throne and the deity of Sri Ganesha. He gifted Lord Sri Sri Jagannatha Mahaprabhu the throne. Sri Ganehsa was placed near the Western Gate. Sri Ganehsa is called as Bhakta Sri Ganehsha or Kanchi Sri Ganehsa.

Afterwards Raja Purushottamdeva married Padmabati Devi, the daughter of the King of Kanchi. In the marriage the role of Manika milkmaid is remembered till date.[3]

References

1. Sri Sri Goudiya Vaishnava Abhidhaan – Edited by Sri Haridas Das Babaji, 2nd, 3rd, and 4th Parts, 2nd Edition, 501 Chaitanyabda, Publisher – Haribol Kutir Poraghat, Nabadwip, Printer – Radha Press, Delhi 110031, p. 1286).
2. *Ibid.*
3. *Ibid.*

58

Malini Devi

(Wife of Sri Sribaas)

Sri Sribaas was one of the 'Panchatattwa' and he gave to Sri Gouranga Mahaprabhu the place of Sankirtan at his residential house in Nabadwip. Her wife was Malini Devi. She was a chaste woman.

Sri Gouranga Mahaprabhu and Sri Nityananda Prabhu used to see her like a mother. As:-

"… … Gouranga Srimukhe Jare Bolilo Janani,
Mata Boli Sambodhilo Netai Gouranga."[1]

To se Sri Nityananda Prabhu Malini Devi's affection became present. Even from her breasts milk would seen for affection. Sri Nityananda Prabhu sometime used to sleep at her lap. With motherlike Malini Devi, Sri Nityananda Prabhu used to play as Gopa Child as in Braja in earlier life. Malini Devi was aged enough. Sri Sribaas also had parental affection for Sri Nityanandaprabhu. .

Sometime Sri Nityananda Prabhu was mistaken in his mad like moods. He used to take the wearing cloth on his head instead of wearing under the waist. To see this uncommon practice Sri Gouranga Mahaprabhu used to dress him properly. But it appeared that Sri Gadadhara Pundit, Sri Sribaas and Sri Haridas who were present there would not find him dress less. Perhaps this was the glory of Sri Nityanandaprabhu.

Sri Nityananda Prabhu once brought back a small pot of oil from a crow by calling it. All present were astonished that a mere crow listened to him.

Sri Gouranga Mahaprabhu had started the Sankirtan Movement from the house of Sri Sribaas Pundit. Many of his notable Lilas were also performed at the Sri Sribaas Angan (yard). Sri Krishnadas Kaviraj expressed:-

SriBaas Angane, Sachira Randhane, Nityanandera Nartane and Raghab Bhawane Mahaprabhu Sri Gouranga remains all the time.[2]

Mahaprabhu directed Sri Nityananda Prabhu to live at the house of Sri Sribaas. With the fortune all the dwellers including sevakas and sevikas of the house of Sri Sribaas have seen Netai and Goura and the Sankirtan Movement every day. Sri Gouranga Mahaprabhu blessed little girl sevika whose name was 'Dukhi' changed her name as 'Sukhi'. When the mother of Vrindabandas was only six years' old and crying at the door of the Angan Mahaprabhu Gourangadeva blessed her by giving his eaten food and told – Do not cry, if you cry, cry for Sri Krishna." Later her son Vrindabandas became a prominent writer of Life Sketch of Sri Gouranga Mahaprabhu.

While the Sankirtan was running with dances of Sri Gouranga Mahaprabhu, Sri Nityananda Prabhu, Sri Gadadhara Pundit, Mukunda and others the only son of Malini Devi and Sri Sribaas suddenly expired. But in view of any disturbance may cause stop both Malini Devi and Sri Sribaas did not inform it to anyone, they just waited for the completion of the Sankirtan. However Sri Gouranga Mahaprabhu failed to continue and found breaks of musical measure many a time and so he enquired the cause inside the inner rooms. Sri Sribaas calmly replied that his only son has expired and so he and others of the family were waiting for completion of the Sankirtan. Sri Gouranga Mahaprabhu was stunned to hear it and came to the lying dead son and asked him - Why you are going to leave this world?" The son as if replied – My time is over so, I cannot exist in this world."

Malini Devi and Sri Sribaas were so tolerant and lover of Sankirtan that they for some time forgot the grief.[3]

Both Sri Gouranga Mahaprabhu and Sri Nityananda Prabhu consoled the mother Malini Devi that they are her sons and so she need not cry.

Malini Devi was also a company of Sachimaa. At the marriage of Sri Nityananda Prabhu with Basudha Maa and Janhaba Maa Malini Devi was highly pleased and she welcomed them cordially too.

References

1. Sri Sri Gourabhaktamrita Lahari – Edited and published by Sri Kishoridas Babaji, printed at Sri Prankrishna Bhakti Press, Sri Chaitanyadoba, Halishahar, 2nd Edition, 1411 BS, 10th Lahari, p. 116,
2. Sri Sri Chaitanya Charitamrita – Sri Krishnadas Kaviraj, Edited by Sri Sri Madbhakti Sri Roop Maharaj, Published from Gaudiya Mission (Rgd.) by Tridandi Bhikshu Sri Bhakti Gunakar Goswami, Printer – Radha Press, Gandhinagar, Delhi – 110 031, 6th Edition, Published in 1990).
3. *Ibid* p. 307.

59

Malini Devi

(Wife of AbhiramThakur)

This Malini Devi was the wife of Abhiram Goswami who was one of the 'Twelve Gopals'. It is believed that Sridam Sakha of earlier Dwapara Yuga has come to Nabadwip from Vrindaban. He at the time of Sri Krishna's disappearance played hide and seek and ultimately was hiding in the cave of the Gobardhana hill and thereafter in this Kali Yuga he came to Nabadwip.[1]

It is also believed that Thakur Abhiram Goswami brought Malini Devi from his body. She in Dwapar Yuga was thrown in a chest and dropped it in the Yamuna River and thereafter the chest was recovered from the garden at Kazipur near Krishnanagar.[2]

And here Thakur Abhiram Goswami met Malini Devi. The characters of both of them were splendid, wonderful and amazing.

Having found the chest the gardeners presuming gold and other riches opened it but a girl Malini Devi appeared at their front. They informed the amazing thing to the Kazi. Kazi by knowing the all the narrations as given by the gardeners decided to keep the girl as his own daughter and seeing some signs of Hinduism he decided to feed the girl not their rice but only sweets.[3]

Later, Malini Devi came to Kazi and Kazi received her cordially as a daughter and found 'Mahashakti' in her.

Thakur Abhiram Goswami having set up Seva at Vikrampore near Banshuli where Poet Jayadeva and Pdmabati Devi met came to Kazipur. There he met his Malini Devi. Afterwards Thakur Abhiram from Khanakul reached at the bank of river Billok village and sat there. To find them there the men of Kazi criticized Thakur Abhiram Goswami saying:-

"Boiragi Haiya Kena Na Chinah Aapana,
Yabaner Kanya Keno Karile Baasana."[4]

But they were surprised to note that a fallen piece of wood at the bank of the river what all of them could not move a single inch but Thakur Abhiram Goswami having touched with one finger lifted it easily. Again he called Malini Devi who in turn did the same. They considered Malini Devi and Thakur Abhiram were not human beings, they might be divine personalities.

Malini Devi on the request of the men to bless named Khanakul as Kazipur. Thakur Abhiram Goswami hid Malini Devi in the wood made flute for several years. Afterwards Malini Devi was released by Thakur Abhiram and they set Sri Sri Gopinath at their Sripat at Khanakul-Krishnanagar where the Vaishnavas usually come and were cordially received by the couple.

Thakur Abhiram used to test the divinity in new born children. The ordinary children could not tolerate the Pranam of Thakur Abhiram and they had to die. The same thing happened while he was testing the earlier new born children of Sri Nityananda Prabhu and they could not tolerate the 'Pranam' and died. But only Birbhadra son of Sri Nityananda Prabhu as a child could survive. Later after the birth of Ganga Devi daughter of Sri Nityananda Prabhu the same incidence happened and Ganga Devi survived.

References

1. Sri Sri Abhiram Lilamritam – Sri Tilak Ram Das, Krishnadas Kaviraj, Collected Edited and Printed by Kishoridas Babaji, 2nd Edition, 1399 BS, printed at Sri Durga Press, 1st Chapter, p.'Bhumika' 'Ka').
2. *Ibid* p.'Gha'
3. *Ibid* p. 20,
4. *Ibid* p. 39.

60

Mother of Mukunda

Actual name is not traceable but the lady was known as Mukunda's Mother. She was the wife of Parameshwar and both of them were devotees of Sri Gouranga Mahaprabhu (Sri Chaitanyadeva). Parameshwar was a sweet-meat seller. They were neighbourers of the house of Sri Gouranga Mahaprabhu (Sri Chaitanyadeva). And from the very childhood Nemai or Sri Gouranga used to meet them off and on. He and Mukunda were also friends. They preferred to offer sweet-meat to this wonder child Nemai.

Mukunda's Mother and Parameshwar were running family but simultaneously their minds were full of thoughts of wonder child Nemai i.e. Sri Gouranga Mahaprabhu (Sri Chaitanyadeva).

Mukunda's Mother and Parameshwar had the attraction of wonder child Nemai. And so, out of affection once they ran to Puri to meet the wonder child Nemai who became Sri Chaitanyadeva. Among the thousands of visitors, Parameshwar informed self-identity saying 'Parameshwara Muin'. He also informed that Mukunda's Mother who had affection to Sri Gouranga accompanied him in Puri. Sri Chaitanyadeva could easily recognize them and accepted them cordially. He being an ascetic did not hesitate to interact with Mukunda's Mother from whom once he got affection.[1]

Sri Chaitanyadeva was not like other ascetics. He and Sri Nityananda-prabhu, Sri Gadadhar Pundit and all other associates knew to give the women their due respect and necessary freedom and also scope of self exposition in the fields of education and the society.

Mukunda's Mother knew only her God in every respect Sri Gouranga Mahaprabhu. She was very pious lady whom we should also remember.

Reference

1. Sri Sri Chaitanya Charitamrita – Sri Krishnadas Kaviraj, Edited by Sri SriMad Bhakti Sri Roop Maharaj, Published from Gaudiya Mission (Rgd.) by Tridandi Bhikshu Sri Bhakti Gunakar Goswami, Printer – Radha Press, Gandhinagar, Delhi – 110 031, 6th Edition, Published in 1990, Antya Lila, 12th Chapter, Shloka 55-56, p. 1058).

61

Menaka Devi

(The Mother-in-Law of Sri Adwaitaprabhu)

Menaka Devi, the Mother-in-Law of Sri Adwaita Acharya is a famous lady amongst the Goudiya Vaishnavas. Sri Nrisinha Bhaduri was her husband. He was in earlier life was the Himalayas.[1]

She was married with Nrisinha Bhaduri at Narayanapur near Saptagram. They had two daughters Sita Devi and Shri Devi both of themwere married to Sri Adwaita Acharya.

Menaka Devi unfortunately expired before the marriage of her daughters. It has been known that at first she gave birth of Shri Devi, a little female baby and thereafter Sita Devi was born.[2]

It is true that at the time of their marriage Sri Adwaita Acharya was aged enough as a bridegroom but afterwards they had six sons viz. Sri Achyutananda, Sri Krishna Mishra, Sri Gopal Mishra, Sri Balarama Mishra and then twin sons Swarup and Jagadananda.

At the time Sita Devi gave birth to her second son Sri Krishna Mishra and almost at the same time Shri Devi also gave birth to a son who could not survive. On the son's demise Shri Devi was shocked and she could not resist her crying. To see the elder sister's shock Sita Devi gave her son in the lap of Shri Devi in the same labour room advising her to feed the son as her own son and also to forget the sorrows. Thus Shri Devi could check herself and brought the child up as her son. This incidence remained a mystery. Only the mothers, Sri Adwaita Prabhu, the writer Ishan and his mother knew the person Padmanava Chakraborty, father of Lokenath Chakraborty was informed.

" Choudda Shata Astadash Shaka Abasheshe,
Madhu Mase Krishna Trayaodashi Nishi Sheshe,

Henakale Shuna Eka Doibera Ghatana,
Sri Shrithakuranir eka Hoilo Nanadan."[3]

Sita Devi was so pure heart that she easily donated her son to her grief-stricken sister. Both of them were followers of Sri Gouranga Mahaprabhu (Sri Chaitanyadeva). And their mother Sri Menaka Devi was a beautiful lady who should be remembered for ever by the Goudiya Vaishnavas.

References

1. (Sri Sri Goudiya Vaishnava Abhidhaan – Edited by Sri Haridas Das Babaji, 2nd, 3rd, and 4th Parts, 2nd Edition, 501 Chaitanyabda, Publisher – Haribol Kutir Poraghat, Nabadwip, Printer – Radha Press, Delhi 110031, p. 1276).
2. *Ibid* p.1899,
3. Sri Adwaita Prakash–by Sri Ishan Nagar, 11th Chapter.

62

Ratnabati Devi

(The Wife of Pundarik Vidyanidhi)

The mother of Sri Gadadhar Pundit, one of the important members of 'Panchatattwa' was Ratnabati Devi and the same name was of the wife of Sri Pundarik Vidyanidhi who was the Preceptor of Sri Gadadhar Pundit. The two Ratnabatis were intimate friends who took the oath of friendships by plunging half of the bodies into the water of the Ganga and thus became 'Gangajal Sakhi'. These friendships had once in Bengal with love, devotion, belief, magnanimity and cognizant with each other.

Sri Pundarik Vidyanidhi and Sri Madhab Mishra were also fellow-students.

The husband of this Ratnabati Sri Pundarik Vidyanidhi was a landlord (zaminder) of Chakrashala or Chati Village in the district of Chittagong or Chattragram (now in Bangladesh). Like the wives Sri Pundarik Vidyanidhi and Sri Madhab Mishra, husband of Ratnabati Devi whose son was Sri Gadadhar Pundit were friends. Sri Pundarik Vidyanidhi had another residence in Nabadwip. He used to travel form Chittagong or Chattragram to Nabadwip of and on.

"Pundarik Vidyanidhir Nadiaya Eka Badi,
Nadiayay Chattragrame Aasa Jaoya Kori."[1]

The names of father-in-law and mother-in-law were Baneswar Brahmachari and Ganga Devi respectively of Ratnabati wife of Sri Pundarik Vidyanidhi. They were of Brahmin in Barendra branch.[2]

Both of them were disciples of Sri Pad Madhabendrapuri. We know that Sri Pad Madhabendrapuri was considered as the 'Kalpataru' from whom everything can be had. He was the 'Kalpataru' of devotion to Lord Sri Krishna. He was the introducer of devotion to Lord Sri Krishna.[3]

Both the two Ratnabatis were pious and sicere devotees of Sri Sri Radhakrishna.

This Ratnabati also liked Sri Gadadhar Pundit as her son also.

Sri Gadadhar Pundit was from the very beginning became a perfect worshipper of Lord Sri Sri Radhakrishna and Sri Gouranga Mahaprabhu (Sri Chaitanyadeva).

Sri Gouranga Mahaprabhu used to call Sri Pundarik Vidyanidhi as 'Bap' (father) and also'Premnidhi' (mine of love). He was also a friend of Swarup Damodar.

Before initiation Sri Gadadhar Pundit finding very luxurious life of Sri Pundarik Vidyanidhi as a zemindar could not recognize him as a Vaishnava. Afterwards with the Kirtan sang by his company Mukunda, the singer of Sri Krishna Sri Pundarik Vidyanidhi danced madly in love of Lord Sri Krishna ignoring own dresses and ornaments including other luxurious articles. To see this kind of madness Sri Gadadhar Pundit with the advice of Mukunda and approval of Sri Gouranga Mahaprabhu took initiation from Pundarik Vidyanidhi.

Like other women Ratnabati Devi did not expose herself in the Goudiya Vaishnava Movement but she inspired the family to serve Lord Sri Krishna and Sri Gouranga Mahaprabhu. So, let us remember Ratnabati Devi and bow our heads to her.

References

1. Prem Vilas – by Nityananda Das, Revised and edited by Dr. Bijon Goswami, Pub, in 1405 BS, 1999 AD, 1st Mahesh Edition, Printed at Printing Publicity, 24 Vilas, p. 252.
2. Sri Sri Goudiya Vaishnava Abhidhaan – Edited by Sri Haridas Das Babaji, 2nd, 3rd, and 4th Parts, 2nd Edition, 501 Chaitanyabda, Publisher – Haribol Kutir Poraghat, Nabadwip, Printer – Radha Press, Delhi 110031, p.1283,
3. Sri Sri Gour Ganoddesh Deepika – by Sri Kavi Karnapur, Edited by Sri Asoka Kumar Bandyopadhaya, publisher- Sandesh, Printer- Orient Press, Pub in 2007 AD, Shloka – 22-25 and Sri Sri Chaitanya Charitamrita– Sri Krishnadas Kaviraj, Edited by Sri Sri Madbhakti Sri Roop Maharaj, Published from Gaudiya Mission (Rgd.) by Tridandi Bhikshu Sri Bhakti Gunakar Goswami, Printer – Radha Press, Gandhinagar, Delhi – 110 031, 6th Edition, Published in 1990, Adi Lila, 9th Chapter, Shloka 7-14.

63

Ratnabati Devi

(The Mother of Gadadhara Pundit)

Ratnabati Devi, wife of Sri Madhab Mishra whose son was Sri Gadadhara Pundit. Sri Madhab Mishra was friendship with Sri Pundarik Vidyanidhi. Their wives having the same name as Ratnabati Devi were also friends as 'Gangajal'.

Ratnabati Devi, mother of Sri Gadadhara Pundit was in earlier life as 'Kirtida' and afterwards in the present life she had another name as 'Nabakumar Devi'.[1]

Sri Madhab Mishra and Ratnabati Devi both the husband and wife were pure soul sincere devotees of Lord Sri Krishna. He was also scholar as we found in the 'Premavilas':-

"Parama Pundita Hoilo Madhab Acharya,
Pundarik Vidyanidhi Tar Sakha Barshya".[2]

Sri Pundarik Vidyanidhi and Sri Madhab Mishra were fellow-students too.

They were Brahmins in Barendra branch. The name of father of Sri Madhab Mishra was Vilas Acharya. He was appointed as the Pundit in the court of Raja Chitrasen of Chattagram. Madhab Mishra was in earlier life in Braja as the Raja Brishavanu and his son Sri Gadadhara Pundit was Srimati Radha, the daughter of Raja Brishavanu at Barshana Village in Braja.

In Chittagong a son of Madhab Mishra and Ratnabati Devi was born and he was named as Jagannath or Baninath:-

"Madhabera Eka Putra Chattagramey Hoy,
Jagannath aar Baninath Tnar Naam Rakhoya."[3]

Afterwards Sri Madhab Mishra and Ratnabati Devi with their son left Chattagram and settled in Nabadwip in order to enhance the practice and culture of education. Their son Jagannath or Baninath was also a wise student with wisdom.

"Tnar Bhai Jagannath Acharya Bijnabara."[4]

Sri Madhab Mishra and Ratnabati Devi took initiation from Sripad Madhabendrapuri there.

"Chattagram Chhadiya Madhab Nadiyaya Bas Koilo,
Madhabendrapuri Hoite Gopal Mantra Nilo."[5]

Sri Gadadhara Pundit was Srimati Radharani in earlier life in Brajalila was born in Nabadwip and stayed always with Sri Gouranga Mahaprabhu (Sri Chaitanyadeva).

"Madhabera Aar Putra Nadiya Majhare,
Boishkhera Kuhu Dine Janmalav Kore,
Rakhila Tahar Naam Srila Gadadhara."[6]

Sri Gadadhara Pundit was was born in 1408 Shaka (1486 AD). His mother Ratnabati Devi also worshipped Sri Gopala and also Sri Sri Radhakrishna 'Yugal'. She was expert in cooking and used to take Harinaam all along.

Sri Chaitanya Mahaprabhu once from the heap of sands discovered a lovely deity of Sri Sri Gopinath and gifted it Sri Gadadhara Pundit. Sri Chaitanya Mahaprabhu used to meet Sri Gadadhara Pundit at the temple at Tota Gopinath almost daily. He used to take the deity in his lap and would cry for love of Sri Krishna. He used to listen to the reading of Srimad Bhagawata from Sri Gadadhara Pundit and tears from the eyes of both used to drench the pages of the holy Srimad Bhagawata. The appearance of Sri Sri Gopinath also attracted Sri Nityanandaprabhu while in stayed in Neelachal.

We must bow our heads to Ratnabati Devi who gave birth of Sri Gadadhara Pundit and also elder son Jagannath or Baninath.

Reference

1. Sri Sri Goudiya Vaishnava Abhidhaan – Edited by Sri Haridas Das Babaji, 2nd, 3rd, and 4th Parts, 2nd Edition, 501 Chaitanyabda, Publisher – Haribol Kutir Poraghat, Nabadwip, Printer – Radha Press, Delhi 110031, p.1199 and 1329).
2. Prem Vilas – by Nityananda Das, Revised and edited by Dr. Bijon Goswami, Pub, in 1405 BS, 1999 AD, 1st Mahesh Edition, Printed at Printing Publicity, 24 Vilas, p. 252).

3. (Ref *Ibid*).
4. Sri Sri Chaitanya Bhagawata – Sri Vrindabandas, Ed. Srila Bhakti Siddhanta Saraswati, 4th edition, 1984 AD, (1391 BS) Kolkata Gaudiya Mission Antya Khanda, 7th Chapter)
5. *Ibid.*
6. *Ibid.*

64

Laksha Hira

(Blessed by Thakur Haridas)

Laksha Hira as a woman who was nothing but a prostitute in earlier life but ultimately she became a serious and sincere devotee of Lord Sri Krishna with the inspiration of Thakura Haridas.

Sri Haridas was widely known as Yaban Haridas. He was a pure devotee of Lord Sri Krishna. He was ultimately given the name as Haridas Thakura.

One zaminder named Ramchandra Khan was so envious to devotee for his fame that he appointed a prostitute to destroy the fame of Thakur Haridas. The prostitute was known as Laksha Hira as her daily rate was almost the value equivalent to one lakh (one hundred thousand) of diamond pieces. Although she was deputed her all efforts to spoil the purity of Haridas resulted in vain. Ultimately that prostitute became a pure devotee and was named as Krishnadasi.[1]

According to History in the book (at p. 364 & 365) 'Jashohar Khulnar Itihas we find that Ramchandra Khan used to go regularly to the prostitute through a canal by boarding on his boat 'Mayurpankhi'. The signs of the canal still exist.[2]

The prostitute used to earn one lakh of rupees from Ramchandra Khan and so she was named as Laksha Hira.[3]

Sri Krishnadas Kaviraj has expressed in the Sri Sri Chaitanya Charitamrita –

"Haridas yabe nij griha tyag koila.
Benapoler bonamadhye katodin rahila.
Nirjana bone kutir kori Tulsi seban.
Ratri dine teen laksha naam samkirtan."[4]

Benapol is situated under the Bongaon Police Station in the District of North Twenty-four Parganas. For a few days Haridas Thakur stayed here and used to take name of God Sri Krishna one lakh times a day. And so he was loved by Sri Chaitanyadev. In addition the veteran devotee and worshiper Sri Adwaita Acharya also lovingly blessed Sri Haridas.

One day Sri Chaitanyadev (Sri Gouranga Mahaprabhu) asked Haridas– What would be the remedy of the Koli Yuga?

Haridas replied – It is true that in Koli Yuga people are mostly sinful. But God's name can wipe out their sin.

> *"Naamoikang yasya baachi smaranapathagatang shrotramulang gating ba.*
> *Suddhang ba Suddhabarnang byabahittang taarayateyva satyam.*
> *Tachchoihdrabinang janataloashandya madhye*
> *Nikshiptang syana falajanakang shighramebatra bipra."*[5]

Only one name (Sri Krishna) whoever utters or remembers or touches the ears that always would help the Creations irrespective of purity or not.

The devotees normally may not be successful by uttering Lord's name if anybody for the publicity or for any kind of greed. However one day in future the result might be seen.[6]

It is clear that the Kali Yuga is full of vices but it has one hope that if anybody once utters the name of Lord Sri Krishna he would get the benefit. Even a sinner may get the favour of Lord Sri Krishna.

Not only that the person guilty of any sin may be free from sin if the person takes shelter of Harinaam. But the person who acts sin at the feet of Lord cannot get any concession. Umadasi a composer states in her composition:-

However, Sri Haridasa's role in the publicity of Harinaam and Mahaprabhu was much important. He could win over Laksha Hira was also for the influence of devotee of Lord Sri Krishna and Sri Chaitanya Mahaprabhu. Once while Mahaprabhu asked how the creation of this world would be free from sorrows and pain Sri Haridas humbly answered – "Prabho (Sir), with your causeless mercy all have been rescued. This is because you have started the Sankirtan for Lord Sri Krishna loudly and that they listened to.[7]

We know that Haridas Thakur erected a hut and started to sing Lord's name. He used to sing and beg alms from the village. His charming nature and devotion would please all the people he met. So, many of villagers were also happy to circulate his devotion and behave. Thus Thakur Haridas got much publicity in the Country. This could not satisfy the local owner of lands the zaminder Ramchandra Khan. He was envious for fame of an ordinary beggar.[8]

Sri Krihnadas Kaviraj has expressed in the Sri Sri Chaitanya Charitamrita –

Sei Deshadhyakshya naam Ramchandra Khan.
Vaishnav bidweshi bada pashanda pradhan.
Haridas loke puje sahite na pare.
Taar apaman korite nana upaay kore.[9]

According to Sri Sri Chaitanya Charitamrita it is known that Ramchandra Khan sent a prostitute to Sri Haridas Thakur in order to defame his glory.[10]

He sent a very beautifully looking prostitute to spoil his Sadhana and fame.[11]

Ramchandra Khan tried a couple of days but could not destroy Sri Haridas. He sent the most beautiful and having highest rate prostitute in a midnight to Sri Haridas. Sri Haridas humbly requested her to please wait till his memorizing God's name as determined three lakhs a day is completed. But his prayer in memorizing did not complete in the night. It was dawn and the prostitute had to return. Again on the next evening she went to Sri Haridas and in the same manner Sri Haridas requested her to wait. Laksha Hira by observing pious Sri Haridas in taking God's name found that night also ended. But she was attracted and inspired. On the third occasion Sri Haridas finding almost changed advised Laksha Hira Harinaam.[12]

Beshya kahe – kripa kari kara upadesh.
Kee mor kartabya yate jaay sarba klesh.
Thakura kahe parer drabya brahmane karo daan.
Ei ghare aasi tumi karaha vishram.
Nirantar naam laha Tulsi seban.
Achirate paabe tobe Krishner Charan.

To see the glorious character and devotion Laksha Hira was changed. She became disciple of Sri Haridas and gave to poor and Brahmin everything she had earlier earned. She left her life style and having fully shaved her hair came to Sri Haridas.[13]

Sri Chaitanya Mahaprabhu tried to tie all from Brahmin to Chandal in one string by inviting them all under an umbrella of Harinaam. He also side by side wanted to show the right paths to the women who were oppressed, tortured and fallen. From that time socially fallen women found their shelter at Vaishnavas Akhra. Thus they would get the scope of their cleansing themselves.

Actually Sri Haridas was satisfied to note the complete changes in Krishnadasi. With honesty, purity, modesty and kindness anyone can change his/her image. And lastly the person can attain the higher path of devotion. Simultaneously the person needs a contact with a perfect preceptor, the Guru. Sri HaridasThakur with his inner vision could observe Laksha Hira the possibility in her so he blessed her to become Haridasi who always used to remain by praying in rosary Harinaam. The women who remained at the front of the Movement of Lord Sri Chaitanyadev, Laksha Hira was one of them. It has also a connection with the kindness of Srimati Radharani. She had also soft corner for the fallen ladies.

Anaradhya Radhapadambhoja renu
Manashritya Vrindabating tat padamkam
Asang bhasya tatbhavgambhira chittam
Kutah Shyamsindho rasasyabagahah." [14]

Afterwards Sri Haridas giving initiation settled her at his Gompha (Bhajan Kutir) and went to Chandpur. The total changed Laksha Hira living at the Ashram started to take three lakh of name of Lord Sri Krishna daily. She was then named as Krishnadasi for her sincerity and devotion. Other Vaishnavas became eager to have a Darshan (visit) of Krishnadasi.[15]

In this connection we may recollect the same incidences as Sri Haridas could easily overcome all the obstacles with his remembering Harinaam. However according to Puranas we find many episodes. Among them one is story of sage Vishwamitra. The sage was in deep austerities. The other gods were envious too. Indra the King of Paradise was frightened if his right of Paradise be snatched and so, beautiful and much attractive Apsara (Nymph) Menaka from heaven was sent to break the deep sadhana of sage Vishwamitra. Menaka with her aromatic gestures and postures started to dance in front of the sage. The sage Vishwamitra could not continue his meditation with the sounds arisen from the dance with strings of small bells worn out at the ankles and when he looked up he found the beautiful nymph almost half dressed dancing in amorous gesture. The sage was highly bewildered and could not avoid his attraction for the nymph. Ultimately their daughter Sakuntala was born. Another hermit Kanwa brought up the female baby left on the ground and guarded by a vulture with its wings.[16]

When Sakuntala was grown up she with her two confidantes Anasua and Priyangbada made the hermitage cheerful with their plays and nourishing the trees and creepers, the flowers, the deers of the forest. All the inhabitants of the hermitage including birds and beasts of the forest became very fan of Skuntala and her confidantes. However this daughter of Vishwamitra and Menaka had to leave the forest to start for bridegroom's place. At the time of roaming in search of preys in the forest by chance King Dushmanata saw Sakuntala and the King was infatuated with the beauty of Sakuntala. Ultimately she was married to King Dushmanta.[17]

But in the Koli Yuga with many of sacrificed associates Sri Chaitanya Mahaprabhu could win over all worldly attachments. His one of the associates Sri Haridas with the help of remembering Lord Sri Krishna was succeeded to win over sex-urge, anger, greed and infatuation. However Ramchandra Khan tried to defame Haridas as well as Sri Chaitanya Mahaprabhu. He sent Laksha Hira at the hut of Haridas. But the woman with beauty and youth became a devotee of Lord Sri Krishna instead of alluring Haridas. This was possible only because Harinaam. How nice Laksha Hira was transformed as Krishnadasi.

Laksha Hira leaving back her identity of prostitute was transformed as Krishnadasi. With company of a Vaishnava like Sri Haridas and with Harinaam all the time she became a real Vaishavi - Mohanti very soon.[18]

It is known that after giving up all her belongings to the Brahmins she as a destitute became a sincere Vaishnavi and at her old age went to Sri Sri Jagannath Dham, Puri.

Laksha Hira although was sent by Ramchandra Khan for spoiling Sadhana of Sri Haridas she heard the utterance of Lord's name from him. With his open heartedly behavior and reciting God's name she left all her ill plan and ultimately became a Vaishnavi. It is an example of changes of any person who commits sin but with the contact of a real devotee the person may become a sincere Bhagawata.[19]

She was blessed by Sri Haridas. The theory remains that without mercy from Srimati Radharani, not taking shelter of Vrindadevi (Tulsi) and not having contacts with the devotees who have completely keep the dust of the holy feet of Radharani one cannot worship and decorate God. It is impossible.[20]

Mainly the Goudiya Vaishnavas are interested to have contacts with real devotee Vaishnava. Thus Laksha Hira could elevate from her heinous profession to a Vaishnavi as well as a Mohanti. For her changes and transformation as Krishnadasi a house was erected at Gayrha – Rajapur near Kagajpuria.[21]

By donating all her belongings to distressed and poor Brahmins Laksha Hira alias Krishnadasi she attained special mention.[22]

Sri Haridas Thakura leaving Benapol lived on the bank of river Nao Ganga just 2/3 miles away in the district of Jessore (now in Bangladesh). The place has now been named as Haridaspur in the tune of the name of Sri Haridas Thakura.

The hut at the curve of Shaibalmoyee River by the side of Jessore Road is also a nice and pleasant spot.[23]

It is also said that a road from Benapol to Sri Sri Jagannath khetra Puri in the State of Odisha was built out of funds of Laksha Hira alias Krishnadasi. It was famously known as 'Hirar Jangal'. Later this sincere devotee she engaged in philanthropic work for thousands of people. She also at the last stayed in Puri for service to Lord Jagannath. Thus Laksha Hira or Krishnadasi has become immortal.

References

1. Sri Sri Sri Goudiya Vaishnava Abhidhan, Edited by Sri Haridas Das Babaji, 2nd, 3rd & 4th Khanda ; 2nd Edition; Published from Haribol Kutir, Printer – Radha Press, Delhi – 110 031, Page 1190.
2. *Ibid* Page 1422.
3. *Ibid.*
4. Sri Sri Chaitanya Charitamrita by Krishnadas Kaviraj, Ed.President Acharya Sri Sri Madbhaktisri rup Bhagawata Maharaj, Published by Tridandibhikku Sri Bhaktigunakar from Goudiya Mission (Regd.), Printed at Radha Press, Gandhinagar Delhi – 110 031, 6th Ed. In 1990 (1396 Beng.), Antya Leela, 3rd Chapter, Sloka – 99-100, Page 942.
5. Sri Sri Gourasundar arthat Sri Krishna Chaitanya Mahaprabhu'r Charit – Compiled by Sri Shyamlal Goswamiprabhu and with comment edited by Vaishnavacharya Sripad Goursundar Bhagawatdarshanacharya, Published by Sri Kashinath Vedanta shastri and Sri Krishnadev Bhattacharya; printed by Sri Jitendranath De, Sri Krishna Printing Works in 412 Chaitanyabda, Antya Leela, Page 528.
6. *Ibid* P.528-529 (Original sense).
7. *Ibid*, Adi Leela, P.55 (Original sense).
8. Sri Sri Goudiya Vaishnav Tirtha Paryatan -1st Khanda, Ed. & Pub. By Sri Kishoridas Babaji, 3rd ed., in Chaitanyabda 512 (1405 Beg.), Printed at Sri Prankrishna Bhakti Press, Chaitanyadoba, P.168-69.
9. Sri Sri Chaitanya Charitamrita by Krishnadas Kaviraj, Antya Leela, 3rd Chap. Sloka 101-102. P. 942.

10. *Ibid* (Original sense)
11. As no.8 above P.169
12. *Ibid.*
13. *Ibid.*
14. Sri Sri Karnananda by Jadunandan Das Thakur, Ed.Sri Haribhakta Das, Pub. By Sri Giridharilal Goswami Vyakarantirtha in 506 Gourabda, 4th Nirjyas, Sloka 50, p. 146
15. As No.8 above, p. 169.
16. Samsad Bangla Abhidhan – Ed. & Revised by Sri Sailendra Biswas, Dr. Sashibhushan DasGupta & Dineshchandra Bhattacharya, 9th ed.1991, Pub from sishu Sahitya Samsad (P) Ltd. Printed at Nataraj Offset, P.630
17. *Ibid*
18. As No.1 above, p. 1422.
19. *Ibid* p. 1353.
20. As above No. 14,
21. As above No.1, p. 1422.
22. *Ibid.*
23. *Ibid* P. 1979 (source: Jashohar Khulnar Itihas, 1/367-68).

65

Laxmipriya Devi

(The First Wife of Sri Gouranga Mahaprabhu)

The first wife of Sri Gouranga Mahaprabhu Laxmipriya Devi was the daughter of Sri Ballavacharya Mishra of Nabadwip. In her earlier lives she was Janaki and Rukmini in the ages of Treta and Dwapara yugas. Some liked to say that at the time of dancing in the court of Indra, the King of the gods and goddesses, somehow broke the rhythm and was cursed to go down to the world. She then entered into Laxmipriya Devi in Nabadwip.[1]

Sri Lakshmipriya Devi was born in 1492 AD (1414 Shaka, 899 BS) in Nabadwip. Some also liked to state that Sri Laxmipriya Devi was herself the Mahalakshmi of 'Boikuntha'.

During the period of adolescence, Nemai nick name of Sri Gouranga Mahaprabhu, at the time of bathing in the 'Ghats' of the Ganga used to play and disturb jokingly the little girls. One of them was Sri Lakshmipriya Devi. Some of the girls also lodged complaint against Nemai to Shachi Devi and Sri Jagannath Mishra. But when Sri Jagannath Mishra used to take up sticks to punish many of the girls shouted that Nemai should not be beaten. Laxmipriya Devi probably complained that Nemai had threatened to marry her.

The beauty of Laxmipriya Devi was incomparable. Her eyes were without blinking and clear. She used to worship Shiba Mahadeva at the 'Ghat' with folded hands and prayed for a bridegroom. It may be that she having shut up her eyes prayed for a bridegroom like Nemai Pundit. And after her meditation she found Nemai Pundit was standing and staring at her.

"Ei Mate Lila Dunhe Kori Gela Ghare,
Gamvira Chaitanyalila Ke Bujhite Pare."[2]

Banamali Acharya was an aged person with the title of 'Kaviraj' could read the emotions of Nemai or Gouranga and also the girl Laxmipriya Devi at the 'Ghat' of the Ganga. Later he acted as a match-maker under advice of Sachi Maa in the marriage Sri Gouranga and Laxmipriya Devi. Banamali Acharya was considered as the beloved 'Sakhi' of Srimati Radharani named Chitra in earlier life in Vrindabanlila. At the first time Sachimaa did not agree to the marriage as Nemai was not enough older to marry and his education was not completed. But Nemai Pundit having known the information from Banamali Acharya asked Sachimaa what happened to him. Sachimaa replied the proposal of marriage was brought by him and she declined as her son Nemai was not ready. But with some interactions between the son and the mother, Sachimaa sent a man to bring back Banamali Acharya.

On hearing his efforts of match making are going to be matured Banamali Acharya ran to the house of Sri Ballavacharya Mishra of Nabadwip who was also a friend of Banamali Acharya. Sri Ballavacharya Mishra a father of Laxmipriya Devi was pleased to the proposal that the life of Nabadwip Sachinanadan Nemai Pundit would be his son-in-law. He considered this was his fortune. And ultimately the marriage was settled.

Afterwards, on an auspicious evening Sri Gouranga (Nemai) having decorated as a bridegroom with his friends and students started for journey by palanquin and other available carts to the house of Sri Ballavacharya. All the roads were decorated with banana trees and leaves and also with illuminatives.

"Shata Shata Sahasra Sahasra Koti Koti,
Nabadwipmoy Hoilo Pradip Deuti."[3]

There on the both sides of the roads thousands of spectators were eagerly waiting for the going of Sri Gouranga (Nemai) having decorated as a bridegroom. Flowers and garlands were sprayed on Sri Gouranga (Nemai). Even some of the writers opined that the gods and goddesses were present in the sky to witness the procession also showered flowers on the decorated as a bridegroom Sri Gouranga (Nemai). The roads of Nabadwip were almost covered with flowers of different colors and fragrances.[4]

Among the companions of the bridegroom there were present Sri Adwaita Prabhu, Sri Chandrasekhar Acharya, Sri Gadadhar Pundit, Sri Sri Baas Pundit, Sri Banamali Acharya and other respectable dignitaries of Nabadwip also.[5]

"Tabu Prabhu Shuvakshne Godhuli-Samaye,
Yatra Kori Aailen Mishrera Aalaye."[6]

On the other side on the occasion of Sri Gouranga (Nemai)'s marriage at the house of Sachimaa there were present Sri Sita Devi wife of Sri Adwaita Prabhu, Sri Malini Devi wife of Sri Sribaas Pundit, sister Sri Sarbajaya Devi wife of Sri Chandrasekhar Acharya, Sri Ratnabati Devi mother of Sri Gadadhar Pundit and wife of Sri Madhab Mishra and also the old mother of Sri Murari Gupta and other dignified women. All of them enjoyed much.

The marriage between Laxmipriya Devi and Sri Gouranga (Nemai) was held in 1502 AD (1424 Shaka, 909 BS). On the next after noon Sri Gouranga (Nemai) and Sri Laxmipriya Devi started to come the house of Sachimaa. There on the both sides of the roads people assembled to see Gour- Laxmipriya combined and considered themselves as fortunate to find the combined Gour- Laxmipriya like Hara-Gouri. Some said Indra-Sachi, some said Laxmi-Narayana and some said Sita-Ram and so on.[7]

Sachimaa received her daughter-in-law cordially with all the rites of women and was satisfied by thinking that her grief for late Purandar (Jagannath) Mishra has now eased. Her house has become again delightful.[8]

The women present at the auspicious night of the unison of Sri Nemai and Sri Laxmipriya Devi decorated them with ornaments and flowers and happy to peruse the united newly bride and bridegroom. There were also present Sri Banamali Acharya and Nemai's lifelong friend Sri Gadadhar Pundit who were satisfied to see the combined 'Yugal' Sri Nemai and Sri Laxmipriya Devi and accordingly they congratulated and worshipped them.[9]

Sri Vrindabandas wrote:-

"Krishna Anugraha Jare, Se E Marma Jaane."[10]

Sri Nemai (Gouranga) also arranged a feast for the Vaishnavas and the poor people in Nabadwip. He did not select deserved or not deserved. Irrespectively all were fed with their satisfaction.[11]

With day to day domestic work Sri Laxmipriya Devi also taken up the work at the temple to worship the deities sincerely.

"Deva Grihe Karen Je Swastik Mandali,
Shankha-Chakra Likhen Hoiya Kutuhali."

And

"Nirabadhi Tulsir Karen Sevan,
Tatohdhik Sachira Sevaya Tnar Mon."[12]

Once Sri Laxmipriya Devi informed her one of the 'Sakhis' that she expressed to her husband that she should not go to paternal house by leaving the sevas of him and the mother. In order to maintain the rites of family customs Sri Gouranga with Sri Laxmipriya Devi went to the house of his father-in-law. There in the evening he used to take lifelong friend Sri Gadadhar Pundit as his shadow and meet others at the 'Ghat' of the Ganga. He used to avoid other women. (Ibid).

However on request of Sri Laxmipriya Devi Sri Gouranga agreed to meet the 'Sakhis' of his wife and talked with humorous subjects with 'Sakhi' Chitralekha, the seniormost 'Sakhi' and some others. Sri Gouranga, the rare personality who was incarnated to please all the 'Jibas' was successful to give happiness to all.

Even after the marriage Sri Gouranga did not ignore the education and he used to carry books in his one arm and used to feel that goddess Saraswati Devi remains all the time with him.:-

"Ei Mata Guptabhabe Aachhe Bipraraj,
Adhyayana Bina Aar Naahi Kono Kaaj."[13]

Sri Laxmipriya Devi on request of Sri Gouranga to Sachimaa took up the responsibility of cooking also. Sachimaa remained only to co-operate her all along. Sri Laxmipriya Devi would bathe in the Ganga and used to enter in the kitchen where Sachimaa and Malinidevi would be present. Sachimaa used to arrange the 'Bhog' for the deities of Lord Narayana and others.

She used to place the Tulsi Leaves with spikes on the 'Bhog':-

"Tulsi Manjari Diya Krishne Nibedilo,
Sari Diya Sakal Vaishnabe Basailo."[14]

Sri Gouranga used to give cloth to all the Vaishnavas. In one occasion Sri Laxmipriya Devi delivered Sri Haridas Thakura with outer clothes and a bag made by her for keeping the rosary. With the practice of charity they spent much but their stock would not be reduced.

Sometime more than twenty Sannyasis or beggars used to meet Sri Gouranga and he used to invite them to have lunch at his residential house. Sachimaa and Sri Laxmipriya Devi would not be surprised to learn the sudden invitation made by Sri Gouranga rather they tried their best to arrange the food and from unknown source the materials in plenty would reach the house.

Nemai Pundit as well as Sri Gouranga now has become famous for his scholarly act as a professor in the town. He was considered as 'Professor-in-Chief (Adhyapak Shiromani).

"Sarba Nabadwipe Sarbaloke Hoilo Dhwani,
Nemai Pundit Adhyapak Shiromani."[15]

During this period a nationwide renowned Pundit Keshab Kashmiri who defeated hundreds of Scholars in Sanskrit arrived at Nabadwip and heard that only a mere young Pundit tops the list of Pundits in Nabadwip named Sri Nemai or Sri Gouranga. He found Nemai Pundit a mere boy of teenaged Professor was teaching the students the Grammar in melodious voice and scholarly expertness. Having been introduced Pundit Keshab Kashmiri and being requested started to recite a poem of one hundred shlokas describing the glory of the Ganga composed by him at the spot. Sri Nemai Pundit detected five faults one of which was 'Bhabanibhartya' but the word 'Bhabani' itself means the wife of 'Bhaba' (Lord Shiva) and then 'Bhartya' i.e. husband of 'Bhabani' becomes useless. At last Pundit Keshab Kashmiri, the conqueror confessed his fault in rhetoric. There were such five faults in only one Shloka cited by Sri Gouranga out of hundred shlokas. Afterwards Sri Gouranga consoled him and advised to take the shelter of Lord Sri Krishna.

To people in Nabadwip and also outside in the country the news was spread like the wind. Nemai Pundit then was more famous.

It was 1506 AD (or 1505 AD) when Sri Gouranga with a few associates and students set for East Bengal by boat. He also wished to see grandmother and grandfather Shova (Kamalabati) Devi and Sri Upendra Mishra respectively at Sylhet. He then went to East Bengal and roamed Sylhet, Dacca, and other places where he taught thousands of interested students. In the district of Dacca Vikrampore-Panchsar was also the famous centre of learning and there he also taught students. Some of the students of East Bengal wanted to learn from him. He also introduced Harinaam Sankirtan from East Bengal. About his travelling in East Bengal the writers wrote as they considered better to uphold the subject.

Sri Vrindabandas:–

"Brihatspati – Dristanta Tomar Jogya Noy,
Ishwarer Angsha Tumi, Hena Mone Loy,
Anytha Ishwar Bine emata Panditya,
Anyera Na Hoy Kabhu, Loy Chitta Bitta."[16]

Sri Jayananda:-

"Sri Gouranga Dekhite Yata Bangadeshera Lok,
Yubati Yubak Sobhar Nai Rog Shok,

Nirabadhi Kirtan Aanandamoy Banga,
Gourachandra Bina Karo Nahika Prasanga."[17]

Sri Krishnadas Kaviraj:-

"Kata Dine Koilo Prabhu Bangete Gamana,
Jaha Jaay, Taha Laoyaya Naam-Sankirtan."[18]

Many people were fortunate to see Sri Gouranga. Many of them were charmed with the oration delivered at different times like the concept of Brahma, the Sadhya and Sadhan Tattwa, the love of Sri Krishna and other topics.

In addition to Vikrampore-Panchasar Sri Gouranga also travelled at Faridpur, Noorpur, Subarnagram, Egar Sindur, Betalgram, Vitadiya and threrafter at Srihatta (Sylhet) and Badaganga Village where his grandparents remained.[19]

Sri Gouranga i.e. Nemai Pundit delivered unsolicited love to all:-

"Chandale, Patit Kiba Sajjan, Durjan,
Savare jachiya Prabhu Dilo Harinaam.
Shuchi Ba Ashuchi Kiba Aachar, Bichar,
Na Manile –Savare Korilo Bhabapaar."

And about the cause of journey to East Bengal:-

"Naam-Sankirtan Prabhu Nouka Sajaiya,
Paar Koilo Sarbajibe Aapani Jachiya.
Je Jan Palaya Tare Dhari Kole Kori,
Kandarir Rupe Paar Kare Gourahari."[20]

Sri Laxmipriya Devi could hardly bear the separation of her husband Sri Gouranga at the time of his absence. Sachimaa was also anxious for only remaining son Nemai. However, she consoled herself that for more earning of her son would be possible. She knew better to run the family earning was an important issue.

Sri Laxmipriya Devi used to discuss everything to her friend Chitra-lekha. She used to cry day after day to Chitralekha and she tried her best to control her. Both of them also understood that Sri Nemai has gone to East Bengal also for more earning. As Sri Laxmipriya Devi was daughter of a rich person she could not realize the wants in running the family in his paternal house as well as at the house of Sri Nemai Pundit.

However, Sri Laxmipriya Devi could not stay for single moment in the absence of Sri Gourangadeva. Sri Laxmipriya Devi aspired only to see his feet all along. She did not like to take daily meals also. But, she continued the necessary service to Sachimaa. She was so controlled herself that she concealed her sorrows in front of her mother-in-law Sachimaa.

Chitralekha the bosom friend of Sri Laxmipriya Devi was also shocked with separation of her 'Pundit Thakur' Sri Gourangadeva and so she was sympathetic to her. She also tried to console Sri Laxmipriya Devi by assuring that Sri Gourangadeva would return shortly. In reply Sri Laxmipriya Devi would just throw a single laugh.

However, Sri Laxmipriya Devi was becoming weak and thin day after day for the last four months and Sachimaa seeing her condition called Sri Murari Pundit, a local physician for necessary treatment. Sri Murari Pundit from a reasonable distance observed her and after presuming the reason understood the illness for the separation with Sri Nemai diagnosed and prescribed some medicine made of creepers and leaves. Thus more than six months passed.

The condition of ill health rather to say ailing Sri Laxmipriya Devi was becoming deplorable. At the house of Sri Gouranga was like a grief-stricken house. The only two inhabitants older Sachimaa and younger Sri Laxmipriya Devi could not wait for return of their Sri Gouranga. They became almost mad for their own Sri Gouranga.

The separation became so shocking to Sri Laxmipriya Devi that it took the shape of a snake and it has bitten her.

"Prabura Biraha-Sarpa Laxmire Danshngilo,
Biraha-Sarpa-Bishe Tnar Paralok Hoilo."[21]

While Sri Laxmipriya Devi was restless with the burning sensation of poision of sanke-bite there came Sachimaa, Malini Devi the wife of Sri Sribaas, Narayani the birth-time nurse of Nemai, the parents of Sri Laxmipriya Devi, the Sakhis like Chitralekha and others in1506 AD (913 BS, 1428 Shaka). Despite the best efforts by available physicians, 'Ojha's etc. no one could ease the burning sensation of poision of sanke-bite and after sometime Sri Laxmipriya Devi expired. Perhaps Sri Laxmipriya Devi at the last moment also was thinking of Sri Gouranga, aspired to see Sri Gouranga and breathed her last with the name of only her God Sri Gouranga.

In Nabadwip at the Ghat of the Ganga all the associates assembled:-

"Thakur Pandit Kanden Ki Hoilore Bidhi,
Gadadhara Jagadananda Kande Vidyanidhi.
Acharyaratna Vidyanidhi Basudeva Acharya,

Laxmira Biyog Shuni Kata Puranari,
Pramad Ganiya Save Bole Hari Hari..."[22]

Sri Gouranga in East Bengal at that time felt something was wrong in Nabadwip. From the very beginning Sri Gouranga was aware of everything and so, perhaps visiualised all the happenings in Nabadwip and soon he decided to come back Nabadwip. He expressed about his return to Sri Banamali Acharya.

In Nabadwip Sachimaa at her sixty-five years of age could not tolerate the sad demise of her only daughter-in-law. She felt everything at the house has become vacant. Her grief was endless.[23]

Sri Gouranga having started in Aswin (Sept.-Oct.) returned Nabadwip in Falguna (Feb.-March). In the same month he was born and married Sri Laxmipriya. Sri Laxmipriya Devi also died in the same month of Falguna (Madhu Mass). Thousands of people gathered at the Ghat of the Ganga to see and receive their own Sri Gouranga. On the Ghat of the Ganga where the boat reached were also present Sri Adwaita Acharya, Sri Gadadhar Pundit, Sri Sribaas Pundit, Bakreswar, Murari and other followers.He was seen as normal as earlier he was. No one wanted to disclose the sad happening that occurred to their own Sri Gouranga.

References

1. Sri Sri Goudiya Vaishnava Abhidhaan – Edited by Sri Haridas Das Babaji, 2nd, 3rd, and 4th Parts, 2nd Edition, 501 Chaitanyabda, Publisher – Haribol Kutir Poraghat, Nabadwip, Printer – Radha Press, Delhi 110031, p. 1355).
2. Sri Sri Chaitanya Charitamrita – Sri Krishnadas Kaviraj, Edited by Sri Sri Madbhakti Sri Roop Maharaj, Published from Gaudiya Mission (Rgd.) by Tridandi Bhikshu Sri Bhakti Gunakar Goswami, Printer – Radha Press, Gandhinagar, Delhi – 110 031, 6th Edition, Published in 1990, Adi Lila).
3. Sri Chaitanya Mongal – Sri Jayananda Ed by Bimanbehari Majumdar & Sukhamoy Mukhopadhaya, Asiatic Society, Pub in 1971, Printer – National Printing Works, Nadia Khanda Sl No.47, Shlokas – 34, Page. 59).
4. Sri Sri Laxmipriya-Charit – by Sri Haridas Goswami, 3rd Chapter, p. 46).
5. *Ibid*, p. 59.
6. Sri Sri Chaitanya Bhagawata – Sri Vrindabandas, Adi Khanda, 10th Chapter, Shloka 90, p. 205).
7. Sri Sri Chaitanya Bhagawata – Sri Vrindabandas, Adi Khanda, 10th Chapter, Shloka 112-114, p. 207).
8. *Ibid.*
9. Sri Sri Laxmipriya-Charit – by Sri Haridas Goswami, 3rd Chapter, p.107).
10. Sri Sri Chaitanya Bhagawata – Sri Vrindabandas, Madhya Khanda, 18th Chapter, Shloka 220, p. 761).

11. Sri Sri Laxmipriya-Charit – by Sri Haridas Goswami, 3rd Chapter, p.110-11).
12. Sri Sri Chaitanya Bhagawata – Sri Vrindabandas, Madhya Khanda, 14th Chapter, Shloka 41, 43, p. 279).
13. *Ibid.*,
14. Sri Chaitanya Mongal – Sri Jayananda Ed by Bimanbehari Majumdar & Sukhamoy Mukhopadhaya, Asiatic Society, Pub in 1971, Printer – National Printing Works, Nadia Khanda, Shlokas – 19, Page. 64).
15. Sri Sri Chaitanya Bhagawata – Sri Vrindabandas, Adi Khanda,).
16. Sri Sri Chaitanya Bhagawata – Sri Vrindabandas, Adi Khanda, 14th Chapter, Shloka 75-76, p. 283).
17. Sri Chaitanya Mongal – Sri Jayananda Ed by Bimanbehari Majumdar & Sukhamoy Mukhopadhaya, Asiatic Society, Pub in 1971, Printer – National Printing Works, Nadia Khanda, Sl No. 57, Shlokas – 8-9, Page.66).
18. Sri Sri Chaitanya Charitamrita– Sri Krishnadas Kaviraj, Edited by Sri Sri Madbhakti Sri Roop Maharaj, Published from Gaudiya Mission (Rgd.) by Tridandi Bhikshu Sri Bhakti Gunakar Goswami, Printer – Radha Press, Gandhinagar, Delhi – 110 031, 6th Edition, Published in 1990, Adi Lila, 16th Chapter, Shloka – 8, p. 279).
19. Sri Sri Laxmipriya-Charit – by Sri Haridas Goswami, 10th Chapter, p. 209).
20. (Both) Sri Chaitanya Mongal – by Sri Lochandas, Madhya Khanda, Shloka 96-97, p. 76).
21. Sri Sri Chaitanya Charitamrita– Sri Krishnadas Kaviraj, Edited by Sri Sri Madbhakti Sri Roop Maharaj, Published from Gaudiya Mission (Rgd.) by Tridandi Bhikshu Sri Bhakti Gunakar Goswami, Printer – Radha Press, Gandhinagar, Delhi – 110 031, 6th Edition, Published in 1990, Adi Lila, 16th Chapter, Shloka 21, p. 281).
22. Sri Chaitanya Mongal – Sri Jayananda Ed by Bimanbehari Majumdar & Sukhamoy Mukhopadhaya, Asiatic Society, Pub in 1971, Printer – National Printing Works, Nadia Khanda, Sl.No.59, Shlokas 4–7, P. 68).
23. Sri Sri Laxmipriya-Charit – by Sri Haridas Goswami, 10rd Chapter, p.213 and 11th Chapter, p. 223).

66

Sachi Devi

(The Mother of Sri Gouranga Mahaprabhu)

She was Sachimaa the mother of Sri Gouranga Mahaprabhu (Sri Chaitanyadeva). Sachi Devi was the daughter of Sri Nilambar Chakraborty a resident of Belpukhuriya in short Belpukur (originally, Bilwapuskarini) in Nabadwip area. It was located on the northern side of the canal of the Ganga named Gudgude Khal.[1]

Sachi Devi was the eldest issue of Sri Nilambar Chakraborty. She had two younger brothers Yogeswar Pundit and Ratnagarva Acharya and another sister Sarbajoya. Sri Nilambar Chakraborty once used to live at Srihatta (Sylhet, now in Bangladesh) and thereafter settled in Belpukhuriya in short Belpukur (originally, Bilwapuskarini) in Nabadwip area.

Sachi Devi was the wife of Sri Jagannath Mishra, son of Sri Upendra Mishra of Srihatta (Sylhet, now in Bangladesh). Sri Jagannath Mishra for the environment of education chose Nabadwip, the centre of plenty of Sanskrit 'Tole' schools and settled there. We can cite a few upper generations as Madhu Mishra – 4 sons, Upendra (wife Kalabati), Rangad, Kirtida and Kirtibaas.

Upendra (wife Kalabati) had seven sons named as Kangsari, Paramananda, Padnava, Sarbeswar, Jagannath Mishra, Janardan and Troilokya Nath.

Upendra (wife Kalabati) Mishra was considered as Parjanya Gopa in earlier life in Brajalila.[2]

Sri Jagannath Mishra had command in various scriptures and was awarded the scriptural title 'Purandar'. He was a fellow professor of Maheswar Visharad, the father of Sarbabhoum Bhattacharya.

Observing the qualities of Sri Jagannath Mishra Sri Nilambar Chakraborty selected him as bridegroom of his elder daughter Sachi Devi. Both of

Sri Jagannath Mishra and Sachi Devi were devotees of Lord Sri Krishna-Lord Sri Vishnu. Sachi Devi always used to co-operate her husband in all rituals. Once she gave births to eight daughters but they did not survive. Thereafter with the Lord Vishnu's mercy the 9th issue one son was born who was named as Vishwarup.

"Vishwarup-Murti-yena Abhinna Madan,
Dekhi Harashita Dui Brahman-Brahmani."[3]

Sri Krishnadas Kaviraj expressed the glory of Vishwarup as:-

"Baladeva-Prakash Paramabyome 'Sankarshan',
Taha Boi Vishwe Kichhu Nahi Dekhi Aar,
Ataeba 'Vishwarup' Naam Ye Tnahar."[4]

With Vishwarup Sri Jagannath Mishra and Sachi Devi once went to Srihatta (Sylhet, now in Bangladesh) in order to show Upendra Mishra and his wife Kalabati and others there. Then the grandmother of Vishwarup told Sachi Devi that she would bear another son and that should be shown to them in future. Ultimately, Sri Gouranga was born and afterwards after being professor of 'Tole' and defeating Kkeshab Kashmiri and also after the marriage with Laxmipriya Devi travelled East Bengal and went to Srihatta (Sylhet, now in Bangladesh). He thus kept mother's promise to her Parents-in-laws.

In the womb of Sachimaa Almighty God as Sri Gouranga Mahaprabhu (Sri Chaitanyadeva) remained for abnormal time of thirteen months. Krishnadas Kaviraj wrote:-

"Chouddashata Chhoy Shake Sesh Magh Mase,
Jagannatha-Sachira Dehe Krishnera Prabeshe."[5]

Sri Gouranga Mahaprabhu (Sri Chaitanyadeva) was born after thirteen months in 'Falgua'. It was 20th Falguna full moon evening and there was a lunar eclips. According to 'Bhaktamal' it was 23rd Falguna full moon and the day of Holi, so all the people were chanting Harinaam in the evening. He was born in order to drive out all the darkness of the world.

"Haribol' 'Horibol' Save Ei Shuni,
Sakal Brahmande Byapilek Haridhwani."[6]

Sachi Devi's father Sri Nilambar Chakraborty was an astrologer too. He whispered to Jagannatha Mishra that it is presumed the new born son of Sri Sachi Devi would be a great man as his signs of body confirm.

Elder brother of the child Vishwarup also was pleased to find his little brother and took him in his lap with affection. Like his name 'Vishwarup' the brother's name was also given by Sri Nilambar Chakraborty as Vishwambhar that too pleased him. And thus Sri Sachi Devi was being called as the mother of Sri Vishwarup and Sri Vishwambhar the two brothers.

Sri Sachi Devi noticed that her youngest son Nemai or Vishwambhar at his boyhood used to play on the dustbin for preaching them that he should given the scope of learning and others. She also was anxious about his tendency to disturb others and also the girls who used to worship gods and goddesses on the bathing ghats of the Ganga. Despite all these Sri Sachi Devi had a strong idea that in her son Nemai Lord Sri Krishna Himself remains all the time.

After a few days suddenly Sri Vishwarup left the family life and went out for becoming an ascetic. Sri Sachi Devi and Sri Jagannatha Mishra were almost mad for the sad departure of their eldest son.

Later after taking Sannyas this Vishwarup was named as Shankararanya. We also came to know that Sri Lokenath Pundit son of Sri Ratnagarva Acharya the younget maternal uncle of Vishwarup and Vishwambhar took initiation from ascetic Shankaranya and they both wandered at various places for a few days.[7]

Observing the aches of Sri Sachi Devi Nemai or Sri Gouranga consoled his mother and assured that the relation of mother and son is unbreakable for births after births. He assured never he would break this relation. He also commented his mother Sri Sachi Devi was fully pious. Moreover he confessed that the debts of mother never could be repaid.

However, Sri Sachi Devi was afraid that someday her only remaining son Sri Gouranga might leave the family following his elder brother Vishwarup. Ultimately, Nemai Pundit i.e.Sri Gouranga also was initiated from Sri Keshava Bharati to beome an ascetic at Katwoa opposite of Nabadwip on the bank of the Ganga but before going for Sannyas he informed mother Sri Sachi Devi and made her understood that each and every 'Jiba' has to leave this earth some days earlier or at old age. She should console herself that her affectioned Nemai will be in this earth but for the benefit of the thousands of devotees he is to go. Sri Sachi Devi could not defy him but nodded her head.[8]

Sri Sachi Devi, however, got Ishan as her helping hand and moreover Sri Vishnupriya Devi was with her to look after and share the sorrows of Nemai's Sannyas. Still Sri Sachi Devi lost her only remaining son forever. It is true that Nemai would come to Goud Bengal and meet his mother Sri Sachi Devi. That was her consolation. She engaged herself in the devotion to Lord Sri Krishna only as advised by Nemai.

Sri Sachi Devi was aware of the work has done by Sri Nemai Pundit as well as Sri Gouranga Mahaprabhu (Sri Chaitanyadeva) was only for the development of innumerable devotees and common people of the country. She somehow was convinced. Yet she was a mother.

Sri Sachi Devi also got Sri Nityanandaprabhu as his eldest son Vishwarup who used to come to her house almost regularly whenever possible and tried to ease the sorrows of her. He also used to supply necessary information to the mother the activities of Sri Gouranga Mahaprabhu (Sri Chaitanyadeva) in Neelachal as he witnessed and collected. Sri Nityananda from the very beginning took her as the mother:-

"Nityananda Bole, Shuna Aai Sarbamata,
Tomare Dekhite Muin Asiyachho Hetha,
Mor Bada Ichha Toma Dekhite Hethaya,
Rahilang Nabadwipe Tomara Ajnaya."[9]

From this we can observe that other than own mother who gave birth the land, the country and also mother of any other person should be regarded as similarly own mother and should bow to them.

There was living Sri Adwaita Acharya who was known as "Goura Aana Thakura" used to take information of Sri Sachi Devi regularly and also supply necessary information regarding the activities of Sri Gouranga Mahaprabhu (Sri Chaitanyadeva) in Neelachal-Puri as he witnessed and also collected. The relation between the families of Sri Sachi Devi-Sri Jagannatha Mishra and of Sri Adwaita Acharya was also friendly like own men since before the birth of Nemai. So Sri Adwaita Acharya was fully acceptable. On one of the occasions about Sri Adwaita Acharya's reaction Sri Vrindabandas wrote:-

"Yar Garve Mohar Prabhura Avatara,
Se Mora Janani, Muin Putra Tnahar.
Ye Aaira Charandhulir Aami Patra,
Se Aaira Prabhab Na Jani Til-Matra."[10]

Sri Sribaas Pundit in whose 'Angan' yard of the house in Nabdwip was given to Sri Gouranga to continue the Sankirtan everyday was also shocked at Nemai's Sannyas. From the very beginning he was associated with the family of Sri Sachi Devi-Sri Jagannatha Mishra as lover of Sri Krishna. He was pleased when Sri Gouranga Mahaprabhu after returning from Gaya and after the initiation of Sri Krishna Mantra from Sripad Ishwarpuri became almost mad for Sri Krishna. He at that time assured Sri Sachi Devi that he should see the matter but told that disease of becoming mad for Sri Krishna is always welcome for Vaishnavas. Sri Sribaas Pundit like earlier days used to exchange information with Sri Sachi Devi almost regularly prior to his changing residence from Nabadwip to Halishahar.

Once Sri Sachi Devi to see the madness of her son Nemai for Sri Krishna she could not control him.Ultimately the one and half months' younger to Nemai Pundit could expertly control him. Observing his ability she advised Sri Gadadhar Pundit not to be separated from her Nemai:-

> *"Aai Bole - Bap Tumi Sarbada Thakiba,*
> *Chhadiya Uhara Sanga Koth Na Jaaiba."*[11]

At that time of advent of Mahaprabhu (Sri Chaitanyadeva) the beautiful women of Bengal used to cover their faces with 'Ghomta' a curtain like obstacle to see the faces by any other men, men of other religion. The women at their eight years' of age were married to person in order to avoid such unwanted situation. Again, in the South some of the women used to wear the bones of boars around their necks so that the Muslim invadaers could hesitate to touch them. As the marriages were completed at their before teen ages naturally the older husbands used to die and they were considered as 'Bidhaba' husbandless. They were forced to die on the funeral pyre with dead bodies of deceased husbands 'Sati Daha' rites were introduced in order to save the chastity of helpless women.[12]

Sri Sachi Devi understood from Nemai's activities and talks that someone is to leave the family life for the welfare of the common men of the outer world. And with mission her son Nemai or Sri Gouranga Mahaprabhu (Sri Chaitanyadeva) left his wife and mother behind. He went out to preach Harinaam to irrespective of persons in the whole country and now millions of people are engaged in the sankirtan that brings unity and integrity among the Mankind. Having understood Sri Sachi Devi controlled herself and became Sachimaa to all.

References

1. Sri Sri Goudiya Vaishnava Abhidhaan – Edited by Sri Haridas Das Babaji, 2nd, 3rd, and 4th Parts, 2nd Edition, 501 Chaitanyabda, Publisher – Haribol Kutir Poraghat, Nabadwip, Printer – Radha Press, Delhi 110031, p.1381, p.1961 and 1356 and Prem Vilas – by Nityananda Das, Revised and edited by Dr. Bijon Goswami, Pub, in 1405 BS, 1999 AD, 1st Mahesh Edition, Printed at Printing Publicity, Seventh Vilas).
2. *Ibid*, p. 1158.
3. Sri Sri Chaitanya Bhagawata – Sri Vrindabandas, Adi Khanda, 2nd Chapter, Shloka 141, p. 82).

4. Sri Sri Chaitanya Charitamrita – Sri Krishnadas Kaviraj, Edited by Sri Sri Madbhakti Sri Roop Maharaj, Published from Gaudiya Mission (Rgd.) by Tridandi Bhikshu Sri Bhakti Gunakar Goswami, Printer – Radha Press, Gandhinagar, Delhi – 110 031, 6th Edition, Published in 1990, Adi Lila, 10th Chapter, Shloka 75-76, p. 261,
5. *Ibid*, Shloka 80, p. 262.
6. Sri Sri Chaitanya Bhagawata – Sri Vrindabandas, Adi Khanda, 2nd Chapter, Shloka 206, p. 89).
7. Sri Sri Goudiya Vaishnava Abhidhaan – Edited by Sri Haridas Das Babaji, 2nd, 3rd, and 4th Parts, 2nd Edition, 501 Chaitanyabda, Publisher – Haribol Kutir Poraghat, Nabadwip, Printer – Radha Press, Delhi 110031, p. 1356).
8. Sri Sri Chaitanya Bhagawata – Sri Vrindabandas, Adi Khanda, 28nd Chapter, Shloka 181, p. 855).
9. *Ibid*, Antya Khanda, 5th Chapter).
10. *Ibid*, Madya Khanda, 12th Chapter, Shloka 39-40, p. 773-74).
11. *Ibid* 2nd Chapter, Shloka 211, p. 473).
12. Maha Biplabi Sri Krishna Chaitanya - Sri Prasanta Basu Thakur p. 7).

67

Sashikala Devi

(The Sakhi of Chandrakala, wife of Raja Pratap Rudra)

Sashikala was one of the beloved 'Sakhi' of Chandralekha, the wife of Raja Pratap Rudra of Odisha. She came to know the influence of Sri Chaitanyadeva on thousands of people. The King of Odisha was also one of them and he was about to leave the pleasure of consuming royal things and food. Queen Chandralekha was so anxious for the King lest he becomes an ascetic.

Sashikala was a woman who had much wisdom and used to give suggestions to her friend Queen Chandralekha. She expressed her knowledge by saying that Sri Chaitanyadeva was a different type of ascetic. His beauty of body would attract anybody and his quality of becoming overwhelmed in thinking God Jagannathaswami what were beyond imagination by anybody.

Sashikala also once got the opportunity of to see Mahaprabhu Sri Chaitanyadeva at the main gate of the temple of Mahaprabhu God Jagannathaswami. She was perplexed to see his eyes were full of tears in love for God. Sri Chaitanyadeva had a rare personality with high qualities of knowledge. No one can be satisfied to see him once and so the devotees preferred to remain with him. Similarly Sashikala also found another chance to see loveable of all Mahaprabhu Sri Chaitanyadeva and duly expressed her emotion to her 'Sakhi' Queen Chandralekha:-

"Aar Ekadina, Jagannatha Darshane,
Daraye Yabe Tini – Nistabdha – Achal, -
'Garooda' Pillar Mule Nirnimesha Nayan,-
Aha Ki Apurba Darashana."[1]

Sashikala also added:-

> *"Saadh Halo Sakhi, Mone Mone*
> *Padi Giye Dandabat Ratula Charane Tnahara,*
> *Gale Bastra Diye Kandite Kandite."*

Sashikala observed tears for love of Sri Krishna as well as Mahaprabhu God Jagannathaswami were coming out of his eyes incessantly. Such emotion can also influence on others to weep. Sashikala also observed the long hands keeping upwards and uttering Harinaam that charmed her. She said to 'Sakhi' Queen Chandralekha:-

> *"Sudhamakha Bole,*
> *Uchcha Kanthe Madhura Hari Hari Bole,*
> *Yaan Yabe Tini Rajpath Diye,-*
> *Dhaya Laksha Loka Pichhu Pichhu Tnar."*

Sashikala expressed gratitude to her Sakhi and the Raja for their attraction to Sri Gouranga Mahaprabhu (Sri Chaitanyadeva). She also inspired them to see Sri Chaitanyadeva and to have mercy from him.

Generally as an ascetic Sri Chaitanyadeva was not interested to meet a king or any person of material outlook. So, Sri Swarup Damodar and Sri Roy Ramananda with other devotees tried their best to convince Sri Chaitanyadeva to give permission of meeting with the King Pratap Rudra. Sashikala knew that Raja was very much eager to meet Sri Chaitanyadeva. Without any positive assurance from Sri Chaitanyadeva Raja became restless and could not sleep well. That influenced on his wife Queen Chandralekha and her 'Sakhi'.

So, being fearless Sashikala decided to meet first the women of Goud Bengal who then were present in Neelachal for the Rathayatra and also for the meeting with Sri Chaitanyadeva. She also talked with aged Sri Sitadevi wife of Sri Adwaita Acharya. She wanted to see her 'Sakhi' Queen Chandralekha satisfied on the satisfaction of her husband Raja Pratap Rudra. She with another 'Sakhi' Indurekha and 'Sakhi' Queen Chandralekha also discussed with Sri Sarbajaya wife of Sri Chandrasekhar Acharya and Sri Malini Devi wife of Sri Sribaas Pundit. She knew that Sri Chaitanyadeva never uttered any name of a woman in tongue other than mother Sachimaa. They can have scopes of perusal of Sri Chaitanyadeva's feet from nearer place. However, how it would be possible to arrange a meeting of Raja with Sri Chaitanyadeva they could not decide. The three women of Goud Bengal were surprised to note the devotion, eagerness and sincerety of

Queen Chandralekha and her two 'Sakhis'. They praised their qualities and assured that the 'Bhakta's eagerness would be prized once.

On the other hand Sri Swarup Damodar and Sri Roy Ramananda with other devotees were trying their best to convince Sri Chaitanyadeva to give permission of meeting with the King Pratap Rudra. They were also trying to find a scope of when Sri Chaitanyadeva would be free to interact with Raja Pratap Rudra.

Refrence

1. Maharaj Gajapati Pratap Rudra (Drama) – by Sripad Haridas Goswami, publisher – Sri Ramnivas Dhandariya, Aryabarta Prakashana Griha, Kolkata -12, printer – Sri Shyamsundar Goswami, Shyamsundar Press, Kolkata – 5, in 1964, 2nd Act, 3rd Scene, p. 74-87.

68

Wife of Sibananda Sen

Sibananda Sen was a dear devotee of Sri Gouranga Mahaprabhu (Sri Chaitanyadeva). He used to take the devotees almost every year from Bengal to Odisha-Puri before every Rathayatra of God Jagannathaswami and to see Sri Chaitanyadeva at Gambhira. He also arranged the residences of the devotees in Puri for the stayal at least four months. His wife, name not known, was a pious lady.

Shibananda Sen was born in Kulingram in the district of Bardhaman but marriage he settled at the house of father-in-law at Kanchrapara. His one of the sons Sri Kavi Karnapur also established the temple and therein Sri Sri Krishnaroyji in 1708 Shaka (1786 AD) what still exists. Devotees from far and near used to assemble every year before the Rathayatra.

Normally in the age before the advent of Sri Gouranga Mahaprabhu (Sri Chaitanyadeva) the women were deprived or tortured or neglected in the society of the whole country. Sri Chaitanyadeva at first taught the society to give due respect to everyone irrespective of caste, creed, religion, rich-poor, learned-illiterate. Sri Chaitanyadeva had also respect for mothers and Sri Nityananda also followed him. The women got much inspiration from the two super personalities. The wife of Shibananda Sen was also one of them.

The wife of Shibananda Sen did not remain behind the invisible curtains and became active in work alongwith the male partner in accordance with the advices and teachings of Sri Chaitanyadeva and his Sripad Nityanandaprabhu.

The wife of Shibananda Sen used to remember the name of Lord Sri Krishna all along even during all the domestic activities as she learnt from the advices and teachings of Sri Chaitanyadeva.

Once the wife of Shibananda Sen and her husband in Puri wanted to feed Sri Chaitanyadeva and advised their son Chaitanyadas a mere boy to invite Sri Chaitanyadeva. Generally Sri Chaitanyadeva did not refuse the children so he accepted the invitation. Whole of the day of Sri Chaitanyadeva's invitation both of Shibananda Sen and his wife prepared various items as preference of Mahaprabhu. The young boy Chaitanyadas also participated in serving different items. Sri Chaitanyadeva was pleased with the feast and expressed as:-

"... *E Balaka Aamar Mata Janey,*
Santushta Hoilam Aami Ihara Nimantraney.[1]

After eating Sri Chaitanyadeva offered the dish of main food to Shibananda Sen. All devotees present there took the Prasad of Mahaprabhu enthusiastically along with all the members of Shibananda Sen and his wife. At the time of parting Sri Chaitanyadeva told Shibananda Sen – Keep the name of your next son Puridas." After a few months of their return the wife of Sri Shibananda Sen was pregnant and in due time a son was born in 1524 AD and he was named Puridas in parity of Paramananda Puri as advised by Sri Chaitanyadeva.

Shibananda Sen and his wife with their three sons (Chaitanyadas, Ramdas and Paramanandadas) used to go to Puri almost every year to see Lord Jagananatha and Sri Chaitanyadeva. Shibananda Sen and his wife were also sponsors of many devotees by meeting up the costs of living and also the fares of the boats.

Paramanandadas was also called as Puridas. Again on hearing a poem composed by him was named as Kavi Karnapur. Let us discuss the fact:-

Once at the age of seven or eight Puridas with his parents went to Puri and met Mahaprabhu Sri Chaitanyadeva at Gambhira. Mahaprabhu Sri Chaitanyadeva was pleased to see him and told – Krishna Bolo". But the boy remained silent. Repeatedly Mahaprabhu Sri Chaitanyadeva tried his best to speak "Krishna Bolo" but no word was spoken by the boy.

At this Mahaprabhu Sri Chaitanyadeva mysteriously told others – See I am successful to others in the world to speak the name of Hari but I failed to this boy".

Swarup Damodar then replied – Prabhu, you have advised him to utter the name of God Sri Krishna. Perhaps this boy considered these esoteric words and so he did not to utter and was reciting silently".

The boy was only continuing of sucking the finger of Mahaprabhu's foot. In the next turn the boy uttered a poem composed by himself:-

"Shrabsoh Kubalaya Makshmo Ranjanmuraso Mahendramanidam,
Vrindabantaruninang Mandalamkhilam Harirjayati."[2]

Meaning is - The personality who is like the earrings of the ears of the young ladies of Braja, who is like collyrium of them, on whom chest remains like a chain of Nilkanta gems and who is the ornaments of them Sri Hari the ornament of this Universe would be victorious".

On hearing this Mahaprabhu Sri Chaitanyadeva made a forecast – My boy, you would be a great Poet in future as you could describe the ornaments of the ears of the Braja Gopies. So, from hence you would be called as Kavi Karnapur."[3]

This son of Shibananda Sen and his wife was the youngest son. Sri Krishnadas Kaviraj wrote:-

"Saat Batsarer Shishu Nahika Adhyayayna,
Oichhe Shloka Kare Lokera Chamatkara Mon."[4]

Ultimately, Kavi Karnapur became a great poet. He wrote the books like Sri Chaitanya Chandrodaya Nataka, Sri Chaitanyacharita Mahakavya, Gouraganoddesh Deepika, Aarya Shataka, Ananda Vrindabanchmpu, Krishnahnika Koumudi, Alankara Koustava and others.

Shibananda Sen and his wife were devotees of Lord Sri Gouranga Mahaprabhu i.e. Sri Chaitanyadeva and also participated in social activities. For these qualities and also for Kavi Karnapur would be remembered by the Vaishnavas in the world.

References

1. Sri Sri Chaitanya Charitamrita– Sri Krishnadas, Edited by Sri Sri Madbhakti Maharaj, Published from Gaudiya Mission (Rgd.) by Tridandi Bhikshu Sri Bhakti Gunakar Goswami, Printer – Radha Press, Gandhinagar, Delhi – 110 031, 6th Edition, Published in 1990, Antya Lila, 10th Chapter, Shloka 150,
2. Sri Sri Gour Ganoddesh Deepika – by Sri Kavi Karnapur, Published by Ramdeva Mishra 4th Edition, Published in 1320 BS,
3. Sri Sri Goudiya Vaishnava Abhidhaan – Edited by Sri Haridas Das Babaji, 2nd, 3rd, and 4th Parts, 2nd Edition, 501 Chaitanyabda, Publisher – Haribol Kutir Poraghat, Nabadwip, Printer – Radha Press, Delhi 110031, p.1279-1280).
4. Sri Sri Chaitanya Charitamrita– Sri Krishnadas Kaviraj, Edited by Sri Sri Madbhakti Sri Roop Maharaj, Published from Gaudiya Mission (Rgd.) by Tridandi Bhikshu Sri Bhakti Gunakar Goswami, Printer – Radha Press, Gandhinagar, Delhi – 110 031, 6th Edition, Published in 1990, Antya Lila, 16th Chapter, Shloka 75, p.1100).

69

Shri Devi

(The another Wife of Sri Adwaita Acharya)

Sri Adwaita Acharya married the two daughters of Nrisingha Bhaduri and they were Shri Devi and Sita Devi. Although the poets preferred to state that the elder was Sita Devi and the youngest was Shri Devi but some other scriptures state that once before the birth of Sita Devi this Nrisingha Bhaduri was collecting lotus flowers for worshipping God Narayana from a nearby pond and found at the centre a female baby in a big lotus having hundred petals. He took it up and found the size of it like a thumb. Then Nrisingha Bhaduri reached home and at that time knew that his wife has already given birth to a beautiful daughter. Secretly he entered the labour room with the thumb sized baby. His wife accepted and started to bring it up. It was publicized that the wife of Nrisingha Bhaduri gave births of twin daughters at a time:-

"Tabe Shuddhachari Sri Nrisinghajaya Biley,
Bachhiya Bachhiya Bahu Padmapushpa Tole.
Tulitei Dekhe Eka Shatadal Padma,
Padma Madhye Kanya Eka Padma Tar Sadma.
Angushtha Praman Kanya Rupe Soudamini.
Krore Kari Bege Ghare Karila Gaman.
Ishwarecchaya Sei Din Nrisingha Mahila,
Shriroopa Namni Eka Kanya Prasabila.
Suti Grihe Varyare Bhaduri Hrishta Mone,
Padma Madhye Kanya Dekhaila Sangopane.
Loke Subikhyata Hoilo Zamaj Duhita. ..." [1]

Sri Adwaita Acharya married both of the daughters and both were confirmed that they were twins, who was elder or younger we need not assess now after more than five hundred years have passed. However Kavi Karnapur wrote:-

"Yogamaya Bhagabati Grihini Tasya Sampratang,
Sitarupenabatirna Shrinamna Tatprakasha."[2]

The meaning of this shloka is with the strength of Yogamaya Bhagabti Sita Devi as life partner of Sri Adwaita and exposed as the name of Shri.

Here we can cite- "Meanwhile, Nrismha's wife had given birth to a lovely daughter whom she named Sri. As soon as Nrismha reached the house, Ishana writes he sneaked into the Child birth room where his wife was confined and showed her baby he had found in the lotus pond. His wife was so charmed by the child that the couplen decided to raise the two girls together as sister."[3]

In childhood, it is learnt, she (Shri Devi) walked on the enlarged Ganga to attend a conference of Harikirtan opposite the river. She was also with the good qualities like Sita Devi and the devotees could understand it. However, as Sita Devi preferred to accompany Sri Adwaita Acharya almost everywhere publicity was given to her. So, the devotees like to call Sri Adwaita Acharya as 'Sitapati' or 'Sitanath'.

At the time of conversation about the settlement of their marriage Sri Adwaita Acharya told Sri Sribaas Pundit as –Sitara Eka Atma Shri Vinna Matra Kaya".[4]

On an auspicious day Shri Devi and Sita Devi were married with Sri Adwaita Acharya at Fulia. Their fatherSri Nrisingha Bhaduri lived at Narayanpur near Saptagram. It has been told that Shri Devi gave birth to a son who was named Shyamdas or 'Younger Shyamdas' like Achyutananda son of Sita Devi. Sita Devi herself brought up the child as her own son. But there remains another story that in 1418 Shaka (1492AD) Shri Devi and Sita Devi both gave births of two sons. Unfortunately the son of Shri Devi died after birth. Seeing the misfortune of Shri Devi the mother of Achyutananda Sita Devi handed her new born child over to Shri Devi saying to her – You bring up this child, don't cry. Your lap is not vacant now."

Excepting Adwaita Acharya, his two wives, Ishana Nagar and his mother and Padmanava Chakraborty knew that Sri Krishna Mishra was the son of Shri Devi.

Shri Devi was also sincere devotee of Lord Sri Krishna as well as Sri Adwaita Acharya. It is true that she was not so humble in nature like Sita Devi but she was a great lady who did not like to disclose herself. She remained at home like a housewife at that time. Her services to Sri Adwaita Acharya and the Vaishnava Movement silently were worth to mention.

References

1. Sri Sri Adwaita Prakash – by Ishan Nagar, Collected Edited and Printed by Kishoridas Babaji, Sri Sri Prankrishna Bhakti Press, (Halisahar, Chaitanya Doba) Published in 1406 BS, 8th Chapter p. 42-43,
2. Sri Sri Gour Ganoddesh Deepika – by Sri Kavi Karnapur, Published by Ramdeva Mishra 4th Edition, Published in 1320 BS, Shloka – 86, p.18,
3. Reconstructing Tradition, Advaita Acarya and Gaudiya Vaishnavism at the cusp of the Twentieth Century – by Rebecoa J. Marning, Columbia University Press, New York, page-196,
4. Sri Sri Adwaita Prakash – by Ishan Nagar, Collected Edited and Printed by Kishoridas Babaji, Sri Sri Prankrishna Bhakti Press, (Halisahar, Chaitanya Doba) Published in 1406 BS, 8th Chapter p. 44.

70

Mother-in-law of Sri Sribaas

Malini Devi was the wife of Sri Sribaas Pundit was blessed by Sri Gouranga Mahaprabhu (Sri Chaitanyadeva) and Sri Nityanada Prabhu. Her mother was also respectable by them.

While Sri Sribaas Pundit remained busy with the Harinaam Sankirtan organized by Sri Gouranga Mahaprabhu at his residence he could not see at any matter in the family, rather all the members of the family were also engaged in the Harinaam Sankirtan. But, one day, mother-in-law coming at the house of Sri Sribaas Pundit, her son-in-law, hidingly wanted to see the Lilas with his associates like Sri Gadadhar Pundit, Sri Nityananda Prabhu, Sri Banamali Acharya, Sri Gangadas Pundit, Sri Mukunda, Sri Murari, Sri Jagadananda Pundit and others. Generally Sri Gouranga Mahaprabhu would get celestial pleasure in the Sankirtan. But, on the day in question Sri Gouranga Mahaprabhu could feel some unnatural things happened there. He looked at everyone in the Sankirtan including the servants in the house and found nothing was wrong as all were regular listeners of the Sankirtan. Then he asked Sri Sribaas Pundit to find the cause behind his dissatisfaction.

Sri Sribaas Pundit searched here and there in the house and at last found that his mother-in-law was listening to the Sankirtan hiding herself without the permission from Sri Gouranga Mahaprabhu and other associates who could allow anybody in the Sankirtan. At once he dragged her from the hiding place, even he touched her hair. He was overwhelmed with running Harinaam Sankirtan, so he had no scope of consideration whomever he was dragging and bringing outside.[1]

Sri Gouranga Mahaprabhu was strict of the Sankirtan and so he also expressed his anger to the intruder whoever he or she was. Ultimately Sri Gouranga Mahaprabhu accepted the woman in the Sankirtan and it continued.

Reference

1. Sri Sri Goudiya Vaishnava Abhidhaan – Edited by Sri Haridas Das Babaji, 2nd, 3rd, and 4th Parts, 2nd Edition, 501 Chaitanyabda, Publisher – Haribol Kutir Poraghat, Nabadwip, Printer – Radha Press, Delhi 110031, p. 1395).

71

Shashti or Shati Devi

(Daughter of Sri Sarbabhoum)

Shati or Shashthi Devi was the name of daughter of Sarbabhoum Bhattacharya. Sri Sarbabhoum was a dignified scholar and settled from Goud Bengal to Odisha at Srikshetra. He was honored by the King Pratap Rudra at his court as 'Raj Pundit' for several years.

He was expert in 'Vedanta' as narrated by Adiguru Shankaracharya. But after coaching seven days at a stretch to Sri Krishna Chaitanya i.e. Sri Gouranga Mahaprabhu (Sri Chaitanyadeva) he asked observing silence whether he learnt anything from his teachings Sri Chaitanyadeva humbly replied that he listened to these but there were no places of devotion to God Sri Krishna. Sri Chaitanyadeva also thus was successful to open the eyes of 'Raj Pundit' Sri Basudeva Sarbabhoum towards 'Bhakti'. He surprisingly became fortunate to see six-handed at Sri Chaitanyadeva and himself painted the picture of six-handed Sri Chaitanyadeva on the wall of the temple of Sri Sri Jagannatha Mahaprabhu.

After a few days Sri Chaitanyadeva was pleased to note the 'Bhakti' to him and his wife. Both of them were sicere devotee of Lord Sri Krishna.

Shati or Shashthi Devi daughter of Sarbabhoum Bhattacharya was married to Sri Amogh Pundit who was one of the critics of Sri Chaitanyadeva. 'Raj Pundit' Sri Basudeva Sarbabhoum was aware of it and so, he was careful so that his loveable and most respectable Sri Chaitanyadeva as the guest could not be fallen in the slanderous comments by Amogh Pundit, the son-in-law.

One day Sri Chaitanyadeva was agreed to take Prasad at the house of 'Raj Pundit' Sri Basudeva Sarbabhoum. After presentation of Prasada of various items as Sri Chaitanyadeva preferred and cooked by the wife of Sri

Basudeva Sarbabhoum there entered Amogh Pundit despite strict guard and saw the heaps of food presented to Sri Chaitanyadeva. Amogha Pundit commented that the food given to Sri Chaitanyadeva can be fed ten to twelve men, then how a Sannyasi can take all these.

"Ei Anne Tripta Hoy Dash Barojan,
Ekela Sannyasi Kare Eteka Bhojana."[1]

Sri Basudeva Sarbabhoum then chased his son-in-law with a stick. His wife was also aggrieved with the sudden behavior of her son-in-law and did not hesitate to curse. However Sri Chaitanyadeva laughingly tried to console both Sri Basudeva Sarbabhoum and his wife, mother of Shati Devi saying not to be worried as it was his simple observation.

"Prabhu Kahe – Ninda Nahe, 'Sahaja' Kahilo,
Ihate Tomar Kiba Aparadha Hoilo."[2]

It was known that within a short period their son-in-law Amogh Pundit was fallen ill with the deadly Cholera and he was to die. Sri Basudeva Sarbabhoum was pleased to know that God has already punished his son – in-law, otherwise Sarbabhoum could not give up his anger to Amogha. His wife, the mother of Shati Devi also commented that such husband should be condemned.

But, Sri Chaitanyadeva unconditionally forgave ailing Amogha. And he touched the chest of Amogha and said – Amogha, please rise and say Krishna, Krishna." Having the touch of Sri Chaitanyadeva Amogha fell at the feet of Sri Chaitanyadeva and said – Please pardon me, I am a sinner, I have done wrong to you. Please pardon Mahaprabhu". Thus Amogha became a Vaishnava. Sri Chaitanyadeva advised him and also Sri Basudeva Sarbabhoum to bathe in the water of the Ganga. Shati Devi did not utter any word but listened to them very patiently.[3]

References

1. Sri Sri Chaitanya Charitamrita– Sri Krishnadas Kaviraj, Edited by Sri Sri Madbhakti Sri Roop Maharaj, Published from Gaudiya Mission (Rgd.) by Tridandi Bhikshu Sri Bhakti Gunakar Goswami, Printer – Radha Press, Gandhinagar, Delhi – 110 031, 6th Edition, Published in 1990, Madhya Lila, 15th Chapter, Shloka 248, p. 629.
2. *Ibid*, shloka 257, p. 629.
3. Sri Sri Goursundar – by Sri Shyamalal Goswami, Madhya Lila, p. 324).

72

Sadanandi Devi

(Mother of Sri Lochandas)

Lochadas was an eminent writer of hagiography of Sri Gouranga Mahaprabhu (Sri Chaitanyadeva) and other Vaishnava Literature. His mother Sadanandi was the daughter of Sri Purushottam Gupta and Srimati Abhaya Devi. Both the paternal house and the house of her husband Sri Kamalakar Das were at the same Kogram in the district of Bardhaman. In the Vaidya (physician) family Sadanandi Devi gave birth to a son in 1445 Shaka (1523 AD). The son was named Trilochan, afterwards he was known to readers of Vaishnava Literature as Lochandas.[1]

At his early age Lochandas was not a sincere student, however his grandmother was of a strict personality and with her endeavour Lochandas could learn the Alphabets. Later his poetic talent and efforts made him an unforgettable poet. He got inspiration from the life of Sri Gouranga Mahaprabhu (Sri Chaitanyadeva). He wrote Sri Chaitanya Mongal in Bengali on the life of Sri Gouranga Mahaprabhu (Sri Chaitanyadeva) as desired by Thakura Narahari Sarkar.[2]

Srimati Sadanandi Devi and Sri Kamalakar Das both were sincere worshippers of Lord Sri Krishna and also Sri Gouranga Mahaprabhu (Sri Chaitanyadeva). They were pure heart so the talents of Lochandas could flourish.

References

1. Sri Sri Goudiya Vaishnava Abhidhaan – Edited by Sri Haridas Das Babaji, 2nd, 3rd, and 4th Parts, 2nd Edition, 501 Chaitanyabda, Publisher – Haribol Kutir Poraghat, Nabadwip, Printer – Radha Press, Delhi 110031, p.1357 and Sri Sri Nityananda Shakti Maa Janhaba – Sri Nemaichand Goswami, Pub. By Sri Sanatan Goswami, Printer – Shyamasundar Press, 1st Pub 1389 BS, 2nd Pub 1401 BS, p. 549).

2. Sri Sri Goudiya Vaishnava Abhidhaan – Edited by Sri Haridas Das Babaji, 2nd, 3rd, and 4th Parts, 2nd Edition, 501 Chaitanyabda, Publisher – Haribol Kutir Poraghat, Nabadwip, Printer – Radha Press, Delhi 110031, p. 1557).

73

Sarbajaya Devi

(Aunt of Sri Chaitanyadeva)

Sarbajaya Devi was the sister of Sachimaa. She was an aunt of Sri Gouranga Mahaprabhu (Sri Chaitanyadeva). She was one of the daughters of Nilambar Chakraborty of Srihatta (Sylhet) and later he settled at Belpukuria in the Nadia district near Nabadwip. Nilambar Chakraborty, an expert in Astrology had two sons and two daughters. They were Yogeswar Pundit, Sachi Devi, third Ratnagarva and fourth Sarbajaya Devi. In his earlier life Nilambar was Gargamuni and Samukha Gopa.[1]

Sarbajaya Devi, the youngest daughter of Nilambar Chakraborty was married to Sri Chandrasekhar Acharya of Srihatta (Sylhet) and on the other hand Sachi Devi earlier was married to Sri Jagannatha Mishra. Sri Gouranga Mahaprabhu (Sri Chaitanyadeva) was the son of Sachi Devi and Sri Jagannatha Mishra. So, Sarbajaya Devi was an aunt of Sri Chaitanyadeva.[2]

In Nabadwip the people who came from Srihatta (Sylhet) used to live at Dakshinpara but only Sri Nilambar Chakraborty lived in Bilwa Pushkarini or Belpukur at the border island of Nabadwip. There were other islands as – Antyadwip, Godrumdwip, Koldwip, Madhyadwip, Ritu dwip, Modrumdwip and Jambudwip. The devotees like to go round all these islands despite the trouble of facing all the obstacles. This going around is considered as a duty by the Vaishnavas.[3]

Sarbajaya Devi was a perfect wife of a Vaishnava. She was also shocked at Nemai's leaving the family world and becoming an ascetic. She also cordially welcomed Sri Nityanadaprabhu after his marriage with Sri Basudha Maa and Sri Janhaba Maa at the house of Sri Nilambar Chakraborty.[4]

After the Sannyas of Sri Gouranga Mahaprabhu all the people, even those used to oppose him were living in shocking situation. On arrival of

Sri Nityanadaprabhu after his marriage with Sri Basudha Maa and Sri Janhaba Maa at the house of Sri Sachimaa all were enthusiastic to live in normalcy.

Sri Sarbajaya Devi and Sri Chandrasekhar Acharya were among them. They also regarded Sri Nityananda Prabhu as the Avatara of God. Sri Nityananda Prabhu was the propagator of love to Lord Sri Krishna like Sri Gouranga Mahaprabhu. They could become enthusiastic to live in normalcy like others in Nabadwip.

Sri Sarbajaya Devi could understand that women are not required to remain inside the walls of their rooms, rather they can participate in the Sankirtan what introduced by Sri Gouranga Mahaprabhu (Sri Chaitanyadeva) and rejuvenated themselves in unity and integrity. The separation of Sri Gouranga Mahaprabhu (Sri Chaitanyadeva) thus they tolerated with the presence of Sri Niyananda Prabhu.

Sri Sarbajaya Devi keeping in mind the Sri Gouranga Mahaprabhu and Sri Niyananda Prabhu participated in propagation of Education, Idealism, Spcialty and also Variety among the other women. So, she is regarded till date.

References

1. Sri Sri Gour Ganoddesh Deepika – by Sri Kavi Karnapur, Edited by Sri Ashoke Kumar Bandyopadhaya, publisher- Sandesh, Printer- Orient Press, Pub in 2007 AD, Shloka -104-105,
2. Prem Vilas – by Nityananda Das, Revised and edited by Dr. Bijon Goswami, Pub, in 1405 BS, 1999 AD, 1st Mahesh Edition, Printed at Printing Publicity, 24 Vilas, p. 237.
3. Vaishnava Tapas Jiban – by Sri Narayana Chandra Mukhopadhaya, published from Sri Krishnachaitanya Mission, Nadia, in 1406 Shaka printed at D.K. Printers p. 40.
4. Sri Sri Nityananda Shakti Maa Janhaba – Sri Nemaichand Goswami, Pub. By Sri Sanatan Goswami, Printer – Shyamasundar Press, 1st Pub 1389 BS, 2nd Pub 1401 BS, p. 116).

74

Sarbani Devi

(Nearer Lady of Sachimaa of Sri Chaitanyadeva)

Jayananda once has written:-

"Narayani Dhatrimata Vaishnavi Sarbani,
Ashtange Tilak Dilo Nimbapatra Aani."[1]

Jayananda also stated that after the Sannyas Yatra of Bishwarup Sachimaa became almost mad and among the women who attended at the house of Sachimaa this Sarbani was also present there in order to console her. Even like other people, mainly women she could not resist her tears to come out.[2]

At the house of Sachimaa then only a child Nemai was keeping mother's cloth in his hand and said – Do not worry, I am here to serve you all like my elder." On hearing this from Nemai Sarbani Devi like other women was satisfied.[3]

Sarbani Devi was also seen at the demise of Sri Jagannatha Mishra with the bereaved family.

Not only that this Sarbani Devi gifted divine ornaments to Nemai or Gouranga at the occasion of wearing sacred thread.

The women before the advent of Sri Gouranga Mahaprabhu (Sri Chaitanyadeva) had no right to enter into the Sankirtan. Afterwards this Sarbani Devi and other women participated in Sankirtan. Mainly at the time of Sri Nityananda Prabhu even the housewives were seen to dance and sing Harinaam in the Sankirtan. Like Narayani Sarbani Devi was attached with the family in all weal and woe position of the family of Sachimaa.

References

1. Sri Chaitanya Mongal – Sri Jayananda Ed by Bimanbehari Majumdar & Sukhamoy Mukhopadhaya, Asiatic Society, Pub in 1971, Printer – National Printing Works, Nadia Khanda, Shlokas – 20, Page.18).
2. *Ibid.*
3. *Ibid.*

75

Sita Devi

(Wife of Sri Adwaita Acharya –for whom he was called as Sitanath)

In the meantime we came to know that Sri Adwaita Acharya married the two daughters of Nrisingha Bhaduri and they were Shri Devi and Sita Devi. They were twin babies and who was younger or older it was not clear to us. However, some like to state that Sita Devi was the eldest. And for her Sri Adwaita Acharya was called as Sitanath or Sitapati.

(Details of the sisters and their parents have been discussed in short in the 'Shri Devi' article earlier at 69th Character).

Their mother Naarasinghi expired before the marriage of daughters Shri and Sita Devi. Sri Nrisingha Bhaduri their father suddenly met Sri Adwaita Acharya while he with his twin daughters were in a boat on the Ganga and reached the ghat where Sri Adwaita Acharya was bathing and playing with his companions.

Afterwards Sri Nrisingha Bhaduri with his twin daughters came to Shantipur on the occasion of the Puja of Bhagawati and met Sri Adwaita Acharya. Sri Sitadevi fell in love at first sight with Sri Adwaita Acharya. Sri Shyamadas one of the disciples of Sri Adwaita Acharya acted as match-maker. Negotiations started but Sri Adwaita Acharya was over aged in case of Sri Sita Devi and Shri Devi. But Sita Devi and also Shri Devi both with seeing the strong, stout, uncommon height, complexion, scholar of high profile, speech and over all with the devotion to God consented gladly to be married with Sri Adwaita Acharya. He was the best bridegroom to them.

And ultimately the match-maker Shyamadas was succeeded in settling the marriage. Although Sri Nrisingha Bhaduri hesitated for not discussing the matter to his relatives match-maker Shyamadas without spoiling time convinced and made Sri Adwaita Acharya agreeable.... Sri Adwaita Acharya also revealed his four armed form. "Nrisimha interpreted this as a sign that Advaita was indeed the proper bridegroom for his daughters."... Sri Nrisingha Bhaduri then proceeded with the betrothal.[1]

The match-maker Shyamadas announced the marriage on the day after tomorrow and all the devotees were pleased to learn that their beloved and respected Sri Adwaita Acharya would marry the two daughters of Sri Nrisingha Bhaduri. In the marriage Sri Jadunandan Acharya, the generation-wise preceptor of Hiranya Das and Gobardhan Das (originally, Majumder) were present. He was also a scholar, a singer and a sincere devotee of Lord Sri Krishna. All the well-wishers within a short period arranged the marriage.

Sri Adwaita Acharya married the two daughters Sita Devi and Shri Devi of Sri Nrisingha Bhaduri. Sita Devi used to cook palatable foodstuff for Lord Sri Krishna as well as for her husband Sri Adwaita Acharya. She remained with the social activities and service to God and also to Sri Adwaita Acharya.Sri Sita Devi got the initiation from Sripad Madhabendra Puri in dream and Sri Adwaita Acharya initiated her with the mantra as advised in the dream. Thereafter Sri Adwaita Acharya advised her to initiate Shri Devi as without initiation no one should cook for Lord Sri Krishna.

Sri Sita Devi was an appropriate female counterpart of Sri Adwaita Acharya. She was also considered as an inspiration for Lord Sri Krishna to Sri Adwaita Acharya. She was also like a mother of Sri Gouranga Mahaprabhu - Sri Chaitanyadeva. Sri Sachimaa and Sri Sita Devi had prestigious friendly relations too.

Afterwards Sri Sita Devi gave births of six sons who were also had some divine power of creating the attraction to God Sri Krishna and also to Sri Gouranga Mahaprabhu (Sri Chaitanyadeva).

They were:-

(1) Sri Achyutananda,

(2) Sri Krishna Mishra,

(3) Sri Gopal Mishra,

(4) Sri Balarama Mishra,

(5) Sri Swarup Mishra and

(6) Sri Jagadananda Mishra. These two were twin sons.

Sri Sita Devi had some disciples two of them were Jungalee and Nandini who passioned to become women to serve Sri Krishna:-

"Sita Debira Dui Dassi Jungalee Nandini,
Krishna Mantre Diksha Sita Dilena Aapani."[2]

Jungalee and Nandini were different personalities and they after the initiation chose separate ways of living and worshipping Lord Sri Krishna under the guidance of Sri Sita Devi.

Nandidni remained in household work and Jungalee left the home and entered into a forest in order to meditate for Lord Sri Krishna.

Rebecca J. Manring has written:-

"SGK (Sita Guna Kadamba) gives full account according to hrisikesh of Jungali and Nandini.

Jungali and Nandini were two mysteriously transsexual devotees who dressed and behaved like women. Their sexual identities throughout Vaishnava literature and ambiguous, but they were in apparent look biologically men desirous of Sita's spiritual instruction. Their story is rich in clues to Sita's theological identity and the ways her movement chose to accommodate and contain that identity…

The text suggests that these two care among the first 'Sakhi Bhava' Practitioners. As the name implies, the Sakhi bhavas adopt the mood and manners of Radha's girlfriends and often take the statement that Krisna is the only male in Vraja to its most extreme conclusion."[3]

Sri Sita Devi witnessed almost all the activities of Sri Gouranga Mahaprabhu-Sri Chaitanyadeva with Sri Adwaita Acharya.

Sri Sita Devi was being worshipped as the mother to the devotees. She was as 'Sarbajanin Mother' to all.

"…the many students who regularly frequented Sri Adwaita Acharya's home would have become quite accustomed to seeing Sita Devi and would probably have treated her with the respect and deference and affection, they would show their own mothers.

Sita is the goddess Lakshmi. Except it, Europeans, Hindus and Muslims all celebrated this remarkable woman's spirituality".[4]

Sri Adwaita Acharya once advised Sri Sita Devi – You are called as 'Kandarpa Sundari', now I being satisfied with your service like to name you as 'Kanakasundari'. Now you should serve Lord Sri Krishna as a (servant) Dassi.

Sri Gouranga Mahaprabhu - Sri Chaitanyadeva always given the respect of a mother to Sri Sita Devi and like Sri Krishna he also preferred her cooking. So, once he requested her:-

"Adwaita Grihini Mahasati Patibrata,
Vishwambhar Mahaprabhu Ja're Bole 'Mata',

Prabhu Bole, - Shighra Giya Karaha Randhan,
Krishnera Noibedya Karo, Karibo Vojana."[5]

We like to quote – In the Advaita Acraya corpus, certain women receive frequent mention because of their relationships with notable men: Saci, Vishnupriya, Janhaba primary wife of Nityananda (one of Caitanya's closest associates), and Sita Devi. Yet sectarian records mention no women among the leaders of the first generation. However, in the next generation leadership shifted to (among others) two women who were so close to the founders that in retrospect their roles seem obvious, although at the time the community itself could not have anticipated their rises to power. These were Advaita Acarya's senior wife Sita Devi and Nityananda's second wife Jahnavi (Janhaba Devi)".[6]

Fourteen months later the disappearances of Sri Chaitanyadeva and Sri Gadadhar Pundit in the Gundicha temple in 1457 Shaka (1535 AD) in the month of 'Agrahayana' at Shukla 4th day of Moon Sri Basudhamaa, wife of Sri Nityananda Prabhu gave birth to a son Birbhadraprabhu at the house in Khardah. Both Sri Adwaita Acharya and Sri Sita Devi attended the house of Sri Nityananda Prabhu in order to greet the child Birbhadra or Birchandra there.

At the same time the grandson of Sri Bangsibadan of Fulia was born in Nabadwip in 1457 Shaka Falguna-Chaitra. He was Sri Ramchandra or in short, Ramai Thakura. With other women and Sri Adwaita Acharya Sri Sita Devi also attended 'Chaitanya Bhawan' in order to see and accordingly greet the son of Sri Chaitanyadas. This child Ramai was adopted by Janhabamaa as her own son. He was brought up by Janhabamaa. Later he established the Baghnapara Sripat.[7]

Sri Sita Devi was a perfect housewife. She fulfilled the customary obligations of a woman of her social class and demonstrated through her behavior that she understood and accepted her traditional role.

However, like other women Sri Sita Devi bore the responsibility of initiating others as introduced by Sri Nityananda Prabhu as in case of Sri Janhaba Maa. She felt for the poor, the socially tortured and deprived women. 'Service to Human Being' was her motto.

Practically, Sri Sita Devi should not be considered as an individual but rather her character is created to conform a desired pattern.

Ishana's identification of Sri Sita Devi as 'Paurnamasi' and 'Yogamaya' are more clear identifications that she is mythologically suited, indeed, to be Sri Adwaita Acharya's wife, 'Paurnamasi' is the old woman in Braja who arranges the secret trysts of Sri Radha and Sri Krishna that epitomize the intense and intimately passionate relationship with the divine that the Goudiyas advocate. 'Yogamaya' is the personification of Sri Krishna's magical powers, who always precedes him into the world. Both characters are essential to Sri Krishna's activities. Thus Sri Sita Devi is perfect mate for the man eventually invokes Sri Krishna to take birth in Nadiya.[8]

In the Eastern region of India during the period of 15th and 16th century the deluge of Vaishnava Movement accepted male and female participants. The aged people were also welcomed in the Movement of Vaishnavas.

Sri Sita Devi by seeing Shasikala, Indurekha and the queen Chandrakala of Raja Pratap Rudra realized the efforts and eagerness to have a 'Darshan' of Sri Chaitanya Mahaprabhu. She consoled by saying that they were sevakas of Sri Sri Jagannatha Mahaprabhu, the motionless Brahma and within a short period they would be satisfied to see the moving Brahma Sri Chaitanyadeva.[9]

Sri Sita Devi also assured that Raja Pratap Rudra would get the opportunity to touch the feet of Sri Chaitanyadeva with blessing too in near future. She could also assure both of them the Queen and the King themselves were really loving devotees of Sri Sri Jagannatha Mahaprabhu and so, their desire would be fulfilled. She wished that they would get Sri Chaitanya Mahaprabhu.

Sri Achyutananda was a perfect and sincere Vaishnava whom the 'Sadachari' Vaishnavas like to follow. He was born in 1414 Shaka. He knew Sri Gouranga Mahaprabhu (Sri Chaitanyadeva) was God Himself. Sri Achyutananda was one of the disciples of Sri Gadadhara Pundit.

"Yata Chaitanyera Priya Paarishadgana,
Achyutera Priya Nahe Hena Nahi Jana,
Nityananda Swaruper Pranera Samana,
Gadadhara Punditera Sishyera Pradhan."[10]

Sri Krishna Mishra was born in 1418 Shaka. At the same period Sri Shri Devi another wife of Sri Adwaita Acharya gave birth to a son and it did not survive. Feeling the shock of Sister Sri Shri Devi, Sri Sita Devi gave her son in the vacant lap of Sri Shri Devi in the usual labour room. Since then Sri Krishna Mishra knew his mother was Sri Shri Devi. He was initiated from Sri Adwaita Acharya and given the responsibility of worshiping the deity of Sri Sri Madan Gopal that established by Sri Adwaita Acharya.

Sri Gopal Mishra was born in 1422 Shaka. He was regarded as Sri Ganesha. Once in the 'Gundicha Marjan' time before the Rathayatra this third son of Sri Adwaita Acharya and Sri Sita Devi fell on the floor of Gundicha Temple while dancing and singing Harinaam with Sri Chaitanya Mahaprabhu and fainted. It was so serious that Sri Adwaita Acharya became restless in fear. However Sri Chaitanya Mahaprabhu at last touched on his chest and said – Gopala of Gokula, rise please, please rise." Gopal rose up and continued to participate in the programme of 'Gundicha Marjan' and Sri Chaitanya Mahaprabhu embraced him and both of them were shedding tears in love of Sri Krishna- Sri Sri Jagannathaswami. The devotees present there also were to shed tears in love of Lord Sri Krishna- Sri Sri Jagannatha Mahaprabhu.

It is known that Sri Gopal Mishra was initiated from his mother Sri Sita Devi.

Sri Balarama Mishra was their fourth son who was born in 1426 Shaka like an incarnation of King of gods and goddesses Indra. Some, seeing the brightness commented that the Moon has come in the house Sri Adwaita Acharya and Sri Sita Devi. Astrologer said that the new born child would be wise like 'Brihaspati' the preceptor of gods and goddesses and like Kuber Avatara he would be preferred by the goddess Lakshmidevi. Moreover this son would be strong enough so he was named as Balarama. He was also one of the followers of Sri Gouranga Mahaprabhu - Sri Chaitanyadeva.

Sri Swarup Mishra and Sri Jagadananda Mishra were twin sons. Both of them were loved by many of the devotees for amiable nature they possessed.

The sons of Sri Adwaita Acharya and Sri Sita Devi were not only followers of Lord Sri Chaitanyadeva but also composers of 'Padas' on Sri Krishna and Sri Gouranga Mahaprabhu (Sri Chaitanyadeva).

Let us quote- "Sita Caritra is probably the first work of Gaudiya Vaishnava Literature whose protagonist is a (mortal) woman.....But no one prior to Sri Lokenath Dass, author of 'Sita Caritra' had taken a mortal female subject. The literary situation obviously reflects prevailing social conditions in the Seventeenth Century in Bengal."[11]

Sri Sita Devi was the comparison to herself only. She was the mother of the Vaishnavas in deed.

References

1. Reconstructing Tradition, Advaita Acarya and Gaudiya Vaishnavism at the cusp of the Twentieth Century – by Rebecca J. Marning, Columbia University Press, New York, page-197).
2. Prem Vilas – by Nityananda Das, Revised and edited by Dr. Bijon Goswami, Pub, in 1405 BS, 1999 AD, 1st Mahesh Edition, Printed at Printing Publicity, 24 Vilas, p. 234.
3. Reconstructing Tradition, Advaita Acarya and Gaudiya Vaishnavism at the cusp of the Twentieth Century – by Rebecca J. Marning, Columbia University Press, New York, Thesis Paper page-203-204,
4. *Ibid* – p. 207,
5. Sri Sri Chaitanya Bhagawata – Sri Vrindabandas, Madhya Khanda, 19th Chapter, Shloka 227-228, p. 743.
6. Reconstructing Tradition: Advaita Acarya and Gaudiya Vaishnavism at the cusp of the Twentieth Century – by Rebecca J. Marning, Columbia University Press, New York, Thesis Paper page-193,
7. Sri Sri Nityananda Shakti Maa Janhaba – Sri Nemaichand Goswami, Pub. By Sri Sanatan Goswami, Printer – Shyamasundar Press, 1st Pub 1389 BS, 2nd Pub 1401 BS, p.128 and 192).
8. Reconstructing Tradition: Advaita Acarya and Gaudiya Vaishnavism at the cusp of the Twentieth Century – by Rebecca J. Marning, Columbia University Press, New York, Thesis Paper, page-198).
9. Maharaj Gajapati Pratap Rudra (Drama) – by Sripad Haridas Goswami, publisher – Sri Ramnivas Dhandariya, Aryabarta Prakashana Griha, Kolkata -12, printer – Sri Shyamsundar Goswami, Shyamsundar Press, Kolkata – 5, in 1964, 2nd Act, 3rd Scene, p.74).
10. Sri Sri Chaitanya Bhagawata – Sri Vrindabandas, Antya Khanda, 4th Chapter).
11. Reconstructing Tradition: Advaita Acarya and Gaudiya Vaishnavism at the cusp of the Twentieth Century – by Rebecca J. Marning, Columbia University Press, New York, Thesis Paper, page-199).

76

Sita Devi

(The Mother of Sri Raghunath Shiromani)

At Panchakhanda in Srihatta (Sylhet) Sri Raghunath Shiromani a renowned scholar in logic and author of various books was born. His mother was also another Sita Devi.

This Sita Devi was married to Gobinda, the youngest son of Vidyutmmali and Ishan of Srihatta (Sylhet). The other elder brothers of Gobinda were Sri Hari, Ramakanta and Ramchandra. Sri Sita Devi and Gobinda had two sons Raghupati and Raghunath.[1]

Raghunath was born at the end of 15th century (1480 AD) in Nabadwip. Their forefather Sridharacharya was invited from Mithila to conduct 'Yagna' by the King of Srihatta Adi Dharmapa in 641AD (51 Tripurabda). Let us quote a comment in Sanskrit Language:-

"Tripura Paarbatisha SriSriTuktadidharmapa,
Smrajnang Datta Ptrancha Moithelishu Tapaswishu.
...Tripurabadebanabde DattaPatrika"[2]

At the premature death of husband Gobinda this Sita Devi fell in the ocean of sorrows to bring up the two sons. Raghunatha was below five years' of age. So, at first she had to choose the begging profession. It was a hard job for her. At last Sita Devi started to serve the domestic work at some of the students of Sarbabhoum Bhattacharya's 'Tole' in order to have the means of food for her and the sons.[3]

Unfortunately since birth Raghunath had vision in only one eye. And so, he was known as 'Kana Bhatta Shiromani'. He was also familiar with the name as 'Kana Shiromani' or 'Kana Bhatta'.[4]

At the age five Sita Devi sent Raghunath to bring some pieces of fire of charcoal from a certain student for her use in cooking. Raghunath accordingly approached the student but the senior student was busy and he was annoyed. He just told him to take it from the burning oven. He did neither thought for any pot nor Raghunath had any pot to carry the fire pieces. With his present-mindedness collected some sands in his palm and thus became ready to collect fire pieces. Sri Basudeva Sarbabhoum Bhattacharya accidentally was present there and noticed the promptness and ready-wittedness of the boy below five years of age. The renowned scholar Sarbabhoum Bhattacharya was surprised to note the promptness and ready-wittedness of the boy and decided to take the boy to educate and to bring him up. He asked for the boy to Sita Devi who in turn took this proposal as her fortune.[5]

Raghunath thus being admitted in the 'Tole' of Sri Basudeva Sarbabhoum Bhattacharya and within a short period became a scholar in various branches of Sanskrit Language. He also during his studentship pointed out some mistakes in the text book 'Chintamoni' and wrote an essay in support of his views to circulate. At this great chaos were aroused in the 'Tole'. Having completed the education from Sri Basudeva Sarbabhoum Raghunath proceeded to learn more from Pakshadhar Mishra in Mithila. He was invited too. But there the existing students out of jealousy uttered the shloka:-

"Aakhandala Sahasraksho Birupaksha Trilochanah,
Anye Dwilochanaah Sarbe Ko Bhabanekalochanah."[6]

The meaning was Indra is with thousand eyes, Mahadeva has the three eyes and others all are having two eyes but who are you one-eyed person?

But in the meantime Sri Basudeva Sarbabhouma was invited by the King Pratap Rudra of Odisha. Raghunath became an unparallel scholar in Nabadwip.

Raghunath the youngest son of Sita Devi also found the mistakes and unusefulness of the 'Tika' on 'Sarbabhouma Nirukta' and did not hesitate to declare its unworthiness. This was written by Sri Basudeva Sarbabhoum.

Once, Sri Gouranga Mahaprabhu (Sri Chaitanyadeva) dropped his writing into the water of the Ganga only to establish the 'Tikka' of Raghunath Shiromani.

Raghunath Shiromani also wrote many books. The notable books were 'Chintamoni – Dadhiti', 'Padartha Khandan', 'Bouddhadikarer Tika' and some others.[7]

This Sita Devi was a fortunate and famous lady who gave birth to a son like Sri Raghunath Shiromani. Let us quote a shloka written by Raghunath Shiromani:-

"Yohandhang Karotyakshimantang Yascha Baalng Prabaodhet,
Tamebaadhyapakang Manye Tadanye Namadharinah."[8]

In this shloka written by Raghunath Shiromani expressed that whoever can give an eye, understands a boy, he is erudite and others are nothing but only bearing a name.

References

1. Sri Sri Goudiya Vaishnava Abhidhaan – Edited by Sri Haridas Das Babaji, 2nd, 3rd, and 4th Parts, 2nd Edition, 501 Chaitanyabda, Publisher – Haribol Kutir Poraghat, Nabadwip, Printer – Radha Press, Delhi 110031, p.1327).
2. Nabadwip Mahima – by Kantichandran Rarhi, Edited by Yagneswar Chowdhury, published by Puratattwa Parishad – Akshar Prakashani, 1st publication in 1291 BS, p.130 rfd from Sahitya Parishad Patrika 1311 BS.
3. *Ibid* – p. 82,
4. Sri Sri Goudiya Vaishnava Abhidhaan – Edited by Sri Haridas Das Babaji, 2nd, 3rd, and 4th Parts, 2nd Edition, 501 Chaitanyabda, Publisher – Haribol Kutir Poraghat, Nabadwip, Printer – Radha Press, Delhi 110031, p. 1327,
5. Nabadwip Mahima – by Kantichandran Rarhi, Edited by Yagneswar Chowdhury, published by Puratattwa Parishad – Akshar Prakashani, 1st publication in 1291 BS, p. 82).
6. *Ibid* – p.83).
7. Sri Sri Goudiya Vaishnava Abhidhaan – Edited by Sri Haridas Das Babaji, 2nd, 3rd, and 4th Parts, 2nd Edition, 501 Chaitanyabda, Publisher – Haribol Kutir Poraghat, Nabadwip, Printer – Radha Press, Delhi 110031, p. 1327).
8. Nabadwip Mahima – by Kantichandran Rarhi, Edited by Yagneswar Chowdhury, published by Puratattwa Parishad – Akshar Prakashani, 1st publication in 1291 BS, p. 85).

77

Sita Devi

(The Mother of Sri Lokenath Goswami)

One of the important characters who followed and acted as Sri Gouranga Mahaprabhu-Sri Chaitanyadeva desired Sri Lokenath Goswami was. His mother and father were Sri Sita Devi and Sri Padmanava Chakraborty respectively. They lived at Talkhadi village of the district of Jessore. Some liked to cite the name of the village as 'Talkhoira' or 'Talgoira'. Sri Lokenath Goswami was as Manjulali Sakhi in Dwapar Lila of Lord Sri Krishna.[1]

Sri Sita Devi and Sri Padmanava Chakraborty had four sons. Their third son Sri Lokenath was born in 1405 Shaka (1483 AD). The upper pedigree of Sri Lokenath is available in 'Sapta Goswami' at p.13 & 14 and "Sri Brajadham' at 2nd Part p. 2 &3 written by Sri Satish Chandra Mitra and Sri Gobardhan Das respectively.[2]

Sri Sita Devi's third son Sri Lokenath was primarily learned basic education from his father Sri Padmanava Chakraborty. He was a talented boy and had sufficient devotion to lord Sri Krishna. Sri Padmanava Chakraborty with an advice of Sri Sita Maa sent Sri Lokenath for learning the Srimad Bhagawata to Sri Adwaita Acharya.

Sri Adwaita Acharya was also a teacher and preceptor of Sri Padmanava Chakraborty. Naturally Sri Adwaita Acharya used to favour and bless Sri Padmanava Chakraborty. At that time one of the 'Panchatattwa' Sri Pundit Sri Gadadhar Mishra was also a student in the 'Tole' of Sri Adwaita Acharya.[3]

Afterwards during living parents Sri Padmanava Chakraborty left the family life and reached Nabadwip in order to serve Sri Krishna with Sri Gouranga Mahaprabhu later Sri Chaitanyadeva and his other associates like Sri Pundit Sri Gadadhar Mishra who remained with Mahaprabhu as a shadow.

The mother of Sri Lokenath Chakraborty Sita Devi was a housewife who remained busy with cooking, receiving the guests and worshipping domestic deities of gods and goddesses. Yet Sita Devi inspired the Vaishnavism Movement actively with heart and soul.

References

1. Sri Sri Nityananda Shakti Maa Janhaba – Sri Nemaichand Goswami, Pub. By Sri Sanatan Goswami, Printer – Shyamasundar Press, 1st Pub 1389 BS, 2nd Pub 1401 BS, 14th Chapter p.410 and Sri Sri Gour Ganoddesh Deepika – by Sri Kavi Karnapur, Edited by Sri Ashoke Kumar Bandyopadhaya, publisher- Sandesh, Printer- Orient Press, Pub in 2007 AD, Shloka -187,
2. Sri Sri Nityananda Shakti Maa Janhaba – Sri Nemaichand Goswami, Pub. By Sri Sanatan Goswami, Printer – Shyamasundar Press, 1st Pub 1389 BS, 2nd Pub 1401 BS, 12th Chapter, p. 411).
3. *Ibid* – p. 412).

78

Sunila Devi

(The Old Grandmother of Sri Ramai Goswami)

The old-grandmother of Ramai Thakura or Goswami Sri Sunila Devi is also to be remembered. Her husband Sri Chhakadi Chattopadhyay or Madhabdas Mishra and his forefathers used to reside at the village of Patuli in the district of Bardhaman. They were of Rarhi Sect with Kashyapa Gotra. The husband of Sunila Devi Sri Chhakadi Chattopadhyay left the residence from Patuli and settled at Fulia in Nabadwip. In the childhood of Nemai they used to visit the house of Sachimaa. So, they were fortunate to become affectionate to child Nemai and could hug him.[1]

Another Researcher commented that the name of wife Sri Chhakadi Chattopadhyay was Bhagwati Devi. He was born in 1416 Shaka. But Tridandibhikshu Sri Bhaktijiban Harijan in Sri Sri Gour-Parshad Charitaboli commented the name of mother was Srimati Chandrakala Devi.

However the year of the birth in 1416 Shaka has been confirmed by the writing of Bansibadan Chattopadhaya:-

"Chouddashata Sholo Shake Madhu Purnimay,
Bansiya Prakatotsab Hoyto Sandhyay."[2]

Once after more than two years after taking Sannyas and toured in the South Sri Chaitanyadeva came to Goud Bengal and pardoned Sri Debananda Pundit at Fulia in Nabadwip at the house of Sri Chhakadi Chattopadhyay. There Sunila Devi had the opportunity of serving Sri Gouranga Mahaprabhu-Sri Chaitanyadeva.

The son of Sunila or Bhagawati Devi Sri Bansibadan Chattopadhaya was also a renowned poet in his time. He was also called by the devotees as Sri Bansibadan, Bansi, Bansidas, Sri Badan and Badananda in five names.

Sri Bansibadan Chattopadhaya the son of Sunila or Bhagawati Devi knew nothing but Sri Gouranga Mahaprabhu-Sri Chaitanyadeva. His all the thoughts and the activities were encircling Sri Chaitanyadeva only. He was fortunate to have affection of Vishnupriya Devi too.

Being the mother of Sri Bansibadan Chattopadhaya Sunila or Bhagawati Devi was a known personality in Nabdwip. She was a sincere devotee of Sri Krishna and a follower of Sri Chaitanya Mahaprabhu.

References

1. Sri Sri Nityananda Shakti Maa Janhaba – Sri Nemaichand Goswami, Pub. By Sri Sanatan Goswami, Printer – Shyamasundar Press, 1st Pub 1389 BS, 2nd Pub 1401 BS, 13th Chapter, p. 178).
2. Bansi Siksha – by Bangsibadan Chattopadhyay, Srila Premdas written glorious book, edited by Edited and Published by Kishoridas Babaji, Sri Sri Prankrishna Bhakti Press, (Halisahar, Chaitanya Doba) Published in 1412 BS, p. 51).

79

Sulochana Devi

(The wife of Preceptor of Mishra Family)

During the 16th century the Movement of Religion, specially was Vaishnavism the role of the Mishra family was a remarkable incidence. All the people of Nabadwip ultimately became united as we seen in the Kazi subdual episode.

Sulochana Devi, the wife of certain Preceptor was one of them. At the time of sacred thread wearing like mother Sachi Devi, nurse-mother Narayani, Malini Devi wife of Sri Sri Baas, and other deserving mothers Sulochana Devi also gave alms to the new Brahmin Sri Gouranga with affection and full satisfaction.

"Narayani Dhatrimata Viksha Dilo Range,
Gurupatni Sulochana Satyabhama Sange."

Again,

"Stree Purush Yata Yata Nabadwipe Boise,
Eke Eke Viksha Dilo Manera Santoshe."[1]

Sulochana Devi like other women became surprised to note the unbelievable dance and singing by Sri Gouranga Mahaprabhu. Sulochana Devi could think herself gratified of the relation with Sri Gouranga Mahaprabhu. The associates used to take these activities of Sri Gouranga Mahaprabhu as exposed as God.

In 15th and 16th century Sri Gouranga Mahaprabhu with his beautiful divine appearance, wisdom, education, thoughts on the reality, debating capacity and a person should have Godlike qualities could easily influence and move all the people he met.

It was the glory of Sulochana Devi that she could understand the future incarnation who could teach all others to inspire to be united in the problem ridden society and to maintain the social rules and other spiritual practices. So, we should bow our heads to Sulochana Devi.

Reference

1. Sri Chaitanya Mongal – Sri Jayananda Ed. by Bimanbehari Majumdar & Sukhamoy Mukhopadhaya, Asiatic Society, Pub in 1971, Printer – National Printing Works, Nadia Khanda - 24, Shlokas – 16, 18 Page. 31).

80

The Mother of Swarup Damodar

Sri Purushottam Pundit or Purushottam Acharya once lived at Bhitadiya village near the Betal village on the bank of the river Brahmaputra in East Bengal. There lived a lot of 'Kulin' Brahmins in the villages of Betal and Bhitadiya. During the period of the tour in East Bengal (now Bangladesh) Sri Gouranga Mahaprabhu also visited villages of Betal and Bhitadiya.

There lived the mother of Sri Purushottam Pundit or Purushottam Acharya. Her husband was Sri Padmagarva Lahiri. There also lived Sri Lakshminath Lahiri who was step brother of Sri Purushottam Pundit or Purushottam Acharya or Swarup Damodar. He despite being capable in debating also begged mercy from Sri Gouranga Mahaprabhu.

Purushottam Acharya lived at his maternal uncle's house as his father Sri Padmagarva Lahiri went to Mithila to learn more.

Having learned in Mithila Sri Padmagarva Lahiri also was initiated in Gopal Mantra from Lakshmipati in Varanasi. Thereafter, Sri Padmagarva Lahiri returned Bhitadiya village and again he married more two. Lakshminath Lahiri was one of the sons of them.[1]

"Sei Padmagarvacharyam Krishna Bhaktottam,
Kramadeepikar Tika Karila Rachan.
Poingi Rahasya Brahmanera Bhasya Koila,
Upanishdera Dwaita Bhasya Tinho Koila.
Adhyayana Sesh Kari Padmagarva Mahamati,
Janmasthan Bhitadiya Karila Basati... ...
Bhitadiya Aasi Aar Dui Bibaha Karilo,
Lakshminath Lahiri Aadi Aneka Putra Hoilo."

Purushottam Acharya since then lived in Nabadwip with his mother and was becoming renowned in different streams of subjects. He also participated in the Sankirtan and charmed others with singing with his melodious tune. He also became a friend and fan of Sri Gouranga Mahaprabhu.

While Sri Gouranga Mahaprabhu set for taking Sannyas informed only the five associates Si Nityananda, life time shadow follower Sri Gadadhar Pundit, singer and composer on Sri Krishna, maternal uncle (husband of mother's sister) Sri Chandrasekhar Acharya and associate Brahmananda and took permission from mother Sachimaa but other associates like Purushottam remained in dark:-

"Sri Abadhutchandra Gadadhar Mukunda,
Sri Chandrasekhar Acharya Aar Brahmananda."[2]

Having known the Sannyas of beloved Sri Gouranga Mahaprabhu he became almost mad and also left the family life and went to Varanasi where he was initiated in Sannyas mantra from Sri Chaitananda and was advised by the Preceptor to coach Vedanta to the disciples of the Preceptor. He was also vastly learned in different scriptures. He did not use the usual costumes of a Sannyasi so, keeping his Sannyas name Damodar he remained in his identity (Swarup) and thus became Swarup Damodar. After more than two years and Sri Chaitanya Mahaprabhu's return from South India he with permission of his Sannyas Preceptor hurriedly reached Puri in order to serve him. He could control Sri Chaitanya Mahaprabhu in several situations as he was capable of doing so. He was:-

Krishnarasa Tattwabetta – Deha Premarup,
Sakshat Mahaprabhur Dwitiya Swarup."[3]

Sri Swarup Damodar knew the 'rasa' of Sri Krishna's love and sufficiently qualified to assist Sri Chaitanyadeva at Gambhira in Puri.

We should keep proper respect for the mother who gave birth of such a son without whom the Goudiya Vaishnava Movement could not flourished little.

References

1. Prem Vilas – by Nityananda Das, Revised and edited by Dr. Bijon Goswami, Pub, in 1405 BS, 1999 AD, 1st Mahesh Edition, Printed at Printing Publicity, 24 Vilas, p.239)
2. Sri Sri Chaitanya Bhagawata – Sri Vrindabandas, Madhya Khanda, 2nd Chapter)
3. Sri Sri Chaitanya Charitamrita– Sri Krishnadas Kaviraj, Edited by Sri Sri Madbhakti Sri Roop Maharaj, Published from Gaudiya Mission (Rgd.) by Tridandi Bhikshu Sri Bhakti Gunakar Goswami, Printer – Radha Press, Gandhinagar, Delhi – 110 031, 6th Edition, Published in 1990, Madhya Lila, 10th Chapter, Shloka -109).

81

Haripriya Devi

(The wife of Dhananjay)

Out of twelve Gopals one of them was Sri Dhananjay Pundit whose wife was Sri Haripriya Devi. Her father-in-law Sripati Bandyopadhyay and mother-in-law was Kalindi Devi. They lived at Jargram in the district of Chittagong where their son Dhananjay was one of twelve Gopals onenajay was born in 1405 Shaka (1484 AD) Chaitra Shukla Panchami.[1]

Another source in 'Sri Gouranga Madhuri' states that near Bolpur in the district of Birbhum at Siyan area Sri Dhananjay was born and his mother was Sri Dayamoyee Devi and father was Sri Adideva Bachaspati.[2]

Sri Dhananjay used to worship 'Tulsi' plant thrice a day. To find the possibility of son's becoming an ascetic Sripati arranged a marriage of Sri Dhananjay with a beautiful girl Sri Haripriya Devi so that the son gets attraction to domestic life. He also arranged the luxurious articles for Sri Dhananjay. However Sri Dhananjay had strong devotion to Sri Krishna and one day leaving the wife and luxurious life behind set for touring in the vast country.[3]

Sri Dhananjay afterwards donated all the wealth to Sri Chaitanya Mahaprabhu and took up the pot of begging:-

"Sri Gouranga Charane Kari Aatma Samaparne,
Prembhanda Grahan Karila."[4]

Haripriya Devi's husband Sri Dhananjay was also associated with Sri Nityanadaprabhu. He was one of the twelve Gopals and in earlier Lila at Braja he was Basu Sudam 'sakha' of Sri Krishna. He accompanied Sri Nityanadaprabhu in circulating the religion of love and engaged in it in the 'Rarh Banga' under advice of Sri Nityanadaprabhu. He after circulating Vaishnavism at Shital and Sanchra-Panchra villages in the district of

Bardhaman settled at Jalandi village nine-ten miles away from Bolpur Rail Station in the district of Birbhum. There remains the sripat of Sanjay Pundit, brother of Sri Dhananjay Pundit. Once he also travelled Vrindaban-Mathura.

There are also Sripats at Shital and Sanchra-Panchra villages of Sri Dhananjay Pundit. In Shital village there lived Bashistha son of Bedagarva who was one of the five Brahmins brought from the King of Kanouj (Kanyakubja) by the King of Adisur who was the seventh generation of King Shashanka (6th century) of Goud Bengal. The renowned Bhabadeva Bhatta was born in this family and his lower generations are called as 'Goshthipati Chowdhury'.

Sri Haripriya Devi's husband Sri Dhananjay Pundit also established New Vrindaban at Jalandi village. His lower generations now are living at Sodepur in the North 24 Parganas. They are sctteredly using the titles as Bandyopadhaya or Choudhury or Adhikari.

The other people of Sri Haripriya's father–in-law's family are living at Jalandi, Maluk, Kumre Veda, Kama, Abjalpur, Kandra, Begun Kedar of Purulia district also.

The date and the place of demise of Sri Dhananjay Pundit are not available, however a base of 'Tulsi' plant at Shital village is being considered as his cremetary.

Sri Haripriya Devi was satisfied with the activities of the husband Sri Dhananjay Pundit and she would get our due respect.

References

1. Sri Sri Dhananjaya Gopal Charit O Sri Sri Shyamchandrodaya – Collected Edited and Printed by Kishoridas Babaji, Sri Sri Prankrishna Bhakti Press, (Halisahar, Chaitanya Doba) Published in 1416, p. 3-4.
2. Sri Sri Goudiya Vaishnava Abhidhaan – Edited by Sri Haridas Das Babaji, 2nd, 3rd, and 4th Parts, 2nd Edition, 501 Chaitanyabda, Publisher – Haribol Kutir Poraghat, Nabadwip, Printer – Radha Press, Delhi 110031, p. 1260, Source Sri Gouranga Madhuri,
3. *Ibid* – p. 1260,
4. Sri Sri Dhananjaya Gopal Charit O Sri Sri Shyamchandrodaya – Collected Edited and Printed by Kishoridas Babaji, Sri Sri Prankrishna Bhakti Press, (Halisahar, Chaitanya Doba) Published in 1416, p. 4.

16th Century AD

82

Indumukhi Devi

(Wife of Srila Byasacharya)

Sri Nityananda Das has written:-

"Sri Nibas Narottam Shyamananda,
Chaitanya Nityanandadwaitera Abesh Avatara,
Sri Chaitanyera Angshakala Sri Nibaas Hoy. ..."[1]

We are familiar with the name of Sri Sribaas Acharya who was one of the 'Panchatattwa' and several times he was called as Sri Nibas. However this Sri Nibas was a different personality. After the disappearances of Sri Chaitanya Mahaprabhu, Sri Gadadhara Pundit, Sri Nityananda, Sri Adwaita Acharya and Sri SriBaas Pundit the three persons Sri Nibas, Narottam and Shyamananda came under the limelight to preach Harinaam and simultaneously Janhaba Devi wife of Sri Nityananda Prabhu and Birbhadra Prbhu son of Sri Nityananda Prabhu have taken up the job of circulating Harinaam in Bengal.

Indumukhi was the name of a disciple of Sri Nibas Acharya and wife of Sri Byasacharya another disciple of Sri Nibas Acharya. She was a talented lady. Her son was Shyamadas Acharya who was also initiated by Sri Nibas Acharya. They were originally titled Chakraborty.[2]

She was considered as a fortunate lady as she got the social and family environment along with neo consciousness. She knew how to lead life with jointly with counterpart. She could overcome all the barriers of ahead.

References

1. Prem Vilas – by Nityananda Das, Revised and edited by Dr. Bijon Goswami, Pub, in 1405 BS, 1999 AD, 1st Mahesh Edition, Printed at Printing Publicity, 20 Vilas).
2. Sri Sri Goudiya Vaishnava Abhidhaan – Edited by Sri Haridas Das Babaji, 2nd, 3rd, and 4th Parts, 2nd Edition, 501 Chaitanyabda, Publisher – Haribol Kutir Poraghat, Nabadwip, Printer – Radha Press, Delhi 110031, p. 1153).

83

Kanakpriyya Devi

(Daughter of Srila Byasacharya)

Kanakpriya Devi was the daughter of Sri Byasacharya of Bishnupur in the district of Bankura. She was also a sister of Sri Krishnaballav Acharya. Bishnupur was being termed as the Lila Kshetra of Sri Nibas Acharya. Sri Krishnaballav Acharya was the first disciple of Sri Nibas Acharya. There still remains the Sripat of Sri Krishnaballav Acharya. He was born at Deuli village on the southbank of the Darakeswar River.[1]

Kanakpriya Devi was not disciple of Sri Nibas Acharya. But she was initiated from Gitagovinda the son of Gourangapriya, the wife of Sri Nibas Acharya. She was an up-to-date lady who accepted the Goudiya Vaishnavism and acted accordingly.[2]

References

1. Sri Sri Goudiya Vaishnava Abhidhaan – Edited by Sri Haridas Das Babaji, 2nd, 3rd, and 4th Parts, 2nd Edition, 501 Chaitanyabda, Publisher – Haribol Kutir Poraghat, Nabadwip, Printer – Radha Press, Delhi 110031, p.1159, 1154, 1192 and 1886).
2. Sri Sri Karnanada – by Sri Jadunandan Das Thakur, ed. by Sri Haribhakta Das, pub.by Sri Giridharilal Goswami, Byakaran Tirtha, 506 Gourabda, second niryas, p. 46).

84

Krishnapriya Devi

(Second Daughter of Sri Nibas Acharya)

Sri Krishnapriya Devi was the second daughter of Sri Nibas Acharya and Srimati Padmabati Devi who was called by many as Gourangapriya. Out of three sisters she was the second and their brother was Govindagati who was called as Gitagovinda also. She was blessed by Sri Birbhadra or Birchandra, son of Sri Nityanandaprabhu. Her son was named Govindagati or Gitagovinda by Sri Birbhadra or Birchandra. He was the first issue of their parents.[1]

Sri Krishnapriya Devi's other sisters were the elder Hemlata Devi and the youngest was Kanchanlatika Devi. Sri Krishnapriya Devi had the strong desire to place herself at the feet of Sri Gouranga Mahaprabhu-Sri Chaitanyadeva.

Sri Gouranga Mahaprabhu-Sri Chaitanyadeva wanted to wipe out all the differences among the people who were tortured, oppressed, neglected in the society. He wanted to see that all the women also could enjoy the rights of living in the society keeping their heads up all the time.

Observing the devotion to Sri Chaitanyadeva Sri Nibas Acharya initiated her in Krishna mantra:-

"Aar Kanya Krishnapriya Naam Thakurani,
Tnar Nija Padashraya Dilo Dayamoni."[2]

Sri Krishnapriya Devi's husband was Sri Chaitanya Chattaraj. His father Sri Kumud Chattaraj was the assistant and also a disciple of Sri Nibas Acharya.[3]

The brother of Sri Kumud Chattaraj was Sri Ramkrishna Chattaraj. Both of them were pious and sincere devotee of Sri Gouranga Mahaprabhu-Sri Chaitanyadeva.

Sri Krishnapriya Devi like other women of Bengal also composed 'Gour Bandana' what has not yet become obsolete.

References

1. Sri Sri Karnanada – by Sri Jadunandan Das Thakur, ed. by Sri Haribhakta Das, pub.by Sri Giridharilal Goswami, Byakaran Tirtha, 506 Gourabda, second niryas, p. 17).
2. *Ibid*, p. 15).
3. Sri Sri Goudiya Vaishnava Abhidhaan – Edited by Sri Haridas Das Babaji, 2nd, 3rd, and 4th Parts, 2nd Edition, 501 Chaitanyabda, Publisher – Haribol Kutir Poraghat, Nabadwip, Printer – Radha Press, Delhi 110031, p. 1175).

85

Ishwari Devi

(The First Wife of Sri Nibas Acharya)

Ishwari Devi or Droupadi Devi was the first wife of Sri Nibas Acharya. She was the daughter of Sri Gopal Chakraborty, a Bhoumik (Landlord) of Jajigram in the district of Bardhaman.

Ishwari Devi or Droupadi Devi had two brothers Shyamdas and Ramcharan Chakraborty. They were also initiated from Sri Nibas Acharya. After a few days Sri Gopal Chakraborty also became disciple of Sri Nibas Acharya. And he engaged himself to circulate Harinaam as advised by Sri Chaitanya Mahaprabhu.[1]

Ishwari Devi or Droupadi Devi was a beautiful and a loveable girl in the village Jajigram. After the demise of mother of Sri Nibas Acharya became alone and his well wisher Vaishnava Sri Raghunandan arranged the match for marriage of Sri Nibas Acharya with this quality girl. At the time of marriage the daughter's name was changed as Ishwari.[2]

After marriage Sri Nibas Acharya initiated his wife Ishwari Devi. She had two sons viz. Vrindaban and Radhakrishna.[3]

However, Sri Nibas Acharya married another girl named as Sri Padmabati Devi who was known as Gourapriya or Gourangapriya whom Sri Ishwari Devi accepted cordially and they both continued friendly relation. Both of them were preferred to worship Sri Krishna God of Love and Sri Gouranga Mahaprabhu-Sri Chaitanyadeva.

Sri Ishwari Devi had some disciples and Sri Rajballav Chakraborty was one of them. He also established Sripat at Borakuli village.[4]

Among their disciples Sri Ramchandra of Vaidya generation is also notable. Sri Ishwari Devi was pleased to Sri Ramchandra also.[5]

Sri Ishwari Devi's husband Sri Nibas Acharya was born to publicise the Vaishnava Scriptures in Goud Bengal under the guidance of Goswamis of Vrindaban. He was possessed by Sri Chaitanya Mahaprabhu in himself.

Sri Ishwari Devi could attain the lofty seat of the Vaishnavas and so she is regarded till today by all the Vaishnavas.

References

1. Sri Sri Goudiya Vaishnava Abhidhaan – Edited by Sri Haridas Das Babaji, 2nd, 3rd, and 4th Parts, 2nd Edition, 501 Chaitanyabda, Publisher – Haribol Kutir Poraghat, Nabadwip, Printer – Radha Press, Delhi 110031, p. 1238.
2. Sri Sri Bhakti Ratnakar – by Sri Narahari Chakraborty, ed.by Pundit Sripad Navinkrishna Paravidyalankar, pub. by Srimat Sundarananda Vidyabenode, printer Sri Ananata Ram Bhakti-Shastri, Nadiya Prakash Printing Works, in 1940, Gaudiya Math Sanskaran, 8th Taranga, Shloka 894, p. 378).
3. Sri Sri Goudiya Vaishnava Abhidhaan – Edited by Sri Haridas Das Babaji, 2nd, 3rd, and 4th Parts, 2nd Edition, 501 Chaitanyabda, Publisher – Haribol Kutir Poraghat, Nabadwip, Printer – Radha Press, Delhi 110031, p. 1392).
4. *Ibid* p. 1333).
5. Sri Sri Karnanada – by Sri Jadunandan Das Thakur, ed. by Sri Haribhakta Das, pub.by Sri Giridharilal Goswami, Byakaran Tirtha, 506 Gourabda, second niryas, p. 73).

86

Gourangapriya Devi

(The Second Wife of Sri Nibas Acharya)

Padmabati Devi was the wife of Sri Nibas Acharya. After marriage with Sri Nibas Acharya her name was changed as Gourangapriya or Gourapriya. She was the daughter of Raghab Chakraborty of West Gopalpur. Some researchers wanted to indicate that he was Sri Raghunath Chakraborty, 'Raghav' or Raghunandan Chakraborty.[1]

While Sri Nibas Acharya was in tour from Vrindaban and in Rarh area the daughter of Sri Raghunath Gourangapriya Devi was attracted to Sri Nibas Acharya and wished to have him as her husband. The father well informed earlier that Sri Nibas Acharya was already married. However, considered himself as fortunate person and arranged the marriage of his daughter Gourangapriya with Sri Nibas Acharya. Srimati Gourangapriya or Padmabati Devi with his father Raghunath was also initiated from Sri Nibas Acharya.[2]

This marriage was possible for the eagerness's of Sri Raghunath Chakraborty, Srimati Gourangapriya or Padmabati Devi and also Sri Janhaba Devi the second wife of Sri Niyanandaprabhu.

This marriage ceremony was fully sponsored by the King and the Queen of Bishnupur. They also invited the bride and the bridegroom to stay at the palace of the King.[3]

Sri Govindagati son of Srimati Gourangapriya and Sri Nibas Acharya was a good writer. He has written 'Biraratnaboli' on the life of Sri Birbhadra or Sri Birchandra son of Sri Nityanandaprabhu and also 'Janhabatattwa Marmartha' on the life of Janhaba Maa, the second wife of Sri Nityananda-prabhu.[4]

References

1. Sri Sri Goudiya Vaishnava Abhidhaan – Edited by Sri Haridas Das Babaji, 2nd, 3rd, and 4th Parts, 2nd Edition, 501 Chaitanyabda, Publisher – Haribol Kutir Poraghat, Nabadwip, Printer – Radha Press, Delhi 110031, p.1325 and Prem Vilas – by Nityananda Das, Revised and edited by Dr. Bijon Goswami, Pub, in 1405 BS, 1999 AD, 1st Mahesh Edition, Printed at Printing Publicity, 24 Vilas, p. 148).
2. Prem Vilas – by Nityananda Das, Revised and edited by Dr. Bijon Goswami, Pub, in 1405 BS, 1999 AD, 1st Mahesh Edition, Printed at Printing Publicity, 24 Vilas, p. 148).
3. Sri Sri Nibas Charitamrita – Ed. by Sri Krishnachaitanya Das Babaji, pub. by Sri Nabanirod Dasgupta and Sri Achyutananda Babaji, printed by Sri Shukdeva Upadhyay, 2nd Edition, 1396 BS, p. 200-201).
4. Sri Sri Goudiya Vaishnava Abhidhaan – Edited by Sri Haridas Das Babaji, 2nd, 3rd, and 4th Parts, 2nd Edition, 501 Chaitanyabda, Publisher – Haribol Kutir Poraghat, Nabadwip, Printer – Radha Press, Delhi 110031, p. 1198).

87

Kanchanlatika Devi

(The Youngest Daughter of Sri Nibas Acharya)

During the ages after the disappearances of the leaders of Goudiya Vaishnavism the Bhaktaavatara Sri Nibas Acharya's family was glorious in circulating the art of living in Vaishnava environment. The role of youngest daughter Kanchanlatika of Sri Nibas Acharya and Gourangapriya cannot be ignored. They were three sisters Srimati Hemlata, Sri Krishnapriya and herself and the brother Sri Govindagati or Gitagovinda were active in those activities that enhanced the Vaishnavism in Bengal. Being lame i.e. physically handicapped Sri Govindagati or Gitagovinda had immense love for Sri Chaitanya Mahaprabhu and so he was more enthusiastically to perform the rites of Vaishnavism.

Kanchanlatika of Sri Nibas Acharya and Gourangapriya had also similar respect to Sri Chaitanya Mahaprabhu. And so, she was initiated in Sri Krishna mantra by Sri Nibas Acharya.

"*Aar Kanya Kanchanlatika Yar Naam,*
Tnare Nija Padashraya Dilo Dayaban."[1]

She was also known as 'Kanchan Thakurjhi' or 'Yamuna Thakurjhi' among the Vaishnava devotees.

Reference

1. Sri Sri Karnanada – by Sri Jadunandan Das Thakur, ed. by Sri Haribhakta Das, pub. by Sri Giridharilal Goswami, Byakaran Tirtha, 506 Gourabda, second niryas, p. 15.

88

Chandramukhi Devi

(The Daughter-in-law of Sri Nibas Acharya)

Opinion of Sri Sri Karnananda that Srimati Chandramukhi was the eldest daughter-in-law of Sri Nibas Acharya being married to Sri Vrindaban Ballava eldest son of Sri Nibas Acharya but it differs as in Goudiya Vaishnava Abhidhan that Srimati Chandramukhi was the second daughter-in-law of Sri Nibas Acharya being married to Sri Radhakrishna Acharya.[1]

However, Srimati Chandramukhi had friendly relation with Srimati Stayabhama wife of Sri Vrindaban Bllava who was her elder brother-in-law. Her youngest brother-in-law Sri Govindagati or Gitagovinda had lot of qualities in preaching the name of God as well as Sri Chaitanya Mahaprabhu.

Srimati Chandramukhi and Srimati Stayabhama had many disciples like Sri Radhaballava Chakrabory, Sri Vrindaban Chakraborty, Sri Radhabenode Chakraborty, Sri Kishore Chakraborty and others after initiations became satisfied to circulate Sri Krishna naam in Bengal.[2]

It is also learnt that Srimati Chandramukhi Devi had also women disciples one of them was Vrindabati Thakurani who also participated to circulate Sri Krishna naam in Bengal. All of them were directed to take the name of God and to lead the family life in the path as Sri Chaitanya Mahaprabhu advised from time to time.

References

1. Sri Sri Karnanada – by Sri Jadunandan Das Thakur, ed. by Sri Haribhakta Das, pub.by Sri Giridharilal Goswami, Byakaran Tirtha, 506 Gourabda, second niryas, p.43 and Sri Sri Goudiya Vaishnava Abhidhaan – Edited by Sri Haridas Das Babaji, 2nd, 3rd, and 4th Parts, 2nd Edition, 501 Chaitanyabda, Publisher – Haribol Kutir Poraghat, Nabadwip, Printer – Radha Press, Delhi 110031, p. 1227).

2. Sri Sri Karnanada – by Sri Jadunandan Das Thakur, ed. by Sri Haribhakta Das, pub.by Sri Giridharilal Goswami, Byakaran Tirtha, 506 Gourabda, second niryas, p. 44).

89

Indurekha

(The Sakhi of Chandrakala Devi)

Like Shasikala Indurekha was also an intimate Sakhi of Srimati Chandrakala Devi the wife of Raja Pratap Rudra.

We may know a glimpse of the mindset of Indurekha from the drama Maharaj Gajapati Pratap Rudra written by Sripad Haridas Goswami.

In the drama we can be aware of the efforts to please the Rajmata Chandrakala Devi, the wife and the Queen of the King Pratap Rudra by discussing the glory of Sri Chaitanya Mahaprabhu. Sri Pratap Rudra was very much eager to meet Sri Chaitanya Mahaprabhu but he in order to maintain the rules of a Sannyasi was not ready to meet any king or people who were materialistic. Sri Indurekha tried to console the Rajmata by narrating that the associates and devotees from Goud Bengal reached Neelachal Dham to witness the Rathayatra of Lord Jagannatha and also their beloved Sri Krishna Chaitanya Mahaprabhu. See also informed her that most of them have brought their wives with them. Sri Indurekha consoles her also assuring that their dreams of meeting the King would be fruitful shortly.[1]

This indicates that the victorious advancement of Sri Chaitanya Mahaprabhu has started to reach the hearts of the women who remain behind the curtains. Without the seeing Sri Chaitanya Mahaprabhu his glory could affect the hearts of the women who compulsorily were bound to stay behind the curtains as the social obligation. Sri Chaitanya Mahaprabhu thus could overcome all the people of the world of men and women. He was considred as full of vitality for all the devotees and followers or not followers who have heard something about Sri Chaitanya Mahaprabhu.

The Rajmata Chandrakala Devi informed Indurekha that she also wanted to meet the women who have come over Puri with their husbands.

They are getting the essence of love and affection of Sri Chaitanya Mahaprabhu and Sri Chaitanya Mahaprabhu also consider them as his own people. If they are so fortunate then what should be the reason of not getting blessings from Sri Chaitanya Mahaprabhu? So, she expressed the desire to Indurekha and Shasikala to see Sri Chaitanya Mahaprabhu for his divine form at least once and her husband to touch the divine feet.

The glory of Indurekha and Shasikala was that they have seen the divine feet several times as they usually go outside the King's palace.

Indurekha was well aware of the strength and lovely behavior with all the Bhaktas and the people whoever they were. Like the Sakhis of Braja who always wanted the pleasure of their own Srimati Radharani Indurekha also wanted to see that the desire of the Rajamata's husband would bc fulfilled one day sooner. She with Rajmata also wished to see a glance at the divine feet of Sri Chaitanya Mahaprabhu.

Reference

1. Maharaj Ganapati Pratap Rudra (Drama) –by Sripad Haridas Goswami. Pub by Sri Ramnivas Dhandariya, Aryabarta Prakashan Griha, printed by Sri Shyamasundar Goswami, Shyamsundar Press, Kolkata-5, pub on 4/6/1964, 2nd Act 1st Scene, p 49.

90

Kadambamala

(The Daughter-in-law of Birchandra)

Kadambamala was the daughter-in-law of Birchandra or Birbhadra, son of Nityanandaprabhu. The members of her family were sevak of Jagannatha Mahaprabhu. Her siter was Gunjamala and brother was Rajiblochan.

Sri Birchandra or Birbhadra, son of Nityanandaprabhu initiated the match-maker Sri Debibar Visharad who was present at the time of marriage of Sri Ramchandra with Sri Kadambamala.[1]

Four sons were born to them. They were Ramdev, Krishnadev, Vishnu-dev and Radhamadhav. They had one daughter Tripura Sundari by name. This Tripura Sundari was married to Rameswar Mukhopadhyay, a lower generation of Kamdev Pundit who was disciple of Sri Adwaita Acharya. They were Rarhi 'Kulin' and residence of Khardah. Chand Sharma, the son of grandson of Kamdev established Sri Sri Radhakanta in Khardah.[2]

Sri Kadambamala wife of Sri Ramchandra was a mere housewife but assisted her husband to spread the Harinaam Movement in the whole Bengal.

References

1. Srimannitya Bangshaballi O Gangadevir Bangshaballi ebang Vaishnavdigera (Purba O Uttarbhag) – written and published by Sri Khirode Behari Goswami, printed by Sri Shachindra Kumar Dasgupta in 1321 BS, p. 57-60).
2. Sri Sri Goudiya Vaishnava Abhidhaan – Edited by Sri Haridas Das Babaji, 2nd, 3rd, and 4th Parts, 2nd Edition, 501 Chaitanyabda, Publisher – Haribol Kutir Poraghat, Nabadwip, Printer – Radha Press, Delhi 110031, p. 1169).

91

Ganga Devi

(The Daughter of Sri Nityananda- Basudhamaa)

Ganga Devi the only daughter of Sri Nityanandaprabhu and Srimati Basudhamaa was born in 1458 or 1459 Shaka (1536 or 1537 AD) just more than one year after the birth of Sri Birchandraprabhu (1457 Shaka).

Like Sri (Birbhadra) Birchandraprabhu (1457 Shaka) the female baby of Basudhamaa could easily tolerate the 'Pranam' of Sri Abhiram Thakura. It is also said that Sri Abhiram Goswami bowed his head for 'Pranam' to this child twelve times but no harm was caused to her and survived.

Generally, no ordinary children could tolerate the 'Pranam' of Abhiram Thakura but only the children who possessed the special power of God or gods or goddesses could survive. To find this baby was alright even after twelve times 'Pranam' by him, Abhiram Thakura then and there himself composed a poem of twenty shlokas in praising goddess Sri Ganga – 'Sri Gangastrotra'.

Ganga Devi was initiated by another mother Janhaba Devi, the second wife of Sri Nityanandaprabhu in the labour room and after the initiation the new born female baby Ganga Devi started to suck breast milk from mother Sri Basudha Devi.

Before Sri Nityanada's disappearance his daughter Gnaga Devi was married in 1463/1464 Shaka (1541/1542 AD) to Sri Madhabacharya, son of Sri Bishweswar Acharya and Srimati Mahalakshmi Devi at Nanyapur near Katwoa in the district of Bardhaman. They were 'Kulin' Brahmin of 'Rarhi' sect. Sri Madhabacharya was the 16th lower generation of Sri Ratnakar Bipra brought from Kanyakubja by King Adisur in Bengal.

However, the mother of Sri Madhabacharya suddenly died keeping child son behind. Mahalakshmi Devi had a friendship 'Sai' with Jai Durga

Devi the wife of Bhagirath Acharya at Nanyapur village. Both Bishweswar Acharya and Bhagirath were also intimate friends. Jai Durga Devi was present at the time of sudden death of Mahalakshmi Devi. So, Jai Durga Devi was shocked to see 'Sai's demise.

On the other hand Mahalakshmi Devi before her death expressed that responsibility of looking after her only son would be borne by Jai Durga Devi. But Mahalakshmi Devi understood that with mother's irresistible death her son like Madhab would become almost helpless. So, she requested Jai Durga to take the son and to bring him up as another son with her two sons.

Jai Durga Devi then started to bring up three sons Sri Nath, Sri Pati and Sri Madhab carefully.[1]

We know that without proper nourishment a small plant cannot get maturity and becomes unable to give fruits. Likewise without the necessary care and nourishment no possibility, no talent can mature. Jai Durga Devi and Sri Bhagirath both were equal careful and gave equal love to the three sons to grow. So, Madhab Acharya was considered as the third son of Sri Bhagirath and Srimati Jai Durga Devi.

Sri Madhab Acharya was a follower of Sri Nityanandaprabhu and he was among the members of Nityananda branch.

"Pitamabar, Madhabacharya, Das Damodar,
Shankar, Nukunda, Jnanadas, Manohar…."[2]

He was a man of high quality and knew how to play with Mridanga and other musical instruments as we find the writer of 'Prem Vilas' Nityanandadas also learnt to play musical instruments from Sri Madhab Acharya.

"Madhab Acharya Sthane Baadya-Shiksha Koilo,
Kripa Kari Tinho Morey Baadya-Shiksha Dilo."[3]

Sri Nityanandaprabhu was affectionate to Sri Madhab Acharya and he saw his devotion, meditation and other qualities for which he selected Sri Madhab Acharya for his daughter Gnga Devi and the marriage was settled. He did not differentiate that he was a 'Rarhi' Brahmin and the bridegroom was of 'Barendra' Brahmin sect. As 'Rarhi' Brahmins and 'Barendra' Brahmins two brothers may be sons of a father. This was nothing but the results of inhabitances at different places/areas in Goud Bengal. However, Like Sri Chaitanya Mahaprabhu he hardly could differentiate Caste-System that jeopardized the society.

Sri Madhab and Sri Gangamaa had two sons whose names were Sri Premananda and Sri Goplalballav.

Sri Gangamaa usually was engaged with the circulation of Harinaam and of the glory of Sri Gouranga Mahaprabhu-Sri Chaitanyadeva.

Sri Gangamaa or Ganga Devi branch of disciples was one of the three important branches. Her generations are called as 'Ganga Bangsha'. It was a rare effort to uplift the parental identities instead of father-in-law's identities by a housewife. As a woman Gangamaa had the courage to do it.

References

1. Sri Sri Nityananda Shakti Maa Janhaba – Sri Nemaichand Goswami, Pub. By Sri Sanatan Goswami, Printer – Shyamasundar Press, 1st Pub 1389 BS, 2nd Pub 1401 BS, p. 153).
2. Sri Sri Chaitanya Charitamrita– Sri Krishnadas Kaviraj, Edited by Sri Sri Madbhakti Sri Roop Maharaj, Published from Gaudiya Mission (Rgd.) by Tridandi Bhikshu Sri Bhakti Gunakar Goswami, Printer – Radha Press, Gandhinagar, Delhi – 110 031, 6th Edition, Published on 11 March 1990, Adi Lila, 12th Chapter, Shloka 52, p. 242).
3. Prem Vilas – by Nityananda Das, Revised and edited by Dr. Bijon Goswami, Pub, in 1405 BS, 1999 AD, 1st Mahesh Edition, Printed at Printing Publicity,)

92

Kanaklata-Aai Chaturbhuja

(The Grand Daughter-in-law of Sri Shankardeva)

Like Goud Bengal the Vaishnava Movement was also in action in Assam where Sri Shankardeva introduced Vaishnavism. During the tour in the country he met in Neelachal with Sri Adwaita Acharya and probably with Sri Chaitanya Mahaprabhu and also Sri Guru Nanak.

In Assam in the year 1590 AD (1512 Shaka) Sri Kanakalata Devi was incarnated. She used to be called as Kanakalata Aai Chaturbhuj or 'Lakshmi Aai' in the society of the devotees. She had deep respect for Sri Krishna. With the worshipping Sri Krishna she also tried to learn more and more. Her eagerness for knowing more and learning education in the period of 16th century made her remarkable. In marital status she was grand daughter-in-law of Sri Shankardeva.

Sri Shankardeva according to Vaishnava Abhidhan was one of the disciples of Sri Adwaita Acharya.[1]

But he found the path of 'Jnan' and Sri Adwaita Acharya advised him to come back in the path of 'Bhakti'. Sri Shankardeva established Neo Vaishnavism for the devotees of Assam.

Sri Kanakalata Aai Chaturbhuj or 'Lakshmi Aai' was the first woman who came forward to highlight the theory and teachings of grandfather-in-law Sri Shankardeva among the devotees of Assam.

She was noble-hearted lady and had thoughts for the development for the women in the country. She had own personality for which she could convince others, mainly women. Like Sitadevi, Janhaba Devi and Hemlata Devi in Goud Bengal this noble-hearted lady Sri Kanakalata Aai also initiated many people. She also selected women who could keep the flow of Neo Vaishnavism in Assam. All these women teachers or the wives of teachers of scriptures remained engaged with sincerely worshipping Lord Krishna and to circulate Neo Vaishnavism as introduced by Sri Shankardeva.[2]

She also allocated the works in different groups like Sri Chaitanya Mahaprabhu as he did at the time of 'Kazi Daman'. She believed in teamwork procedure to be observed in order to succeed in the Movement.

She expired in 1668 AD (1705 Shaka) but her name would be remembered for ever for her untiring efforts in moving the Vaishnvism in Assam.

References

1. Sri Sri Goudiya Vaishnava Abhidhaan – Edited by Sri Haridas Das Babaji, 2nd, 3rd, and 4th Parts, 2nd Edition, 501 Chaitanyabda, Publisher – Haribol Kutir Poraghat, Nabadwip, Printer – Radha Press, Delhi 110031, p. 1380,
2. Radhakrishna Bhaktakosh – Edited by Dr. Bhagawati Prasad Singh, published by SriKrishna Seva Sansthan, Mathura in 1987AD, 1st Part, p.11).

93

Kanaklatika Devi

(Narottam Shakha)

Here we can again remember the portion of another article many a time- "After the disappearances of Sri Chaitanya Mahaprabhu, Sri Gadadhara Pundit, Sri Nityananda, Sri Adwaita Acharya and Sri SriBaas Pundit the three persons Sri Nibas, Narottam and Shyamananda came under the limelight to preach Harinaam and simultaneously Janhaba Devi wife of Sri Nityananda Prabhu and Birbhadra Prbhu son of Sri Nityananda Prabhu have taken up the job of circulating Harinaam in Bengal."

Kanaklatika Devi the wife of Sri Ramkrishna Chakraborty who was also known as Sri Ramkrishna Acharya who belonged to the branch of Sri Narottam Thakura.[1]

Kanaklatika Devi was initiated from her husband and gave births to two sons Radhakrishna and Krishnarama. In the atmosphere of devotion to God this housewife could easily understand the service to own family was also an urgent need.

In the path of progress of the women their co-operation was simultaneously important to run the family and also society of Goudiya Vaishnavism. Kanaklatika Devi did so accordingly.

Reference

1. Sri Sri Goudiya Vaishnava Abhidhaan – Edited by Sri Haridas Das Babaji, 2nd, 3rd, and 4th Parts, 2nd Edition, 501 Chaitanyabda, Publisher – Haribol Kutir Poraghat, Nabadwip, Printer – Radha Press, Delhi 110031, p. 1160)

94

Kanchana Devi

(The wife of Lochandas)

The resident of Ko-gram near Mangalkot Sri Kamalakardas and Srimati Sadanandi had only one son named Trilochan or Lochan married a girl of Kakutia-Adampur. This girl was Kanchana. Her father-in-law was from a Vaidya (physician) family.[1]

Lochandas the husband of Kanchana was initiated from Sri Narahari Sarkar. Lochandas although was married but his academic learning was not achieved. However, he learnt the Alphabet from his grandmother and accompanying her he reached Sri Khanda where he received the contact with Sri Narahari Sarkar. There he used to know the Goura Katha from his Preceptor Sri Narahari Sarkar almost every day.

The stream of Sri Khanda was to consider Sri Gouranga Mahaprabhu as the only male and all human bodies are females. All the male persons as female devotees worship Sri Gouranga Mahaprabhu:-

"Gour Chhara Purush Nai,
Naari Boi Manush Nai."[2]

Afterwards the Preceptor Sri Narahari Sarkar having informed that Kanchana has become matured advised Lochandas to meet his wife and to settle the family life.

He, keeping in mind the feet of Sri Gouranga Mahaprabhu-Sri Chaitanyadeva all the time started for his father-in-law's house but could not recognize the house exactly. Then he took rest under a tree on a bank of a pond and there he accidentally met a young lady whom he addressed 'Mata' and asked for the house of his father-in-law. But this lady was herself Kanchana, his married wife.

Srimati Kanchana's husband Sri Lochandas then regarded her as the Mata – Mother and continued rest of his life and did not accept her as wife. He returned Sri Khanda and informed his Preceptor Sri Narahari Sarkar. He explained the Rasatattwa of Sri Gourasundar and ordered him to go back to Ko-gram near Mangalkot with his wife Kanchana and start the writing of life sketch of Sri Gouranga Mahaprabhu-Sri Chaitanyadeva whatever he realized. Thus Sri Chaitanya Mongal was written by him and the regular listener was Kanchana Devi. She became the main inspiration of Lochandas.

"Pranbhasha Nibedeu Nibedeu Nijakatha,
Aagey Aashirbad Maago, Yata Yata Mahabhaga,
Tabe Se Gaahibo Gunagataha."[3]

The conjugal life of Sri Kanchana Devi and Sri Lochandas was with earthly happiness and woes but everything would be transformed into eternal pleasure only in thinking the coloured and fragrant feet of Sri Chaitanya Mahaprabhu.

"Grihete Ba Banetey Thako Ha Goranga Bole Dako,
Narottam Magey Taar Sanga."[4]

Practically Srimati Kanchana Devi was a pious devotee having patience, sincerety and ability to become a deserving counterpart of of Lochandas. She was indeed a religious wife of writer Sri Lochandas.

We must confess that Sri Lochandas was highly fortunate as he got the assistance of a deserving wife Srimati Kanchana Devi who had no desire of earthly pleasure and used to work efficiently by remaining shoulder to shoulder. The importance of work done and devotion of Srimati Kanchana Devi are yet to be revalued.

References

1. Sri Sri Nityananda Shakti Maa Janhaba – Sri Nemaichand Goswami, Pub. By Sri Sanatan Goswami, Printer – Shyamasundar Press, 1st Pub 1389 BS, 2nd Pub 1401 BS, p. 549).
2. *Ibid.*
3. Sri Chaitanya Mongal – by Sri Lochandas, Sutra Kahnda)
4. Sri Sri Nityananda Shakti Maa Janhaba – Sri Nemaichand Goswami, Pub. By Sri Sanatan Goswami, Printer – Shyamasundar Press, 1st Pub 1389 BS, 2nd Pub 1401 BS, p.551 and Narottam Vilas – Sri Narahari Chakraborty, Collected Edited and Printed by Kishoridas Babaji, Sri Sri Prankrishna Bhakti Press, (Halisahar, Chaitanya Doba) Published in 1314 BS.

95

Mother of Kanhaiya

(Vraja)

The Mother of Kanhaiya had affection for Sri Sanatana and Sri Roop Goswamis. In Braja as well as in Vrindaban this lady was from a Brahmin family. She used to extend affection to Sri Sanatan and Sri Roop Goswamis as her own sons. She was called as the mother of Kanhaiya. This Kanhaiya in Braja as well as in Vrindaban was also from a Brahmin family.

"Kanhaiya Namete Eka Bipra Brajabasi,
Krishney Aaradhaye Sei Brikshataley Bosi."[1]

In Vrindaban Sri Nibas Acharya once got the opportunity to meet Kanhaiya. While after seeing off Sri Shyamanada and Sri Narottam Sri Nibas Acharya became restless and could not stop to shed tears from his eyes. At that time he found Kanhaiya sitting under a tree alone and bowed his head to Kanhaiya.

The mother of Kanhaiya used to collect flowers and sandal woods for Sri Sanatana Goswami and Sri Roop Goswami. She also used to invite the two goswami brothers at her house for giving alms:-

"Sri Roop- Sanatane Parama Aadarey,
Madhye Madhye Viksha Karayen Loiya Ghare,
Phal Mool Shakadi Milaye Yabe Jaaha,
Dnohar Basaya Ati Yatne Den Taha."[2]

One day Sri Sanatana Goswami attended the house of the mother of Kanhaiya but there was none in the house. But Sri Krishna Himself in disguise of Kanhaiya gave alms. And thus Kanhaiya became a loved one person by the Vaishnavas in Braja.

We also can note that at the demises of Sri Sanatana Goswami and Sri Roop Goswami this Kanhaiya also was shocked.

At last Kanhaiya took the shelter under a tree on the bank of the Yamuna. Although we could get no further information about Kanhaiya and the mother of Kanhaiya both of them of Vrindaban would be remembered with due respect by the Vaishnavas.

Refrences

1. Sri Sri Bhakti Ratnakar – by Sri Narahari Chakraborty, ed.by Pundit Sripad Navinkrishna Paravidyalankar, pub. by Srimat Sundarananda Vidyabenode, printer Sri Ananata Ram Bhakti-Shastri, Nadiya Prakash Printing Works, in 1940, Gaudiya Math Sanskaran, Shloka 373, p. 313).
2. *Ibid.*

96

Krishnadassi

(The Wife of Haribansa)

Krishnadassi was one of the two wives of Haribansa or Hitaharibansa who introduced the "Radhaballavi Sampradaya".[1]

Krishnadassi was born in Brahmin family in Chattathabol village. Her sister was Manohara. Both of them were married to Haribansa Mishra a Brahmin of Goud. The father-in-law and the mother-in-law of the sisters were respectfully Vyas Mishra and Tara Devi. The husband of Krishnadassi Haribansa was initiated from Sri Gopal Bhatta of Braja.

Although Sri Sanatana Goswami explained in details the 'Haribhakti Vilas' but gladly announced that this book was written by Sri Gopal Bhatta.

However once the husband of Krishnadassi Haribansa was abandoned by his Preceptor on an occasion that in the day of Ekadashi took the Betel from the Bhog offered to Srimati Radharani what was not in order to take rice Prasad or its touched Betel leaf in the day of Ekadashi. His Preceptor advised him not to do the same thing. But Haribansa was mistaken again at the second time. Then Sri Gopal Bhatta became offended.

At the last Haribansa established the deity of Sri Sri Radhaballava alone himself. Afterwards he gave the responsibility of worshipping to his two sons Krishnadas and Suryadas. He had more two sons Bonchandra and Vrindabanchandra as information we have collected.

In the year 1551 AD in the Ashwin month Haribansa expired. His wife Krishnadassi got importance in the Vaishnava Literature.

Reference

1. Sri Sri Goudiya Vaishnava Abhidhaan – Edited by Sri Haridas Das Babaji, 2nd, 3rd, and 4th Parts, 2nd Edition, 501 Chaitanyabda, Publisher – Haribol Kutir Poraghat, Nabadwip, Printer – Radha Press, Delhi 110031, p. 1418).

97

Gourangadasi

(The Second Wife of Shyamanandaprabhu)

Here we are to remember the portion of another article many a time- "After the disappearances of Sri Chaitanya Mahaprabhu, Sri Gadadhara Pundit, Sri Nityananda, Sri Adwaita Acharya and Sri SriBaas Pundit the three persons Sri Nibas, Narottam and Shyamananda came under the limelight to preach Harinaam and simultaneously Janhaba Devi wife of Sri Nityananda Prabhu and Birbhadra Prbhu son of Sri Nityananda Prabhu have taken up the job of circulating Harinaam in Bengal."

This Shyamanandaprabhu was the son of Sri Krishna Mondal and Srimati Durika Devi of the village of Dandeswar (Dharanda) in the district of Medinipur on the bank of the river Subarnarekha. His second wife was Srimati Gourangadasi.

Srimati Gourangadasi's husband Sri Shyamanandaprabhu originally was in the name of 'Duhkhi' or 'Duhkhini' or 'Krishnadas'. Afterwards Sri Jib Goswami in Vrindaban has changed his name as Shyamananda.[1]

Gourangadasi's husband Sri Shyamanandaprabhu was born in 1456 Shaka (1534 AD). His father Sri Krishna Mondal used to live in Goud area. Afterwards he changed his residence at Dharenda-Bahadurpur within Dandeswar in Utkal. He is also referred in 'Shyamananda Prakash', 'Abhiram Lilamrita', 'Prem Vilas' and 'Bhakti Ratnakar' scriptures with dignity and respect. He was also considered as Adwaita Acharya in new form by the Vaishnavas.[2]

Sri Jib Goswami in Vrindaban not only changed his name but also he with his supervision and teachings along with Sri Sri Nibas and Sri Narottam enlightened him to become also an expert teacher. Srimati Janhaba, the second wife of Sri Nityanandaprabhu also confirmed this.[3]

Gourangadasi's husband Sri Shyamanandaprabhu with the permission from parents went to Ambika-Kalna and was initiated from Sri Hridaya Chaitanya, the brother's son of Sri Gadadhara Pundit. After the permission from the Preceptor Sri Hridaya Chaitanya he travelled Nabadwip and other Vaishnava places and thereafter went to Vrindaban.

Gourangadasi's husband Sri Shyamanandaprabhu had divine character. With his divinity of character and amiable behave Gourangadasi also was pleased and became a perfect Vaishnava woman.

The whole family including their followers used to paint and bear 'U' shaped 'Tilak' signs at twelve spots on their bodies. This 'U' shaped 'Tilak' sign was as a result of Srimati Radharani's 'Kripa' showered on him.

During the stayal in Vrindaban once Sri Shyamananda in mind visualized:- "*........that Sri Krishna and Srimati Radharani and other thousands of 'Sakhi's were engaged in divine dancing and singing. By chance from the left foot anklet of Srimati Radharani fell on the ground but with the air leaves from the trees fell and covered it. After the programme the 'Sakhi's searched but did not find the anklet of Srimati Radharani.*"

Sri Shyamananda also visualized in mind:- *"On the next morning at the time of sweeping out the leaves at the divine place of Lila of Sri Sri Radhakrishna with their 'Sakhi's he found the beautiful anklet studded with gems. He was sure it owned by Srimati Radharani. He informed Sri Jib Goswami and asked what he should do. Sri Jib Goswami advised him to keep the anklet at the place from where he got it. He went there to return the anklet. At the same time Lalita Sakhi and Srimati Radharani in disguise came there to find the lost anklet. They finding Shyamananda asked him if he has gotten it he should hand over it to them. He replied – Yes, I've got it but I shall not hand over, rather I like to put on the foot from where it was detached". Then Srimati Radharani Herself forwarded her left foot and thus satisfied the devotee Shyamananda. At the time of returning the anklet he touched it on the head and also on the nose. And so an impression of* 'U' shape *was marked on his nose....*"[4]

Gourangadasi's husband Sri Shyamanandaprabhu was one of them who advanced the Goudiya Vaishnavism in Utkal (Odisha) and also Goud Bengal.

Gourangadasi always used to inspire him to spread the Harinaam as advised by Sri Chaitanyadeva all along.

References

1. Sri Sri Goudiya Vaishnava Abhidhaan – Edited by Sri Haridas Das Babaji, 2nd, 3rd, and 4th Parts, 2nd Edition, 501 Chaitanyabda, Publisher – Haribol Kutir Poraghat, Nabadwip, Printer – Radha Press, Delhi 110031, p.1224 and 1387.

2. *Ibid* – p. 1388.
3. Sri Sri Nityananda Shakti Maa Janhaba – Sri Nemaichand Goswami, Pub. By Sri Sanatan Goswami, Printer – Shyamasundar Press, 1st Pub 1389 BS, 2nd Pub 1401 BS, p. 232-235.
4 Sri Sri Goudiya Vaishnava Abhidhaan – Edited by Sri Haridas Das Babaji, 2nd, 3rd, and 4th Parts, 2nd Edition, 501 Chaitanyabda, Publisher – Haribol Kutir Poraghat, Nabadwip, Printer – Radha Press, Delhi 110031, p. 1388).

98

Hemlata Thakurani

(The Eldest Daughter of Sri Nivas Acharya)

In the families of domestic Goudiya Vaishnavas the chastity, affection, love to children, giving due respect to the respectable and sincerity in worshipping God - all these good qualities were observed in the lives of women.

Sri Nivas Acharya was considered as the second incarnation of Sri Chaitanya Mahaprabhu in the post- Sri Chaitanya period. His daughter and also a disciple was Srimati Hemalata Devi. He also educated properly to her. His eldest son Geetagovinda was also initiated and educated by him.[1]

Srimati Hemalata Devi could easily attract others with her personality and good behaved character. Swarup Damodar expressed:-

"Acharyera Kanya Hemalata Naam,
Lachhima Sundari Purbe Tahara Aakshyan,
Sri Nivas Prabhu Hon Acharya Thakura,
Purbe Chhila Vidyapati Kavi Ratnapur."[2]

The mother of Hemalata Devi was Padmabati Devi or Gouranagpriya. She had more two daughters Krishnapriya and Kanchanlatika and a son Geetagovinda or Govindapati.

Srimati Hemalata Devi was married to Sri Gopijanaballava, son of Sri Ramkrishna Chattaraj of Budhuipara in the district of Murshidabad. According to 'Manava Vilas' this Budhuipara or Budhuri was under the Saidabad Pargana in the district of Murshidabad. Sri Gopijanaballava was an actual gentleman and well behaved personality. He was also known to Sri Nivas Acharya before the marriage.[3]

Srimati Hemalata Devi had no issue. Her husband Sri Gopijanaballava would like to treat her like a goddess as later Sri Ramkrishna once worshipped Sarada Maa. Hemalata ultimately adopted Radhamadhava, the fifth son of her brother Geetagovinda or Govindapati who had more four sons Krishnaparasad, Sundarananda, Sri Hari and Subal.[4]

Srimati Hemalata Devi used to serve her husband all the time and keep the thoughts of Sri Gouranga Mahaprabhu. She loved Mahaprabhu Sri Chaitanyadeva and the Goudiya Vaishnavas from any caste. She also used to visit her parental house at Bon Bishnupur. There still remains the banyan tree under which Sri Nivas Acharya took rest later returning fron Vrindaban. The place is called 'Bishramtala'.

Srimati Hemalata Devi also arranged to bring Sri Sri Radharaman deity and established at Bon Bishnupur. One Ramsundar Munsi erected a temple there what was demolished due to earthquake in 1304 BS. In the hands of the priest the deity was also broken and now another duplicate deity is found. The place was named as Kankila or Kankhal wherefrom the manuscript of 'Sri KrishnaKirtan' was discovered from the shed of the room for dwelling the cows. The deity of Sri Sri Radharaman is now being worshipped by the members of the family of Sri Nivas Acharya at their residences.[5]

Srimati Hemalata Devi used to worship the deity of Sri Sri Radharaman as mother and son relation. She had a good quantity of disciples. She should be remembered as a prominent leader in spreading the Harinaam all along.

References

1. Sri Sri Gouranga Parijan – by Sri Nityagopal Goswami, pub. By Jayadeva Goswami, in 1417 BS, printed at Graphix, Bankura, p 38, (original mode),
2. Manav Vilas – by Sri Pradip Kumar Sinha, pub. by Sri Maniklal Sinha in 1387 BS, Bishnupur, Bankura, printed at The New Minarva Press Sri Suchand Chandra Biswas, Bhumika p x, xii.
3. Sri Sri Goudiya Vaishnava Abhidhaan – Edited by Sri Haridas Das Babaji, 2nd, 3rd, and 4th Parts, 2nd Edition, 501 Chaitanyabda, Publisher – Haribol Kutir Poraghat, Nabadwip, Printer – Radha Press, Delhi 110031, p. 1957).
4. Manav Vilas – by Sri Pradip Kumar Sinha, pub. by Sri Maniklal Sinha in 1387 BS, Bishnupur, Bankura, printed at The New Minarva Press Sri Suchand Chandra Biswas, Bhumika p x, xii.
5. Sri Sri Goudiya Vaishnava Abhidhaan – Edited by Sri Haridas Das Babaji, 2nd, 3rd, and 4th Parts, 2nd Edition, 501 Chaitanyabda, Publisher – Haribol Kutir Poraghat, Nabadwip, Printer – Radha Press, Delhi 110031, p. 1957).

99

Putlibai

(Mother of Mahatma Gandhi)

Mahatma Gandhi was born on the 2nd October 1869. His mother was Putlibai and father was Karamchand Gandhi. Almost all the Indians are well aware that 'Gandhiji' or 'Bapuji' was the most prominent political and spiritual leader of India. Original name of Bapuji was Mohandas Karamchand Gandhi.

Putlibai was born in 1839 in a wealthy family belonging to the caste of tradesman. It was the tradition in the 19th century girls were not allowed to have formal education. From the very beginning of life she had to obey family tradition and religious rites at home. Her husband Karamchand Gandhi, son of affluent parents, in his early forties, had to marry three times and was left with two daughters from previous marriages. At the age of twenty years he was selected as the Chief Minister in a small state of Porbander in Gujarat.

Putlibai gave birth to her the fourth and the last son Bapuji at her thirty in a dark windowless ground-floor room in the Porbander city. Putlibai came from a Pranami Vaishnava Hindu family. She was a pious lady. She used to maintain usual rites of Vaishnavism. Not only that, she used to observe the 'Chaturmasya', the four months' long vow in the rainy season as the saints, the sages and other devotees used to observe due to non passable of roads to move from one place to another. She used to take food once in a day and devote to Almighty the whole days. She was also strict to honesty and sincerity in her all the deeds. Bapuji once commented about his mother – I do not remember her having ever missed the 'Chaturmasya". Without seeing the Sun she did not take food in a day of 'Chaturmasya' and so Bapuji and his fellows used to find the Sun in the rainy season on the clouded sky and inform inside the house where his mother Putlibai remained in worshipping God. Whenever she used to come outside the house unfortunately the Sun would become covered with clouds and she remained in fasting in several days. The whole Gandhi family was strict Vaishnava. Putlibai used to visit the temple of God regularly. She also served her husband as a nurse during his death bed in 1885 while Bapuji was then only a boy of sixteen.

'Gandhiji' for his political activities and love for all irrespective of castes and creed was and is considered as the 'Father of the Nation' and so he was named 'Bapuji' by almost all the people of India. From the very beginning Bapuji used to sing by humming songs on Lord Sri Ram. The song he liked most was as:-

"Raghupati Raghava Raja Ram,
Patita Pabana Sita Ram,
Ishwara Allah Tero Naam,
Sobko Sanmati De Bhagwan…"

He also used to sing by humming song on Vaishnavism as:-

"Vaishnava Janoto Tene Kahiye Ye,
Peer Parai Janere
Para Dukkhe Upkar Kare Koi,
Maan Apamaana Na Maanere.

Mohandas Karamchand Gandhi and his elder brother were fond of the dramas 'Harishchandra' and 'Shravana Pitribhakti. Both of them had immense respect for their father Karamchand Gandhi and mother Putlibai. Mainly the Gandhi family was purely Vaishnavite.

The holy and pious character of Putlibai would always influence on and inspire her son to become perfectly honest and sincere in every respect of life and deeds. We are sure the major portion of the character of the greatest national leader 'Gandhiji' was built by the family and specially to mention for his noble mother Putlibai. She died at her 52 in 1891. We bow our heads to her with respect.

References

1. The Story of My Experiments with Truth – An Autobiography: Mohandas Karamchand Gandhi, - Publisher: Future, Howrah, Published in 2013-14, 1st Chapter. p. 1 – 21.

16th Century AD

100

Meera Bai

(A Lady who Loved Sri Krishna and Sang for Him)

Meera Bai of Rajasthan had the ability to give a picture of Lord Sri Krishna by singing in the minds of all the devotees of the country. She was born at Merta village.[1]

Someone has written that Meera was a Rajput princess born about 1498 AD in Kudaki, Rajasthan, India. Someone has also written that, Meera Bai on the 3rd Baisakh in 1555 Sambat (1503 AD) in Jodhpur kingdom at Kudki village was born. Someone also commented that "She was born in Bajoli Nagaur, Rajasthan, India.

Whatever the opinions are we can stick to the information as received that Meera Bai was the only daughter of Ratan Singh and Srimati Kusum Kubari.[2]

Her father Ratan Singh (a devotee of Lord Krishna) was the youngest son of Rao Duda (grandfather of Meera) ruler of Merta, and son of Rao Jodha ruler and founder of Jodhpur. Ratan Singh belonged to the Rathore clan. And he died in January 1528 in a Battle with the Mughal Emperor Babur. On the other hand, Meera's mother Veer Kumari (Kusum Kubari) died during childbirth when Meera was around eight. Meera was then sent to her grandfather, Rao Duda and father's elder brother, Rao Viram Dev at Merta where she was educated. From her age of 7 she was joined by her childhood friend, Mithula, who stayed with Meera till the end. In her new family there remained the family deity Tulaja Bhawani (Parvati – the goddess of Strength). Meera loved Sri Krishna.

Meera Bai was a beautiful girl in outer appearances and also in inner personality with various qualities above all, her heart was full of love for Sri Krishna what made her more loveable by Lord. She was married with the eldest son of Rana of Mewar Bhojraj who was inheritance of the throne of Mewar in 1516 AD.[4]

However, Meera Bai being married to Bhoj Raj (Kumbh), Ruler of Chitt or also became the owner of plenty of wealth. As she was follower of Lord Sri Krishna her wealth was nothing but the unconditional love for Sri Krishna. There were no children from this marriage, and in any event she took no interest in her earthly spouse, since she believed herself to be married to Krishna.

Meera Bai being the devotee of Lord Vishnu i.e. Sri Krishna used to spend her time in thinking and singing of Lord Sri Krishna, because, she learnt to worship Lord from the very beginning of the life. However, her father-in-law Rana Sangha respected her devotion and protected her.

But in the Battle of Khanua in 1527 AD her father-in-law Rana Sangha was defeated and survived only for another year with broken heart. Afterwards his second son Rana Ratan Singh was enthroned and he also died after three years. Then the third son Rana Vikramjit occupied the throne.

Despite all these political changes Meera Bai continued to sing on Lord, to the deity of Lord in the temple erected by her husband, the company of the chanting Kirtana by Sadhus and Vaishnavas, distributing Prasad to all. These activities of women living behind the curtain were detrimental to the extant rules of the royal family, mainly of Rana Vikramjit, the Ruler opposed her.

The members of her royal family could not tolerate her devotion to these ascetics in order to discipline her they frequently chased her, looked her up, and even tried to kill her.

It is believed that Meera's husband Bhoj Raj Kumbh had also the fascination in writing poems, drama etc. in Cannad, Maharashtra (Marathi) and Mewari languages. In the initial stage he also guided in writing poems and songs to Meera. Remembering the wife Meera and his Shyamsundar he erected a pillar of Victory and named it as Kumbhashyam wherein the both names of Lord Sri Krishna worshipped by Meera and Kumbh the husband of Meera exist. He also built a temple for Lord Sri Krishna nearer to the palace. However, with approval from Meera Bhoj Raj Kumbh married the princess of Jhalawar....... On different occasions he used to leave Meera and again accepted her. He fascinated Meera. Once Emperor Badshah or Akbar in disguise, some liked to state, being engrossed with the Bhajana of Meera and wanted to give gift a necklace to her. She refused it and told –

Better you give it to 'Ranachhorji' (Krishna)." On hearing this incidence her husband sent a message – Now better you die". Meera did so but somehow she was saved. She did not return and started to travel by singing Lord's name.[5]

In 1512 AD Meera's husband died in a Battle or killed by his notorious son Uda while Meera was in Dwarka.

Meera Bai left Chittor and went to Merta and thereafter left for Vrindaban the centre place of Vaishnavism for Sri Krishna.

Meera Bai also considered herself to be a Gopi, Lalita and she was mad for her 'Ranachhorji' (Krishna).

'Ranachhorji' (Krishna) lover Meera Bai expressed her desire to have a discussion about authentic matters with Sri Roop Goswami, a directly taught by Sri Chaitanyadeva and one of the foremost saints of Vrindaban at that time. Sri Roop Goswami, however, being a celebrated renounced and sincere follower of Sri Chaitanyadeva, refused to meet her as she was a woman.

In reply Meera Bai sent a message to Sri Roop Goswami that there is only one male man (Purush) in the Universe Lord Sri Krishna. All others are 'Prakriti' the women. Whether any other 'Purusha' in Vrindaban is found?

Sri Roop Goswami was ashamed of for his mistake and requested her to visit the 'Ashram' once.

"Kripa Kori Aasi Jeno Den Darshaney".[6]

Thereafter Meera Bai met Sri Roop Goswami who was a highly learned personality in Vrindaban and was also one of the Six Goswamis in the line of Sri Cahitanya Mahaprabhu in preaching Vaishnavism in the world. Sri Roop Goswami and his elder brother Sri Sanatan Goswami once were dignified and important personalities next to the Nawab in the Royal Court of Hussein Shah in Goud Bengal. They could easily left their positions and after giving away all the wealth and property they had joined with Sri Chaitanya Mahaprabhu and lived in Vrindaban in order to revive the lost temples and deities and engaged themselves in composing necessary scriptures for Vaishnavism.

Their discussion between Meera Bai and Sri Roop Goswami was only on Sri Krishna and of Sri Krishna and for Sri Krishna, nothing else.

"Duijane Paraspara Krishnakatha Rasey,
Magan Hoilo Prem-Ananda-Ullasey."[7]

In another source expressed the opinion that Meera Bai had discussed the subject of Lord Sri Krishna with Sri Jib Goswami brother's son of Sri Sanatan and Sri Roop. His father was Ballava or Anupam, the youngest brother of Sri Sanatan and Sri Roop.[8]

Meera Bai once declared herself a disciple of Raidas or Ravidas.

Meera Bai while-heartedly used to spend money received from husband for establishing guest houses for the pilgrims and opened the centres to co-operate the orphans and the poor.

Afterwards Meera Bai travelled pilgrimages in the country with singing for Lord Sri Krishna. About thirteen hundred sacred songs might have been composed by Meera Bai. These were clinging to the tongue and lips of her all along. With these Meera Bai continued her pilgrimage by advancing one village to another village in the country. Once she met and received divine company of Kabir in Kashi.

Meera Bai went to Gujarat and visited Dwarka where Lord Sri Krishna full of wealth with precious ornaments was in the temple.

Then Rana Udai Singh who had succeeded Rana Vikram Singh sent a team of delegations comprising Brahmins to bring her back to Mewar. Meera Bai was reluctant to return however, she sought for a night for staying in the temple of Lord. Unfortunately she was found to have disappeared.

We still can hear her song:-

"Mere To Giridhara Gopala Dusro No Koi,
Jaake Sira Mora Mukuta Mero Pati Soi."[9]

From another source of information we could know that Meera Bai was born probably in 1505 AD. —— At her age of 4 years she with her mother noticed a colourful marriage procession and asked who her bridegroom was? Her mother just showed the deity of Sri Giridhariji as her bridegroom. Since then Meera Bai became fascinated to Lord Sri Giridhariji and used to worship the deity regularly. After her marriage at her twelve with Bhojraj son of Maharaja Sang at Chittor she was ordered by her mother-in-law to leave Sri Giridhariji and to worship the deity of Shakti Devi at the house. She could not obey it and so she had to live at a corner of the palace. Ultimately, her husband built a temple of 'Ranachhorji' Lord Giridhariji there for her worshipping. — Sri Roop Goswami hearing her comments that in Vrindaban there is only one male is Lord Sri Krishna was pleased and later he initiated her in Sri Krishna mantra.[10]

References

1. Brihat Sri Sri Bhaktamaal – Original in Hindi by Sri Navaji, Bengali Trans. by Sri Laldas Babaji, edited by Sri Dilip Mukhopadhyyay and published by Benimadhab Seals Library, printed by A B C Printers, re-printed in 1416 BS (2009AD) p. 633.
2. Turki O Afgan Yuge Bharat – by Asit Kumar Sen, pub. by K.P.Bagchi & Co., typesetting – the Hall Mark, printer- Unique India, 1st edition, 1998 AD, 2nd print - 2011 AD, Discussion on Bhakti, 12th Chapter, p. 353.
4. Brihat Sri Sri Bhaktamaal – Original in Hindi by Sri Navaji, Bengali Trans. by Sri Laldas Babaji, edited by Sri Dilip Mukhopadhyyay and published by Benimadhab Seals Library, printed by A B C Printers, re-printed in 1416 BS (2009AD) p. 633.
5. Bairer Daak Bhetarer Sara (RAJASTHAN) – by Radhu Goswami (Radhakrishna), pub. by Patha Parikrama, B.E.386 Salt Lake City, Calcutta –'64, on 23rd January, 1997 AD, printer – Himadri Roy, Ramkrishna Press, 9A, Ramdhan Mitra Lane, Cal.- '4, p. 52-54.
6. Brihat Sri Sri Bhaktamaal – Original in Hindi by Sri Navaji, Bengali Trans. by Sri Laldas Babaji, edited by Sri Dilip Mukhopadhyyay and published by Benimadhab Seals Library, printed by A B C Printers, re-printed in 1416 BS (2009A D) p. 400.
7. *Ibid*,
8. Sri Sri Goudiya Vaishnava Abhidhaan – Edited by Sri Haridas Das Babaji, 2nd, 3rd, and 4th Parts, 2nd Edition, 501 Chaitanyabda, Publisher – Haribol Kutir Poraghat, Nabadwip, Printer – Radha Press, Delhi 110031, p.1314 & 1602.
9. *Ibid* and Sl.No. 56 – Meera Bai Shabdaboli.
10. Amiya Asim Charit – 16th year Beginning 2010 Radhaballav Dey, Ed. Sachidulal Chakraborty, p. 45. Original in H.

101

A Fortunate Lady of Odisha

One day Sri Chaitanya Mahaprabhu was looking at the deities of Sri Sri Jagannatha Mahaprabhu, Sri Sri Subhadra Devi and Sri Sri Balarama as usual daily schedule. Almost every day Sri Chaitanya Mahaprabhu remained standing by the side of the Gadur Stambha looking at Sri Sri Jagannatha Mahaprabhu used to shed tears without any stop the floor were drenched with eye drops. He could not stare at anything around him. On the very day the inside temple was full of crowd of visitors. One certain lady tried her best to look at Lord but failed due to rush. At last she found some higher position on the shoulder of Sri Chaitanyadeva and succeeded to have 'Darshan' of Sri Sri Jagannatha Mahaprabhu. Aide Govinda noticed it and he requested her to come down to the floor. Perhaps he also rebuked her. Sri Chaitanyadeva then laughingly said to Govinda not to disturb the lady while she was looking at Sri Sri Jagannatha Mahaprabhu and allow her to quench the thirst of seeing the deity of Lord.

"Adi Bashya Ei Streekey Na Kara Barjan,
Karuk Jathesta Jagannatha Darshan."[1]

We should note that the very word 'Adi Bashya' means very loveable in Tamil Language. Sri Chaitanyadeva understood the eagerness of looking at Sri Sri Jagannatha Mahaprabhu with plenty of love for God made her unconscious about the place from where she wanted to peruse the faces of Sri Sri Jagannatha Mahaprabhu, Subhadra Devi and Balarama.

The name of the lady of Odisha was not known to us but her pure and sincere devotion made her immortal to the Goudiya Vaishnavas.

Reference

1. Sri Sri Chaitanya Charitamrita– Sri Krishnadas Kaviraj, Edited by Sri Sri Madbhakti Sri Roop Maharaj, Published from Gaudiya Mission (Rgd.) by Tridandi Bhikshu Sri Bhakti Gunakar Goswami, Printer – Radha Press, Gandhinagar, Delhi – 110 031, 6th Edition, Published on 11 March 1990, Antya Lila, 14th Chapter, Shloka 26, p. 1076.).

102

Narayani Devi

(The Mother of Poet Sri Vrindabandas)

Narayani Devi was one of the blessed women by Sri Gouranga Mahaprabhu at her childhood when she was only a four/six years' girl. She was crying at the gate of Sribaas Angan while inside Sri Gouranga Mahaprabhu was busy with Kirtan and dancing in love for Si Krishna with all other associates. Sri Gouranga Mahaprabhu was taking some food and he gave the residual to the child by saying – Do not cry, if you prefer to cry then cry for Sri Krishna only."

She was Narayani, the daughter of Nalin Pundit, the elder brother of Sri Baas. But at the age of one year her parents died and all her responsibilities were taken on the shoulders of Sribaas Pundit and his wife Malini Devi.[1]

Sri Gouranga Mahaprabhu could realize that once this girl would be famous in future for her son. Really afterwards this Narayani was married to one Baikunthadas Bipra who died in a premature stage and at that time Narayani was carrying. Thinking this situation of Narayani Sribaas Pundit and Malini Devi brought her with them. After her husband's death. Narayani Devi's son was born in 1419 Shaka (1497 AD) in the month of Baisakh 12th day of black moon. This son was named Sri Vrindabandas who wrote the life sketch in lucid Bengali Payar rhythm what was probably the first poem in Bengali literature. Narayani Devi at the age of five of her child started to settle at Mamgachhi under the supervision of Sri Basudeva Dutta, a follower of Sri Gouranga Mahaprabhu.

About this Sri Basudeva Dutta we should cite Goura Ganoddesh Deepika as:-

"Brajey Sthitou Gayake Zou Madhu Kantha-Mashubratou.
Mukunda-Basudevou Tou Duttou Gouranga-Gayakou."[2]

In the earlier life in Braja Lila the singers named as Madhukantha and Madhubrata are now in the Nabadwip Lila of Sri Gouranga Mahaprabhu Mukunda and Basudeva. We can be confirmed that Mukunda-Basudeva Dutta were the singers who followed Sri Gouranga Mahaprabhu all the time.

We also find the name of Basudeva Dutta in other scriptures one of them is Vaishnava Abhidhan.[3]

Basudeva Dutta used to worship Sri Sri Madan Gopal at his village Mamgachchi near Purbasthsali. The Deity is still being worshipped.[4]

It was possible for Narayani Devi to bring up her son with proper education for the full co-operation of Basudeva Dutta with care to the child. Without Basudeva Dutta we could not get the first poet in Bengali Literature.

Narayani Devi's son Vrindabandas wrote the Sri Sri Chaitanya Bhagawata that elaborately described the life sketch of Sri Gouranga Mahaprabhu and the Nabadwip Lila. It was first named as Chaitanya Mongal but after reading the manuscript the learned people living in Vrindaban named the book as Sri Sri Chaitanya Bhagawata in parity of Srimad Bhagawata and Narayani Devi also admitted the change of name of the first book of the hagiography in Bengali Language.

We generally call Durga as Narayani, the power of Sri Sri Narayana. Narayani is also the name of Laxmi, the wife of Sri Sri Narayana. This Narayani mother of Vrindabandas was also a woman of highly praiseworthy for her devotion, sincerity and also sacrifice.

References

1. Prem Vilas – by Nityananda Das, Revised and edited by Dr. Bijon Goswami, Pub, in 1405 BS, 1999 AD, 1st Mahesh Edition, Printed at Printing Publicity, p. 218 & 219).
2. Sri Sri Gour Ganoddesh Deepika – by Sri Kavi Karnapur, Edited by Sri Ashoke Kumar Bandyopadhaya, publisher- Sandesh, Printer- Orient Press, Pub in 2007 AD, Shloka -187.
3. Sri Sri Goudiya Vaishnava Abhidhaan – Edited by Sri Haridas Das Babaji, 2nd, 3rd, and 4th Parts, 2nd Edition, 501 Chaitanyabda, Publisher – Haribol Kutir Poraghat, Nabadwip, Printer – Radha Press, Delhi 110031, p.1364).
4. *Ibid* p. 1365.

103 & 104

Satya Bai & Lakshmi Bai

(Both the two women were from brothel to the shelter under the Holy Feet of Lord Sri Chaitanyadev)

Mahaprabhu Sri Chaitanyadev travelled most of the major parts of India in the South, some portion of the West and also the North. He wanted to circulate Harinaam all over India. While in Mathura Sri Chaitanyadev went to a Banyan tree. His intention was to visit Bateswar Shiba Mahadeva.

"...Bateswar name Shib aachhen tathay,
Bhakti kori seikhane Gorachand dhay,
Bhakti saha Bateswar Prabhu Pranamila,
Anahare seikhane Rajani jaapila........"[1]

Mahaprabhu Sri Chaitanyadev wanted to uplift the extremely wicked and hard hearted people wherever He met. One of the reasons of getting Sannyas was to uplift those people.

"...Ataeba abasya Aami Sannyas koribo......
Nirmal Hridaye Bhakti karaibo uday.....
Esob Pashandir taube haibe nistar,
Aar kono upay nahi ei yukti sar....."[2]

Mahaprabhu was firm to do the betterment of the oppressed and fallen people. Among them were also two women in Mathura.

In the morning, one day, after having bath Mahaprabhu went to receive alms from doors to doors as needed. In the Kadcha of Govindadas we find–

"....Bhiksha maagi aailam Madhyahna smaye,
Pak kori seba kore mor Gora Raye,
Prasad paamu muhi amrita saman..."[3]

Mahaprabhu Sri Chaitanyadev's incarnation was also for emancipation for the oppressed and neglected. However, Mahaprabhu did not discriminate between good or bad characters to deliver Harinaam and to advise to live pure and simple without vanity. So Mahaprabhu was considered as 'Patit-Pawan'.

He also used to note the ill motivation of the people and could solve easily. He had to fight all known or unknown enemies with His foreseeing capability and love.

".....Henokaale aaila setha Tirtha dhanaban,
Duijan beshya sange aaila dekhite,
Sannyasira bhari-bhuri pariksha korite,
Satyabai Lakshmibai name besyadaya
Prabhur nikate aasi koto katha koy........."[4]

We can recollect that the nymph Menaka was sent from Paradise to spoil the meditation of sage Vishwamitra and she succeeded to do it.

Sri Chaitanya Mahaprabhu's physical form and beauty were so beautiful that these were beyond imagination of anybody. The writers and poets from the past and still today whenever get chance utilise to describe these aspects. As an example we can cite from Lochandas –

"....Koto koti kaamer nripati Gourahari,
Kulabati kalankabithaar dehadhari..."[5]

Dhanram Tirtharam brought the two prostitutes to stumble Sri Chaitanya Mahaprabhu. The two women at first tried to captivate the mind of beautiful looking youth new Sannyasi Sri Chaitanyadev with their cleverness of speeches. The wicked character Tirtharam wanted to defame Chaitanyadev with these women-

"Sannyasira tez ebe hare lobo chhale".[6]

Govindadas described in the kadcha –

"...Kato ranga kare Lakshmi Satyabala haase,
Satyabala hasimukhe base Prabhu paase,
Kanchali khulia Satya dekhaila stan,
Satyare korila Prabhu Matri sambodhan..."[7]

Sri Chaitanyadev addressed them as mothers. Referring this respectable Khudiram Das wrote – "We can guess that He never slept with Vishnupriyadevi and His desire of Sannyas originated from here."[8]

Sri Chaitanyadev had unbelievable control over Himself but the abandoned women had no idea of it. However, they could understand that Mahaprabhu possessed an extra ordinary personality. We find:-

"...Thar thar kaape Satya Prabhura Bachane,
Iha dekhi Lakshmi bada bhoy pay mone,
Kichhui Bikaarnaahi Prabhura Monete,
Dheye gia Satyabala pade charanete..."[9]

Sri Chaitanya Mahaprabhu without any deviation from normal state humbly said to them – Oh, Mothers please do not consider me guilty:-

" Keno aparadhi kara aamare Janani,
Ei matra boli Prabhu padila dharani."[10]

Actually Sri Chaitanyadev's ecstatic state caused by profundity of Love for Lord Sri Krishna made him more and more dear personality to all. He called them 'Mother' what made them mad and they also followed His endless Love for Sri Krishna. We can also say Sri Chaitanyadev was also a great teacher for the people.[11]

His madly expression has been described elaborately;-

"...Sob elo thelo holo Prabhura aamar,
Kotha Lakshmi kothay Satya naahi dekhi aar,
Nachte lagila Prabhu boli Hari Hari,
Romanchita kalebar ashru dardari...
...Harinaame matta hoye nache Goraroy,
Anga hote adbhut tez baahiray..."[12]

Satya Bai and Lakshmi Bai observed the dance and singing Harinaam by Mahaprabhu and were not only surprised but also attracted to the reaction on the body of Sri Chaitanya Mahaprabhu with tears, trembling, perspiration etc the 'Asta Sattwik' signs. They were nothing but prostitutes. They liked their profession only to earn money more and more. They, generally, had no any intention to defame Sri Chaitanyadev, nor they had any idea how deep of the Love for Sri Krishna Mahaprabhu had. However, they were rented and supposed to obey their then present owner Tirtharam. But all on a sudden the sinner Tirtharam then fell at the feet of Sri Chaitanyadev. As we find:-

"...Iha dekhi sei dhani mone chamakilo,
Charantalete padi ashraya chahilo,...
...Harinaame matta Prabhu naahi bahya jnan,
Ghar bhenge paditechhe aakul paran,
Mukhe lala ange dhula naahika basan,
Kantakita kalebar mudita nayan..."[13]

At the first effort these two women were frustrated. But later they with the contact of Sri Chaitanya Mahaprabhu by naam samkirtan could leave all the pasts and properties behind and became sincere Vaishnavites. This Mahaprabhu's Love for Lord Sri Krishna may be compared with the highest peak of the Himalayas or with the depth of Ocean. Sri Chaitanya Mahaprabhu thus used to teach us that with listening, uttering and participating in the Naam Sankirtan any person can awake from dark livelihood and become a Vaishnava, the Bhagawata.

We can conclude that Satyabai and Lakshmibai were transformed to sincere and real Vaishnavis with the causeless mercy of Sri Chaitanyadeva and His huge Love for Lord Sri Krishna.

Refrences

1. Kadcha of Govindadas, Ed. By Madhusudan Karmakar, Pub. Dey's Publishing in 1997, p. 26,
2. Sri Sri Chaitanya Charitamrita by Krishnadas Kaviraj, Ed.President Acharya Sri Sri Madbhaktisri Rup Bhagawata Maharaj, Published by Tridandibhikku Sri Bhaktigunakar from Goudiya Mission (Regd.), Printed at Radha Press, Gandhinagar Delhi – 110 031, 6th Ed. In 1990 (1396 Beng.), Antya Leela, 17th Chapter, Sloka – 265-267, Page 310,
3. Same as No.1 above,
4. *Ibid*
5. Sri Sri Chaitanya Mongal by Lochandas, 3rd ed. Pub. By Goudiya Mission in 1391(Beng. Sal), printed at Sri Bhagawat Press, Ed. Sri Rup Bhagawat Maharaj, Adi Khanda, Sloka – 736, p. 64,
6. Same as No.1 above
7. *Ibid*
8. Sri Chaitanyer Baul-Byactitwa, by Khudiram Das (source: Sri Chaitanya Prasanga, ed.by Jagadish Bhattacharya, p. 31)
9. Same as No.1 above,
10. *Ibid*
11. Jagatprabhu Sri Gouranger Sannyas, by Dr. Uma Bandopadhyay, Pub. Radhamadan Gopal Kunja, Ed. By Sri Jawaharlal Bandyopadhyay and Pradip Mukhopadhyay, 1st ed. In 1416 (Beng. Sal.) printed at N.B.Publicity, p. 42-43,
12. Same as No.1 above
13. *Ibid.*

18th Century AD

105

Annapurna Devi

(The Mother of Harichand Thakur)

Sri Harichand Thakur in post Sri Chaitanya period was one of the known figures of Bengal. His devotion and sincerity could attract thousands of people of Bengal including of East Bengal (now in Bangladesh), Assam, Tripura and some other states of India.

His mother was Annapurna Devi. She was born at Tarail village in East Bengal (now in Bangladesh) in the house of Sri Ramprasad Chowdhury who once shifted to Odakandi with all the members of the family. There he was introduced with Yashobanta, the sixth generation of Sri Ramdas Thakur. Relation between the two families developed so deep and friendly that Sri Ramprasad arranged the marriage of his daughter Annapurna with Yashobanta, generation of Sri Ramdas Thakur:-

"Thakur Chowdhury Bangshey Parama Piriti".[1]

The husband of Annapurna Devi Yashobanta Thakur lived in the district of Faridpur (now in Bangladesh). Originally they were worshippers of Shakti Mantra. But gradually they became interested in Vaishnavism as Sri Gouranga Mahaprabhu or Sri Chaitanyadeva started to bring all the people under one umbrella Harinaam.

Yashobanta Thakur was initiated from Sri Ramkanta Gossainji, sevait at the temple of Sri Sri Basudeva Jiu at Mukdoba in the district of Faridpur and started to reside at Odakandi-Safaladanga. Sri Ramkanta Gossainji, the 'Siddha' in Sadhana would believe that Sri Chaitanyadeva Himself would incarnate as a son of Yashobanta Thakur.

Let us recollect a brief genealogical table of Yashobanta Thakur as under:-

Sri Ramdas Thakur (a Brahmin of Mithila) – Chandramohan – Shukdeva – Kalidas – Nidhiram, Rabidas and Sri Jib –From Nidhiram –

Mukundaram and Kartik-From Mukundaram – Yashobanta, Sanatan, Prankrishna, Rammohan and Ranakrishna –From Yashobanta – Krishnadas, Harichand, Vaishnavadas, Gouridas and Swarupdas –

A forefather of Annapurna Devi's father-in-law Sri Ramdas Thakur did not care the caste distinction system of the society at the time of his son Chandramohan's marriage with Rajalaxmi, a girl of a father of Namah Shudra caste what was not permitted by the society. So he was outcaste.[2]

We also can cite:-

"Brhmasutah Namah Shudra Gunete Naheto Kshudra
Aar Naki Vir Bangshaboli.
Dekha Giye Sei Ghare Kamala Biraj Karey
Pele Pete Paro Mahakali."[3]

At that period caste distinction demoralized the society. So, the Sadhak of Shakti Chandramohan had to leave own village and began to live in Jessore. Before the demise he directed his son and grand children to adhere to practicing virtuousness generations after generations in every respect. It is also learnt from also the 'Bhaktamaal' that Maa Durga in a dream informed him that a divine personality great man would incarnate in the family.[4]

About Sri Yashobanta we may cite also:-

"Srbashjyesthya Yashobanta Gune Tar Nahi Antya
Asesh Gunete Guna Dham
Hari Chita Hari Katha Hari Sukh Hari Byatha
Hari Deha Hari Mona Pran."[5]

Gradually Annapurna Devi became attracted to Vaishnavism. With the love for God Sri Krishna, sincerity in devotion and service to the public made her a glorious Vaishnava and so we could get her son Harichand a divine character.

References

1. Sri Sri Harililamrita – by Sri Tarak Chandra Sarkar.
2. Sri Sri Harichnd Thakur O Matua Sampradaya – by Sri Netaidassi, pub. by Esha Mukhopadhaya, edited by Pradip Mukhopadhaya, 1st edition, Baisakh 1411 BS, printer – Sodepur Computer Centre, p. 46.
3. *Ibid* and (4) Brihat Sri Sri Bhaktamaal – Original in Hindi by Sri Navaji, Bengali Trans. by Sri Laldas Babaji, edited by Sri Dilip Mukhopadhyyay and published by Benimadhab Seals Library, printed by A B C Printers, re-printed in 1416 BS (2009AD) p. 729.
5. Sri Sri Guruchand Charit – by Acharya Mahananda Haldar, p. 34.

106

Swarnamoyee Devi Thakurani

(The Mother of Bijoykrishna Goswami)

Swarnamoyee Devi, the mother of Sri Bijoy Krishna Goswami who was known to all for his own identity and activities in the path of Devotion and Sadhana in the 19th Century. His father was Sri Ananada Goswami who was later generation of Sri Adwaita Acharya, the person who caused the incarnation of Sri Gouranga Mahaprabhu by his Sadhana with Tulsi Leaves and water of the Ganga regularly as a part of his daily routines.

For giving birth to Sri Bijoy Krishna Goswami, Srimati Swarnamoyee Devi is still remembered in Shantipur as well as in the whole Bengal. Sri Bijoy Krishna Goswami was born in Shantipur on the 16th Shravana 1248 BS (in 1763 Shaka) or on the 2nd August 1841 AD at the inception of Full Moon of Jhulanyatra.[1]

Another opinion is Sri Bijoy Krishna Goswami was born in Full Moon evening in 1258 BS (in 1852 AD) in Shantipur.[2]

The husband of Srimati Swarnamoyee Devi Sri Ananada Goswami was a learned personality with profound knowledge in Srimad Bhagawata. He used to cook for Sri Sri Shyamasundar. He had the practice of washing the dry wood with the water of the Ganga before burning in the oven and thereafter he started to cook. So, he was familiar with the name 'Khari Dhoya' Gossain by the people. In the mood of Sadhana the eight 'Swattik' signs with tears, trembling, pleasure etc were seen on his body. He knew how to distribute 'Prasad' to the devotees with their satisfaction. He also used to distribute all the money he received to his disciples or not without discrimination. He travelled from Shantipur to Puri Dham by bowing head to Lord Sri Sri Jagannathaswami.[3]

Swarnamoyee Devi was the third wife of Sri Ananada Goswami. As advised by the elder uncle's son Gopinath Goswami at his death bed Ananada married third time to Swarnamoyee. He was also requested after giving births two sons the youngest should be given to his widow wife as adoption and the elder would keep the continuity of the generation of Ananda.

Swarnamoyee Devi's father used to live at Shikarpur. Her father Sri Gourikanta Joardar being a widower could manage the marriage of his daughter Swarnamoyee Devi with Ananada Goswami. Later in due time Swarnamoyee gave births to two sons. They were Brajagopal and Bijoykarishna. On knowing these Ananda's elder brother's widow wife Krishnakamini Devi was so pleased that she arranged a 'Vaishnava Seva' with giving away the gifts in charity and worshipping gods and goddesses.[4]

Before the 'Annaprashan' (festival the rites of allowing child to taste rice first before the opening of teeth) mistakenly opium was given and the youngest child Bijoykrishna swallowed instead of village doctor's medicine. The child became ill in tetanus and was to die. Somehow the child was rescued by the grace of God. Afterwards, Swarnamoyee Devi returned to Shantipur at Ananda's house and again the 'Annaprashan' and giving a name at the age of eight months of the child was observed with grandeur.

At the age of two and a half of Bijoykrishna Swarnamoyee Devi and Sri Ananda Goswami could not forget their promise to give the youngest child to the widow and issueless sister-in-law. But all on a sudden at the house of Mukundanarayan Chowdhury at Amlagachhi in Rangpur Sri Ananda Goswami while in delivering and narrating the 'Path' of Srimad Bhagwata and mediating of Lord Sri Krishna, his meditation did not break in reasonable time, nor he returned to normal stage rather he succumbed.[5]

However, Swarnamoyee Devi alone kept the word to hand over the youngest child Bijoykrishna at his five years' of age to Ananda's elder deceased brother Sri Gopi Madhya Go swami's widow wife Krishnakamini Devi. This adoption ceremony was observed by Swarnamoyee Devi with some ached heart in presence of the then Zaminder Motilal Roy, Kanailal Goswami and many other dignified personalities.

Bijoykrishna used to call his adoption mother as 'Maa Janani' and own mother as only 'Maa'. But Krishnakamini Devi his 'Maa Janani' did not survive much and so, Bijoykrishna had to return to his Maa again.

Swarnamoyee Devi used to call her youngest son as 'a son of jungle of taro (Kochu). She in the period of pregnancy was ill with dysentery and had to run nearest jungle, as usual practice at that time in want of any latrine and there at the time of releasing, her labor pain started for the birth of the son. From there the peculiar name 'Kochi' was given to own son for joking only.

Swarnamoyee Devi had to travel to the houses of disciples for earning money etc. regularly and also from Shantipur and Shikarpur own dwelling house and paternal house the education of the sons could not be uninterrupted. However, for the merit that Bijoykrishna possessed he and his elder brother learnt from teacher Bhagawanbabu, Reverend Hessle and Pundit Govinda Bhattacharya at Shantipur.

Once, Bijoykrishna was stolen by some miscreants for sacrificing to Mother Kali. Once he remained whole night at the temple of Shyamchand in Shantipur. Once he dreamt that in the lap of his deceased father Ananda in the land of the moon. Once, he brought one horse without permission to learn riding. Once He had some uncommon behavior that lead to Swarnamoyee Devi to accompany his son outside the home as a shadow.

However, Bijoykrishna used to maintain all the rules and rites as required by the family tradition. But one day he left Shatipur and started to learn treatment in the Calcutta Medical College and Hospital after studying three years participated in a demonstration against the authority. On his request Ishwar Chandra Vidyasagar mitigated the problem arisen. Afterwards he left studying in medical line and got admission in Sanskrit College for studying in the Vedanta.

He also wanted to leave the sacred thread and become a 'Brahma'. But his mother Swarnamoyee Devi warned him by saying that she should die by committing suicide so he kept the scared thread.

Swarnamoyee Devi was a benevolent lady. Whatever she would get from the disciples she could not spend all for ownselves, she used to distribute to the poor and the needy people. She also gave shelter to a needy woman. She liked to feed hungry people throughout her life.

Bijoykrishna the son of Swarnamoyee Devi travelled different places in the country. Once in the Kumva Mela at Prayag he was also selected the Best Sadhu. He had affection to the animals also. Once he protested the inhuman killing of monkeys under Puri Municipality.

His path was for the Hindus, the Brahamas, the Muslims, the Christians above all for everybody to remain calm with the mentality of cooperation with each other.

In brief Swarnamoyee Devi and her son Bijoykrishna Goswami were really humans what the future generation may not believe. We bend our heads to the mother Srimati Swarnamoyee Devi and her son Bijoykrishna Goswami, the real saint of the age.

References

1. Mahatma Bijoy Krishna Goswamir Jiban Brittanta – by Bankabehari Kar, pub. by Swami Dwijeshananda Saraswati, 1st pub 1317 BS, printer Sri Hari Press, p. 1.
2. Brihat Sri Sri Bhaktamaal – Original in Hindi by Sri Navaji, Bengali Trans. by Sri Laldas Babaji, edited by Sri Dilip Mukhopadhyyay and published by Benimadhab Seals Library, printed by A B C Printers, re-printed in 1416 BS (2009 AD) p. 633.
3. Prabhupad Bijoy Krishna Goswami – by Jagatbandhu Moitra, pub. by Allied Book Agency, 1st pub in 1318 BS, printer- Trio Process, 6th edition 1417 BS, p. 9.
4. *Ibid* p. 16 and (5) *Ibid* p. 9.

16th Century AD

107 & 108

Basudha Devi & Janhaba Devi

(The wives of Sri Nityananda Prabhu)

"Now women activities and their glory of successes are being to some extent getting highlights. However, during the last half a millennium ago women's coming up in the society was almost unthinkable. Yet we find rare personalities among the women existed also five hundred years back. Srimati Vasudha Devi and Srimati Janhaba Devi were of such rare women."[1]

Sri Nityananda Prabhu was 'Abadhut' almost a Sannyasi but once Sri Chaitanya Mahaprabhu at Neelachal (Puri) requested Sri Nityananda Prabhu not to attend in Neelachal every year and to remain in Goud Banga in order to spread the Movement of Harinaam Mahamantra to all with continuity. Mahaprabhu clarified to Sri Nityananda that He Himself was a Sannyasi, Sri Gadadhar Pundit remained unmarried for being with Mahaprabhu and lived at Tota for serving the Deity of Sri Sri Gopinathji, Sri Adwyaitacharya the aged one with his utmost capability was already engaged in his style in the Movement of Harinaam Mahamantra to some people, Sribaas does not prefer to go outside and to solicit anything for himself. And so, any capable personality should come forward to maintain the continuity of the flow of the Movement of Harinaam Mahamantra as introduced by Sri Chaitanya Mahaprabhu to all. For this continuity Sri Nityananda should enter into domestic life.

In short, Sri Nityananda Prabhu married Bsudha Maa and Janhaba Maa both the daughters of Sri Suryadas Sarkhel of Shaligram. Their mother was Srimati Bhadrabati Devi.

Bsudha Devi

The daughter of Sri Suryadas Sarkhel and Srimati Bhadrabati Devi Basudha was born rather to say was incarnated on this earth probably on the holy day of Rathayatra, the Shukla Dwitiya of the month of Ashada in 1429 Shaka.[2]

Kavi Karnapur has mentioned Vasudha Devi and also Janhaba Devi as Anaga Manjari in earlier Brajalila in his Sri Sri Goura Ganoddeshdeepika. The Manjaree of Vrindavan Leela here took birth as two sisters Vasudha and Janhaba.

Kechit Sri Vasudhadeving Kalabapi bibrinwate,
Ananga Manjaring kechinJanhabincha prachkshate.

Not only that we find in the same scripture that Srimati Vasudha and Srimati Janhaba were Srimati Baruni and Srimati Rebati the wives of Sri Balaram in the earlier births.

Sri Baruni Rebatyarangsa Samvabe
Tasy priye Sri Vasudha ch Janhaba,
Sri Suryadasakhya Mahatmnah sute
Kukudmi roopasya ch Suryatejasyah.[3]

It was known to all Vaishnavas believe that Sri Nityanada Prabhu was considered as Balarama in earlier life in Braja.

Sri Suryadas Sarkhel of Shaligram to respond to fourth brother Sri Gouridas's call came to Ambika Kalna and settled separately there. However, leaving behind two sons Balaram and Raghunathdas the wife of Sri Gouridas Pundit Srimati Vimala Devi expired. Then Srimati Bhadrabati Devi took up the responsibility of bringing up the two sons Balaram and Raghunathdas with her own children. Her daughters Vasudha and Janhaba thus participated in domestic work as well as the looking after the brother Chandrasekhar and also Balaram and Raghunathdas.

Vasudha and Janhaba the two sisters looked almost same. They seemed to be twin sisters. Both of them had almost same and equal qualities, intellects etc. However, Vasudhadevi was effeminately expert in domestic work specially in cooking palatable dishes with tasting foodstuffs for the household Deity of Lord. And Janhaba Devi was rather a spirited lady.

Both of them were taught by Father Sri Suryadas and Uncle Sri Gouridas with the Scriptures and day to day different things. Thus they were enough educated. Yet Basudha Devi preferred to co-operate mother Bhadradevi at the time of cooking 'Bhog' of Lord as situated in the domestic temple. Janhabadevi also used to forward her hands to quicken the work for Lord.

For plucking flowers, Tusi leaves and other arrangements both Basudha and Janhaba the two sisters had to rise early in the morning before Sunrise.

While plucking flowers, Tusi leaves they used to sing songs of Poets Jaydev, Vidyapati and others as they both have loved one and only one.

Ki Kahaba re Sakhi, Ananada aor,
Chiradin Madhab Mandire mor.
Papa Sudha karo jato dukh delo,
Piya mukh darshane tato sukha velo.[4]

At the time of singing songs before the Deities Vasudha and Janhaba their younger brother Sri Chandrasekhar and also cousins Balaram and Raghunath used to play mridanga, kartaal, etc in order to create an atmosphere filled with music. The two sisters kept nothing secret to each other.

During the period of preaching Harinaam Sri Nityananda as directed by Mahaprabhu among the people of Goud Bengal one day Sri Adwaitacharya reminded that Sri Krishna Chaitanya Mahaprabhu also advised him earlier to settle in domestic life. Sachimaa at Nabadwip also advised him to marry without any delay.

One day taking with Krishnadas Hore and Uddharan Dutta and some other associates Sri Nityananda came to the house of Sri Suryadas Sarkhel at Kalna. He with his companies was welcomed. Uddharan Dutta announced the proposal to Sri Suryadas Sarkhel. As Sri Nityananda was a Rarhi Brahmin with Shandilya Gotra and Suryadas Sarkhel was a Rarhi Brahmin with Batsya Gotra there remains no obstacle. Both the families were matching for marriage.

But the local orthodox society was reluctant to accept Sri Nityananda as a pure Brahmin as he like a Sannyasi travelled whole India and could not maintain the rites of a domestic Brahmin. He had to accept food whatever received like the rules of Abadhut. So, his Brahmanism was lost. Sri Nityananda as Sri Chaitanyadeva did not fight against extant rules of Society and again he arranged to bear the sacred thread.

The followers of Sri Nityananda selected Basudha Maa as a suitable bride for him. However, Sri Suryadas Sarkhel could not confirm the proposal of his daughter's marriage with Sri Nityananda in fear of orthodox society. Understanding this, the followers like Krishnadas Hore and Uddharan Dutta and some others requested him to show the divine real wealth to the members of family Suryadas Sarkhel and the villagers of the society.

"Karaha Oishwarya Prakash Ati Paripati"[5]

In the meantime Sri Nityanandaprabhu heard a loud crying by some of the members inside the house of Suryadas Sarkhel. He on way to the river

Ganga with associates halted for a moment but did not stop and did not express any eagerness on it. He went on to the river side. It was river Ganga that flows with sweet breeze smoothly there.

Sri Nityananda prabhu was completely free from any tension. Like other unpleasant incidences the news came to him that all on a sudden Vasudha Devi was fallen ill with almost incurable disease like epilepsy. The members of the family became hopeless for the life of Vasudha Devi. The village physicians and older experienced persons advised Suryadas to arrange to carry the affected girl near the holy Ganga and to wait till the daughter breathes her last at holy Ganga. Suryadas generally called his men to arrange accordingly.

At that time Sri Gouridas Pundit arrived and advised – It is better to approach Sri Nityananda prabhu first. Let us observe whether he can anyhow save our child. If he can, we should offer our daughter to him".

Sri Suryadas however, discussing the pros and cons with his wife Bhadrabati Devi and next brother Sri Gouridas, at last decided to depend on God or on Sri Nityananda prabhu.[6]

Sri Gouridas Pundit with Suryadas hurriedly reached the place where with all the associates Sri Nityananda prabhu was chanting Harinaam concentratedly. The two brothers confessed – For the customs of society we could not recognize you and so we did not dare to accept your proposal. Please pardon us. If you remain with us we need not care for the various customs of the society."

Sri Gouridas Pundit added – Prabhu, our daughter is ill, there remains little scope of her life. Please come to our house and save our child. Prabhu, do not hesitate, and come along us immediately".

Sri Gouridas Pundit with Suryadas fell on the feet of Sri Nityananda prabhu.

With a short smiling Sri Nityananda prabhu with his associates came to the spot where Vasudha Devi was lying senselessly. Her body was fully covered with a piece of bed sheet. Seeing this Sri Nityananda prabhu advised the women standing nearby to uncover the face. After doing the same miracally Basudha Devi's nose got fresh air with divinely fragrances that came out from the body of Sri Nityananda prabhu. It made Vsudha Devi alive. She after being seated on the floor looked around and found Sri Nityananda prabhu was standing in front of her. To see him, she felt shame and then and there hided herself inside the room.

The associates and the assembled people in the crowd started to chant Harinaam and the glory the name of Sri Chaitanyadev. All the people of the village approved the marriage of Vasudha Devi with Sri Nityanandaprabhu.

At last the marriage was settled at Ambika Kalna and it took place at Shaligram where most of the closed relatives of Sri Suryadas Sarkhel used reside. But according to 'Bhakti Ratnakar' the marriage took place at Kalna.[7]

In the year 1442 Shaka or 1520/1521 AD in an auspicious afternoon of the marriage day in the royal palace of Krishnadas Hore Sri Nityananda prabhu was seated in the balcony of Sri Vishnu. Afterwards he was nicely decorated with necessary dresses, ornaments, flowers, available cosmetics and also a garland of fragrant flowers as a suitable and beautiful bridegroom by the follower Sri Gouridas Pundit. Sri Gouridas Pundit was Subal Sasha in earlier life in Brajalila. There this was his duty to dress up Sri Krishna and Balarama.

"Nityananda Bose Vishnumandap Upare.
Gouridas Aasiya Barabesh Kare.[8]

The cost of expenditure of the marriage was borne by Krishnadas Hore and Uddharan Dutta. Sri Uddharan Dutta himself paid Rupees ten thousand at that time and Sri Krishnadas Hore paid all other expenditures unlimitedly from the royal chest and kept the palace open for the marriage for the days of arrangements and completion.[9]

From Bargachhi the Palace of Sri Krishnadas Hore a palanquin well decorated with various kinds of gems Sri Nityanandaprabhu in the dress of bridegroom moved towards Shaligram. It was followed by a long procession of his followers with songs and music and also dances, with illuminative lights and fireworks in the sky. It looked like a prince in the palanquin was approaching Shaligram where the parents of Basudha Maa with hundreds of relatives and villagers were waiting for Sri Nityanandaprabhu, the bridegroom. All the moving participants in the long procession were also chanting Harinaam and Sri Nityanandaprabhu in the palanquin could not but thinking of his beloved and respected Sri Chaitanya Mahaprabhu.[10]

After the all rituals of marriage like the sounds of conch, 'Hulu' from the mouths of the present women, seeing each other, exchanging of garlands of beautifully decorated bride and bridegroom and the necessary mantras of the Vedas recited by the bride and bridegroom conducted by 'Purohit' priest the marriage of Basudha Maa and Sri Nityananda Prabhu was completed. Suryadas Sarkhel, the father handed over Basudha Maa along with all the necessary articles to the bridegroom. The people who were invited and assembled including the persons accompanying bridegroom were well fed in a feast. After the 'Kushundika' the 'Jajna' unmarried Sri Nityananda Prabhu was married with Basudha Maa. Both of them were also given palatable dishes at that night.

Thereafter Sri Nityananda Prabhu having married the youngest daughter of Suryadas Sarkhel Janhaba Devi roamed Barogachhi, Saptagram, Nabadwip, and Shantipur with two wives Basudha and Janhaba. And then reached Khardah he was gifted the house by Sri Purandar Pundit at Khardah for his dwelling permanently.

Basudha Maa since 1442 gave births to seven sons but none of them could survive after offering 'Pranam' of Abhiram Thakura what the new born babies could tolerate. Afterwards, in 1457 Shaka in Shukla Chaturthi (4th day of Moon of 'Agrahayan'November or December) the eighth son of Basudha Maa was born and he could easily tolerate the 'Pranam' by Abhiram Thakura. Sri Adwaita Acharya learnt it and he hurriedly even at the 102 years of age reached Khardah to welcome the child as his Sri Gouranga after fourteen months of disappearances with Sri Gadadhar Pundit has taken rebirth in the family of Sri Nityananda Prabhu. The son was named as Birbhadra or Birchandra.

Afterwards within one and a half years of Birchandra's birth Basudha Maa gave birth of a daughter calm and quiet like the holy river Ganga. She was so named as Ganga Mata.

Janhaba Devi

After the disappearances of Lord Sri Krishna Chaitanya Mahaprabhu, Sri Gadadhara Pundit, Sri Swarup Damodar in Neelachal and Sri Nityananda Prabhu, Sri Adwaita Acharya the whole condition of the Vaishnava Society became confused and witnessed disorderliness. To unite all the Vaishnavas in Bengal the efforts that done by the Vaishnavas under the leadership of Janhaba Devi was a unique example in the history of Bengal.[11]

Janhaba Devi, another daughter of Sri Suryadas Sarkhel and Srimati Bhadrabati Devi was born about two years later of Basudha Maa. She was incarnated on the Shukla Navami of the month of Boisakha in 1431 Shaka or 1509 AD.

After a few days of the marriage of Basudha Maa with Sri Nityananda Prabhu an incidence was occurred at the house of Sri Suryadas Sarkhel when Sri Nityananda Prabhu proposed to marry the sister in law Janhaba Maa. It was at the time of taking 'Prasad' the lunch by Sri Nityananda

Prabhu when different foodstuffs were served by Srimati Bhadrabati Devi along with her daughters. Basudha Maa, newly married and Janhaba Maa, not yet married were co-operating their mother in forwarding different foodstuffs to Sri Nityananda Prabhu one after another. But the ladies both married and unmarried were wearing new sharees with veils as the procedures of the time and for which none of them were accustomed to wear as daily habits and so, by chance the veil of Janhaba Maa fell in front of Sri Nityananda Prabhu and others elderly present male personalities. At that moment the two hands of her were engaged in holding a pot of foodstuff so she had to control her veil with other two hands for the moment. Sri Nityananda Prabhu noticed it and considered Janhaba Maa as a Supra Woman. He then and there decided to marry this unmarried girl and establish her as his other counterpart.[12]

Sri Nityananda Prabhu thought himself that to circulate the Harinaam Movement in Goud Bengal and also outside Bengal as advised by Sri Chaitanya Mahaprabhu would be a mammoth work for him. He also thought a question that there are more than twelve Gopals and almost one hundred Upa-Gopals who on behalf of him are distributing Harinaam under his guidance but after him who would lead all of them?

Sri Nityananda Prabhu laughingly told Sri Suryadas Pundit – I like to take your this younger daughter also for my work. You can hand her over me as a dowry in the marriage with Basudha."

"Zoutuk Lailam Tomar Kanishtha Duhita"[13]

The word Zoutuk is meant some additional money or valuable articles that are prayed for giving to bridegroom. But Janhaba Maa was neither money nor any valuable article rather she was becoming a strong woman who could fight for any situation. She could not be considered as an inanimate article.

On the other side Janhaba Maa was fully aware of the qualities of Sri Nityananda Prabhu from the day to day discussions with Srimati Basudha Maa all along as both the sisters used to sleep in one bed before the marriage. Janhaba Maa also liked to remember Sri Nityananda Prabhu.

"Suryadaser Kanya Hoyen Basura Kanishtha,
Balyabadhi Nityanandye Tnar Nishtha."[14]

Sri Suryadas Sarkhel and Bhadrabati Devi thought that within one or two years they should arrange a bridegroom for their youngest daughter. And they also thought that like Sri Nityananda Prabhu where they would find other bridegroom? They discussed the matter in the family and also with some neighboring personalities. No one raised any objection rather nodded their heads.

As in the house a marriage festival was taken place a few days earlier there were many things useful to the rituals of another marriage. Most of the guests accompanying the bridegroom were still present with Sri Nityananda Prabhu. It was also a period of marriages as in the 'Panjika' so there was no inconvenience for the marriage of Janhaba Maa with Sri Nityananda Prabhu.

"Lokshatramate Suryadas Bhagyaban,
Nityanandachandrey Dui Kanya Koilo Daan."[15]

Sri Suryadas Sarkhel and Bhadrabati Devi were very much pleased to find their youngest daughter Janhaba was also enthusiastic to have Sri Nityananda Prabhu as her husband. Newly married Bsudha Maa with Sri Nityananda Prabhu was also pleased to know that her younger sister Janhaba would be with her for the rest of the life having married with Sri Nityananda Prabhu who was mostly preferred by herself and also by Janhaba the loving younger sister. She took up the charge of decorating Janhaba Maa with cosmetics, valuable perfumes, dresses and ornaments. She gave Janhaba her mostly choiced ornaments also.

Sri Gouridas Pundit a strong and sincere follower of Sri Nityananda Prabhu danced and sang with a 'Kirtan':-

"Aaj Ki Ananada Suryadas Ghare,
Basudha Janhaba Saho Nitai Biharey".[16]

Both the wives Bsudha and Janhaba were satisfied with their husband Sri Nityananda Prabhu who sat on a divan took Basudha on the left and Janhaba on the right sides.

".....Aakarshiya Prabhu Bosailo Bam Pashey,
Prabhusparsha Pai Devi (Basudha) Sukharase Bhasey.
......Iha Dekhi Nityananda Kare Aakarshiya,
Basailo Janhabarey Dakshiney Aaniya."[17]

Sri Nityananda Prabhu, thereafter, from Shaligram with two newly wedded wives Bsudha and Janhaba returned to Barogachhi in the royal palace of Krishnadas Hore where the women from Nabadwip were waiting to welcome Sri Nityananda Prabhu with the two newly wedded wives Bsudha and Janhaba. Mainly Malini Devi the wife of Sri Sribaas Pundit came forward to welcome them first.

Then, after a few days Sri Nityananda Prabhu with the wives went to Nabadwip at the house of Sri Chaitanyadeva where Sachimaa and Vishnupriya Devi were waiting to welcome them. Vishnupriya Devi leaving her meditation and sadhana ran towards Bsudha and Janhaba. She embraced them and arranged a divine seat for them. Sachimaa started to shed tears in joy of getting the two wives and also Sri Nityananda. Then Sri Nityananda attended the house of Sribaas Pundit where the Naam Sankirtan was started by Sri Gouranga Mahaprabhu.

Then he with the two wives attended the house of Sri Adwaita Acharya at Shantipur where Srimati Sitadevi was also waiting for them. There Sri Adwaita Acharya and Sri Nityananda Prabhu remembered their earlier lovely quarrel and Sri Adwaita laughingly indicated that as Sri Krishna Chaitanya Mahaprabhu as desired Sri Nityananda Prabhu left the life of 'Abadhut' and entered into domestic life. He was happy.

Sri Nityananda Prabhu with two newly wedded wives Bsudha and Janhaba returned to Saptagram the place of Uddharan Dutta. The members of the family and the relatives including neighbourers also received immense happiness. Uddharan Dutta with various materials and foodstuffs served them with unlimited happiness. He also arranged for the service in charity. All the devotees were satisfied with their presence for some days in Saptagram.

Afterwards from Saptagram Sri Nityananda Prabhu with two wives Bsudha and Janhaba returned to Khardah on the bank of the Ganga. He reached the house of Sri Purandar Pundit.

"Bhaktera Icchchaya Prabhu Khardahey Giya,
Rakhilen Apurba Aagarey Nija Priya."[18]

Sri Nityananda Prabhu was gifted the house at Khardah for permanently residing by Sri Purandar Pundit. The house was named as 'Kunjabati' that still exists.

After the disappearances of Sri Chaitanya Mahaprabhu with lifelong partner Sri Gadadhar Pundit, Sri Nityananda Prabhu did not get enthusiasm to go outside of Khardah. He once came to Nabadwip to meet Sri Jib Goswami of Vrindaban. We find in the writing:-

"Prabhu Kahe Tomar (Sri Jib) Nimitte,
Aailam Shighra Etha Khardah Hoyite."[19]

Sri Nityananda Prabhu had to bear the shock for Sri Chaitanyadev's disappearances for almost eight years as written Ishan Nagar:-

"Kebal Gouranga Naame Ullas Antara,
Henamate Gata Hoilo Astama Batsara."[20]

Janhaba Maa was considered as the mother of the Vaishnavas and she with the inspiration of Sri Nityananda Prabhu also started to initiate the devotees. She initiated hundreds of peasants with their owner of land Chandra Mondal in the district of Bardhaman. Janhaba Maa also initiated Birchandra and Gangamata.

Originally Janhaba Maa had no children. She took the charge of education of Birchndra and Gangamata. However, she adopted five years' old the grandson of one of the followers of Sri Chaitanya Mahaprabhu Sri Bangshibadan Chattopadhaya, the eldest son of Sri Chaitanyadas. Later this son Ram Chandra or Ramai established the Sripat at Baghnapara. Ram Chandra or Ramai also witnessed the Lilas of Sri Chaitanyadeva. He was also initiated by Janhaba Maa.

Janhaba Maa also brought up Nityanandadas who was born in 1537 AD as a son of poet Sri Atmaram or Purushottam Das in the generation of Sadashib Kaviraj of Sri Khanda. This child whose mother was also another Janhaba and she died keeping the son alone. Sri Nityananda Prabhu brought the son in his lap and gave to Janhaba Maa. Janhaba Maa also initiated Sri Nityanandadas who was also known as Kanu Thakura or child Krishnadas. He also travelled twice in Vrindaban with Janhaba Maa.

Sri Nityananda Prabhu's second wife Janhaba Maa gave the leadership to Vaishnavas in her time. She used to love all the Vaishnavas. She knew the equality among them. Her efforts after the Sri Chaitanya Mahaprabhu to unite and integrate all Vaishnavas was a unique endevour in the History of Vaishnavas.

Under the efficient leadership Janhaba Maa presided over the Kheturi Maha Sammelan in 1582 AD at Kheturi village of Rajshahi District of East Bengal (now in Bangladesh). This was a historical conference wherein all sections of Vaishnavas from different corners of the country assembled. There the ways of Sadhana of Sri Radhakrishna and of the 'Panchatattwa' were recommended by Vaishnavas of Bengal and of Vrindaban. After the almost long fifty years the people could breathe fresh air with uttering Harinaam as Sri Chaitanya Mahaprabhu desired.

References

1. The Two Mothers – Basudha Maa and Janhaba Maa – Radhakrishna (Radhu) Goswami, June 25, 2017, On the day of Basudha's incarnation).

2. Full Panjika (in Bengali) – by Sri Benimadhab Seal)
3. Sri Sri Gour Ganoddesh Deepika – by Sri Kavi Karnapur, Edited by Sri Asoka Kumar Bandyopadhaya, publisher- Sandesh, Printer- Orient Press, Pub in 2007 AD,)
4. *Padaboli of Vidyapati)*
5. Prem Vilas – Nityanandadas, Dr. Bijon Goswami, pub. by Mahesh Library, 1405 BS, 1999 AD, printed by Printing Publicity)
6. *Ibid*
7. Sri Sri Bhakti Ratnakar – by Sri Narahari Chakraborty, ed.by Pundit Sripad Navinkrishna Paravidyalankar, pub. by Srimat Sundarananda Vidyabenode, printer Sri Ananata Ram Bhakti-Shastri, Nadiya Prakash Printing Works, in 1940, Gaudiya Math Sanskaran, Sri Sri Nityananda Shakti Maa Janhaba – Sri Nemaichand Goswami, Pub. By Sri Sanatan Goswami, Printer – Shyamasundar Press, 1st Pub 1389 BS, 2nd Pub 1401 BS, 5th Chapter, p.79, Source Nityananda Bangsa Bistar and Sri Sri Adwaita Prakash – by Ishan Nagar, Collected Edited and Printed by Kishoridas Babaji, Sri Sri Prankrishna Bhakti Press, (Halisahar, Chaitanya Doba) Published in 1406 BS).
8. Sri Sri Nityananda Shakti Maa Janhaba – Sri Nemaichand Goswami, Pub. By Sri Sanatan Goswami, Printer – Shyamasundar Press, 1st Pub 1389 BS, 2nd Pub 1401 BS, p.88),
9. The Two Mothers – Basudha Maa and Janhaba Maa – Radhakrishna (Radhu) Goswami, June 25, 2017, On the day of Basudha's incarnation).
10. Sri Sri Nityananda Shakti Maa Janhaba – Sri Nemaichand Goswami, Pub. By Sri Sanatan Goswami, Printer – Shyamasundar Press, 1st Pub 1389 BS, 2nd Pub 1401 BS, p.89).
11. The Two Mothers – Basudha Maa and Janhaba Maa – Radhakrishna (Radhu) Goswami, June 25, 2017, On the day of Basudha's incarnation).
12. Sri Sri Nityananda Shakti Maa Janhaba – Sri Nemaichand Goswami, Pub. By Sri Sanatan Goswami, Printer – Shyamasundar Press, 1st Pub 1389 BS, 2nd Pub 1401 BS, p.88 and The Two Mothers – Basudha Maa and Janhaba Maa – Radhakrishna (Radhu) Goswami, June 25, 2017, On the day of Basudha's incarnation.
13. Nityananda Bangsa Bistar – by Sri Vrindabandas, pub.by Sri Kishori Das Babaji, printed at Sri Sri Prankrishna Bhakti Press, Chaitanyadoba, Halishahar,
14. *Ibid*, and Sri Sri Nityananda Shakti Maa Janhaba – Sri Nemaichand Goswami, Pub. By Sri Sanatan Goswami, Printer – Shyamasundar Press, 1st Pub 1389 BS, 2nd Pub 1401 BS, p.100).
15. Sri Sri Nityananda Shakti Maa Janhaba – Sri Nemaichand Goswami, Pub. By Sri Sanatan Goswami, Printer – Shyamasundar Press, 1st Pub 1389 BS, 2nd Pub 1401 BS, p.100 and also in Sri Sri Bhakti Ratnakar – by Sri Narahari Chakraborty, ed.by Pundit Sripad Navinkrishna Paravidyalankar, pub. by Srimat Sundarananda Vidyabenode, printer Sri Ananata Ram Bhakti-Shastri, Nadiya Prakash Printing Works, in 1940, Gaudiya Math Sanskaran, Shloka -)
16. Sri Sri Bhakti Ratnakar – by Sri Narahari Chakraborty, ed.by Pundit Sripad Navinkrishna Paravidyalankar, pub. by Srimat Sundarananda Vidyabenode,

printer Sri Ananata Ram Bhakti-Shastri, Nadiya Prakash Printing Works, in 1940, Gaudiya Math Sanskaran, 12th Taranga, Shloka 3782, p. 606).

17. Sri Sri Nityananda Shakti Maa Janhaba – Sri Nemaichand Goswami, Pub. By Sri Sanatan Goswami, Printer – Shyamasundar Press, 1st Pub 1389 BS, 2nd Pub 1401 BS, p.81 (Source: Sri Sri Chaitanya Charitamrita).
18. Sri Sri Bhakti Ratnakar – by Sri Narahari Chakraborty, ed.by Pundit Sripad Navinkrishna Paravidyalankar, pub. by Srimat Sundarananda Vidyabenode, printer Sri Ananata Ram Bhakti-Shastri, Nadiya Prakash Printing Works, in 1940, Gaudiya Math Sanskaran, 12th Taranga, Shloka 3959, p. 609).
19. Sri Sri Bhakti Ratnakar – by Sri Narahari Chakraborty, ed.by Pundit Sripad Navinkrishna Paravidyalankar, pub. by Srimat Sundarananda Vidyabenode, printer Sri Ananata Ram Bhakti-Shastri, Nadiya Prakash Printing Works, in 1940, Gaudiya Math Sanskaran, 1st Taranga, Shloka - 767).
20. Sri Sri Adwaita Prakash – by Ishan Nagar, Collected Edited and Printed by Kishoridas Babaji, Sri Sri Prankrishna Bhakti Press, (Halisahar, Chaitanya Doba) Published in 1406 BS and Sri Sri NityanandaShakti Maa Janhaba – Sri Nemaichand Goswami, Pub. By Sri Sanatan Goswami, Printer – Shyamasundar Press, 1st Pub 1389 BS, 2nd Pub 1401 BS, p.131).

Index

A

Aasuri Keshabacharya, 25
Abhiram Goswami, 152
Abhiram Lilamrita, 248
Abhiram Thakura, 237
Abhoya Devi, 48
Acharya Achyutaprakash, 36
Adi Saptagram, 43
Adiguru Shankaracharya, 27
Adwaita Acharya, 103, 192
Adwaita Makaranda, 138
Ambika Kalna, 274
Amiya Asim Charit, 258
Ananda Tirtha, 36
Ananta Basudeva, 111
Ananteswar Temple, 35
Ancient Odisha, 23
Andhra History Research Society, 42
Andhra Pradesh, 52
Anhaba Devi, 240
Annapurna Devi, 267, 268
Antyadwip, 200
Anuman Pariksha, 138
Arber Vishnuchitta Swami, 21
Ashram of Somgiri, 41
Assam, 240
Astrologer, 209
Astrology, 200
Authentic writers, 128
Ayodhya, 43

B

Badagram, 88
Badshah' of Delhi, 88
Bahulul Lodi, 52
Baikunthadas Bipra, 261
Bajoli Nagaur, 255
Balakrishnacrirhakavyam, 41
Balarama, 111
Ballavacharya, 52
Ballavacharya Mishra, 171
Ballavdeva, 21
Bama Devi, 29
Banamali Acharya, 171, 177
Baneswar Brahmachari, 70
Bangladesh, 65, 95, 107, 114, 168, 179, 180, 220, 267
Baninath or Jagannath, 114
Bank of the Yamuna, 19, 246
Baraganga, 44
Bardhaman, 282
Basudha Devi, 274
Basudha Maa, 119, 135, 140, 200
Batsya Gotra, 134
Battle of Khanua, 256
Beautiful girl, 255
Begging profession, 211
Begum of Nawab, 38
Belegram, 35
Belpukuria, 200
Bengal, 209, 232
Bengali Language, 262
Bengali Payar, 261
Betalgram, 175
Bhabadeva Bhatta, 223
Bhabesh Dutta, 43
Bhadrabati, 135
Bhadrabati Devi, 132, 134, 280

Bhagawata Tika, 53
Bhagirath Acharya, 238
Bhagirath Basu, 50
Bhagirathi Devi, 137, 138
Bhajan Kutir, 166
Bhajana of Meera, 256
Bhakti Ratnakar, 248
Bhanumati, 75
Bharadwaj Gotra, 45, 52
Bhattacharya, 212
Bhattanath Swami, 15, 16
Bhoj Raj (Kumbh), 256
Bhojdev and Bama Devi, 31
Bhoumakar clan, 23
Bhumi Peratri, 25
Bidhumukhi Devi, 117
Bijoykrishna, 270
Bijoykrishna Goswami, 272
Bilwa Pushkarini, 179, 200
Bimala Devi, 120
Bishnupur, 225
Bishwarup Sachimaa, 202
Bishweswar Acharya, 141
Biswas Devi, 121
Boikuntha Koili, 96
Bon Bishnupur, 252
Borakuli village, 228
Bouddhadikarer Tika, 212
Brahma Sutranuvasya, 53
Brahmananda, 221
Brahmin culture, 40
Brahmin family, 245
Braja Gopies, 19, 190
Braja Lila, 262
Brajagopis, 19
Brajalila, 37
Buddhimanta Khan, 124

C

Calcutta Medical College, 271
Centre place of Vaishnavism, 257
Chaitanya Bhawan, 207
Chaitanya Mongal, 48
Chaitanyadeva, 144
Chaitanyadeva made a forecast, 190
Champaran district, 52
Chandidas Geeti, 38
Chandra Mondal, 282
Chandrakala, 75, 76, 77
Chandralekha, 185
Charitable institution, 140
Chaste wife, 127
Chattragram, 114
Chaturdash Padaboli, 38
Chhoto Haridas, 144
Chintamoni – Dadhiti, 212
Chitralekha, 79, 81
Chittagong, 65, 114, 175
Chittagong district, 70
Chole King, 26
Chowrasiji, 89
Consort of Mahavishnu, 102

D

Dacca, 174
Dakshinpara, 200
Dandeswar (Dharanda), 248
Dandeswar in Utkal, 248
Darakeswar River, 225
Dasarath Basu, 50
Daughter of Raja Pratap Rudra, 90
Dayamanti Devi, 92, 93
Decorated with various kinds of gems, 277
Dehi Padapallavamudaram, 33
Depth of Ocean, 266
Deva Singha, 46
Dhananjay Pundit, 65, 66
Dhanram Tirtharam, 264
Dibakar Dutta, 132
District of Bankura, 225
District of Bardhaman, 188, 228, 237

District of Jessore, 215
Divya Prabanadha, 16
Divya Singha, 121
Domestic deities, 215
Domestic work, 211
Droupadi Devi, 228
Dukhini Devi, 96
Durgadas Bagchi, 37
Durgadas Mishra, 116
Dwapar Lila, 215
Dwapar Yuga, 152
Dwarka, 27, 258

E

East Bengal, 79, 174, 177, 220, 267
Egar Sindur, 175
Ekchakra village, 109
Emperor Badshah, 256
Energy of the earth, 123

F

Faridpur, 175, 267
Follower of Gour-Nityananda, 139
Forest of Champaran, 53
Fulia in Nabadwip, 216

G

Gadur Stambha, 260
Gambhira, 189
Gandhar Raga, 32
Ganga Bangsha, 239
Ganga Devi, 153, 237, 239
Ganga Mata, 278
Geeta Govinda, 32, 33
Geetagovinda, 251, 232
Glorious Vaishnava, 268
Gnga Devi, 238
Gobardhan Acharya, 43
Gobardhan Das, 205
Gobinda, 211
Goda Devi, 20
Godrumdwip, 200
Gopala of Gokula, 209
Gopijana Ballava, 18
Goshthipati Chowdhury, 223
Goswami Sri Sunila Devi, 216
Goud Bengal, 45, 181, 196, 223, 229, 240, 257, 275, 279
Goudiya Vaishnava Movement, 45, 159
Goudiya Vaishnavas, 156, 157, 251, 260, 233
Goudiya Vaishnavism, 147, 225, 232, 242
Gour Bandana, 227
Gouranga Mahaprabhu, 117
Gourangapriya, 228, 230
Gouri, 75
Gouri Devi, 73, 90
Gouri Sen, 140
Govinda Damodar Stotrang, 41
Govinda Strotam, 41
Goyeedevi, 71
Gunaraj Khan, 50
Gundicha Marjan, 209
Guskara Rly Station, 48

H

Hadai Ojha, 109, 110
Hadai Pundit, 109
Hakimpur, 74
Hanuman Ghat, 53
Hardwar, 27
Haribangsha, 88
Haridas Thakur, 73
Haridas Thakura, 168
Harinaam Movement, 116, 120
Harinaam Sankirtan, 194
Hemlata Devi, 226, 240
Hindu Law, 137
Hiranya Das, 205
Hirar Jangal, 168
History of Odisha, 90
Hitaharibansa, 247

How to play with Mridanga, 238
Hridayananda, 114
Husband Bhoj Raj Kumbh, 256

I

Ikshu River, 44
Indumati Basu, 50
Indurekha, 208, 235
Ishwari Devi, 228

J

Jagananath Mishra, 44
Jagannath Dham, 167
Jagannath Mahaprabhu, 112
Jagannath Swami, 31
Jai Durga Devi, 84, 141, 238
Jalandi village, 223
Jambudwip, 200
Jamun Acharya, 25
Jamunacharya, 27
Janhaba Devi, 224, 248, 274, 278
Janhaba Maa, 135, 140, 207, 230
Janhabi Devi, 86
Jargram, 65
Jayananda, 202
Jessore, 268
Jodhpur kingdom, 255

K

Kalagachhi village, 73
Kalindi Devi, 65, 222
Kamala Devi, 56, 58
Kamalakshya Bipra, 95
Kamdev Pundit, 236
Kana Bhatta Shiromani, 211
Kanailal Goswami, 270
Kanaklatika Devi, 242
Kanakpriya Devi, 225
Kanauj to Goud Bengal, 50
Kanchanlatika, 251
Kanchanlatika Devi, 226
Kanchi Mahraja, 112
Kanchi Sri Ganehsa, 149
Kanchipurna of Kanchi, 26
Kantimoti Devi, 25, 26, 27, 28
Kantimoti Devi Ramanuja, 27
Kari Habibullah, 74
Karnataka, 36
Karnataka State, 45
Kashi Dham, 27, 53
Kavi Karnapur, 60, 190, 274
Kavi Maladhar Basu, 50
Kavindra Billwamongal, 40
Kazipur, 152
Keshab Kashmiri, 174
Keshabacharya, 26
Khersuti Devi, 68
King Adisur in Bengal, 237
King and the Queen of Bishnupur, 230
King Dushmanta, 167
King Lalithar, 23
King Mang, 68
King of Ahom, 68
King of Kanchi, 149
King of Madura, 21
King of Mithila, 121
King of Odisha, 185
King of Pandya, 16
King of Utkal, 112
King of Vijayanagar, 90
King Padma Singha, 121
King Pandya, 16
King Pratap Rudra, 187, 196, 212, 234
King Satrajit, 123
King Shashanka, 223
King Shiva Singha, 46, 47
Kkeshab Kashmiri, 180
Koldwip, 200
Koli Yuga, 167
Kripamoyee Devi, 67
Krishna Ekadasi, 53
Krishna Mongal, 117

Krishna Stotram, 41
Krishnadas, 275
Krishnadasi, 163, 168, 247
Krishnadev, 236
Krishnakamini Devi, 270
Krishnanagar, 152
Krishnapriya, 251
Krishnarama, 242
Kuber Acharya, 102
Kudaki, Rajasthan, 255
Kudki village, 255
Kulin' Brahmin, 237
Kumva Mela, 271

L

Lachhimadevi, 46
Laksha Hira, 163, 168
Laksha Hira Harinaam, 165
Laksha Hira was, 166
Lakshman Bhatta, 52, 53
Lakshmana, 25
Lakshmi Bai, 265, 266
Lakshmi-Narayana, 125
Lakshminath Basu, 51
Lakshminath Lahiri, 56
Lakshmipriya Devi, 79, 81
Lava Devi, 101
Laxmipriya Devi, 170, 171, 172
Lila Kshetra, 225
Lila Shuka, 41
Lilas of Lord Sri Krishna, 21
Lochandas, 48
Lord Govinda, 20
Lord Jagannath, 31, 32
Lord Jagannatha Mahaprabhu, 112
Lord Jagannathdeva, 112
Lord Ranganatha, 17, 18, 19
Lord Ranganathaji, 20
Lord Sri Chaitanyadeva, 72, 86
Lord Sri Giridhariji, 258
Lord Sri Gourangadeva, 116
Lord Sri Krishna, 18, 29, 33, 37, 41
Lord Sri Radha Krishna, 41
Lord Sri Vishnu, 180
Lord Vishnu, 15, 16, 17, 23
Lord. Srimati Tulsidevi, 15

M

Madhab Acharya, 238
Madhab Mishra, 117
Madhabacharya, 84
Madhabendra Puri, 70
Madhabi Dasi, 147
Madhabi Devi, 142, 143
Madhabi Mahiti, 143, 145
Madhiji Bhatta, 35, 36
Madhu Mishra, 44
Madhukar Mishra, 44
Madhwacharya, 35
Madhyadwip, 200
Mahalakshmi Devi, 84, 141, 237, 238
Mahamaya Devi, 139, 140
Mahananda Bipra, 101
Maharaj Gajapati Pratap Rudra, 234
Maharani, 89
Maharastra, 27
Mahendra Singha, 45
Maid Servant of Sita Devi, 82
Maladhar Basu, 51
Malini Devi, 150, 151, 152, 218, 280
Manjaree of Vrindavan, 274
Manohar Chakraborty, 73
Marriage festival, 280
Marriage with Jamamba, 26
Mathura, 38, 88
Mathura Mahatmya, 53
Meera Bai, 255, 258
Meera Bai left Chittor, 257
Meera Bai of Rajasthan, 255
Meera was in Dwarka, 257
Menaka Devi, 156
Mithila, 212

Modrumdwip, 200
Mother of Ballavacharya, 52
Mother Sachi Devi, 218
Movement of Harinaam Mahamantra, 273
Movement of Religion, 218
Mughal Emperor Babur, 255
Mukul Bhatta, 90
Murari Mahiti, 143
Murshidabad, 251
Musical instruments, 238
Muslim person, 73

N

Naam Sankirtan, 266
Naarasinghi, 204
Nabadwip, 45, 96, 116, 123, 170, 171, 172, 177, 179, 200, 281
Nabadwip Lila, 262
Nachchier Tirumourhi, 22
Nadia district, 200
Nadiar Tirumeri, 18
Nag clan, 23
Nakul Bagchi, 38
Nanda Suta, 19
Nandini, 98
Nanyapur village, 238
Narahari Sarkar, 63, 71
Narasingha Nadial, 100
Narayanapur, 156
Narayani, 104
Narayani Sribaas Pundit, 261
Nawab of Goud, 38
Nayayananda, 114
Neelachal, 95, 186
Neelachal (Puri), 273
Neelachal Dham, 31, 234
Nemai Pundit of Nabadwip, 117
Nemai Sarbani Devi, 202
Neo Vaishnavism, 241
Nilambar Chakraborty, 200
Nityananda Padmabati Devi, 110
Noorpur, 175
Nrisingha Bhaduri, 204
Nrisinha Bhaduri, 156
Nrisinha Bhaduri at, 156
Nurse-Mother, 104
Nurse-mother Narayani, 218

O

Odisha, 185, 196, 212
Only daughter of Ratan Singh, 255

P

Padartha Khandan, 212
Padma Singha, 121
Padmabati Devi, 31, 32, 33, 109, 111, 149, 228, 230, 251
Padmabati or Rupambika Devi, 112
Padmamoni Devi, 108
Padmanava, 45
Padmanava Chakraborty, 107
Padmsmoni Devi, 107
Pakshadhar Mishra, 212
Pancham Prakash, 128
Panchshloki, 53
Parjanya Gopa, 44
Paurnamasi, 208
Peak of the Himalayas, 266
Pediya Arber, 15, 16
Plucking flowers, 274
Poet Chandidas, 38
Poet Jaydeva, 31, 33, 135
Poetic talent, 198
Prayag, 27, 271
Prem Vilas, 238, 248
Premature death of husband, 211
Propagation of Education, 201
Puja of Bhagawati, 204
Pundit Gadadhar, 114
Pundit Govinda Bhattacharya, 271
Pundit Srimati Vimala Devi, 274
Puri, 138, 167

Puri Dham, 148, 269
Puri Municipality, 271
Purnapragna, 36
Purnapragna Bosudeva, 36
Purushottam, 220
Purushottam Acharya, 220

Q

Queen and the King, 208
Queen Chandrakala, 208
Queen Chandralekha, 185, 186

R

R Lord Sri Krishna, 40
Raasalila, 19
Raasalila of Sri Krishna, 41
Radhaballavi Sampradaya, 247
Radhaballavi Section, 88
Radhakrishna, 47, 242
Radhamadhav, 236
Raghaber Jhali, 93
Raghunandan Chakraborty, 230
Raghunath, 212
Raghunatha, 211
Raidas or Ravidas, 258
Raj Pundit, 196
Raj Purohit, 52
Raja Chitrasen of Chattagram, 160
Raja Dasaratha, 25
Raja Lakshman Sen, 43
Raja of Kanchi, 148
Raja Pratap Rudra, 75, 90, 112, 185, 208, 234
Raja Purushottam Deva, 112, 149
Raja Rammohan Roy, 73
Rajamalla, 23
Rajmata Chandrakala Devi, 234
Rajpundit, 123
Rajput princess, 255
Ramai Thakura, 207, 216
Ramananda Basu, 51
Ramanuja, 25
Ramanuja propagated Vaishnavism, 26
Ramayana, 25
Ramayana Raja Siradhwaja Janaka, 16
Ramcharan Chakraborty, 228
Ramdev, 236
Rameswar Mukhopadhyay, 236
Rami Rajakini, 38, 39
Rana of Mewar Bhojraj, 256
Rana Ratan Singh, 256
Rana Sangha, 256
Rana Udai Singh, 258
Rana Vikramjit, 256
Rani Lachhimadevi, 46
Rani Viswas Devi, 46
Rao Duda, 255
Rao Viram Dev, 255
Rarhi Brahmin, 275
Ratan Singh, 255
Rathayatra, 209, 274
Rathayatra Festival, 148
Rathayatra of Lord Jagannatha, 234
Ratnabati Devi, 159, 160, 161
Ratnagarva, 200
Renowned Pundit, 174
Ri Banamali Acharya, 194
Ri Byasacharya, 225
Ri Nityananda Prabhu, 58
Ritu dwip, 200
River Padmabati, 80
River Swarna or Salai, 74
Roop Goswami, 245
Royal Court of Hussein Shah, 257
Royal family, 256
Rupambika Devi, 112

S

Sachi Devi, 179, 200
Sachimaa, 200
Sachimaa Vishnupriya Devi, 128
Sage Vishwamitra, 166
Saidabad Pargana, 251

Sakhi Bhava, 206
Samkirtan Movement, 104
Sanchra-Panchra, 223
Sandal wood paste, 124
Sanjay Pundit, 223
Sannyas Mantra, 127, 221
Sannyas Yatra, 202
Sanskrit College, 271
Sanskrit Language, 211, 212
Saptagram, 156
Sarada Mutt of Kashmir, 27
Sarbabhoum Bhattacharya, 196
Sarbabhouma Nirukta, 212
Sarbajanin Mother, 206
Sarbajaya Devi, 200
Satya Bai, 265, 266
Scholars of Mithila, 137
Sea-bank, 148
Sebait Yadav Mishra, 130
Seventeenth Century, 209
Shaka Asada Shukla Dwitiya, 135
Shakti Chandramohan, 268
Shaligram, 58, 274, 277, 280
Shaligram to Ambika Kalna, 119
Shantipur, 100, 118, 269, 271
Shasikala, 208, 235
Shasikala Indurekha, 234
Shati or Shashthi Devi, 196
Shibananda Sen, 190
Shikhi Mahiti, 143
Shital, 223
Shital village, 223
Shiva Singha, 46
Shri Devi, 191, 204
Shudasha Grantha, 53
Shyamananda, 248
Shyamananda Prakash, 248
Singer and dancer, 32
Sister of Kanjilal Dhar, 43
Sita Caritra, 209
Sita Devi, 191, 204, 207, 211
Sita Thakurani, 83
Sobodhani, 53
South India, 23, 25, 55
Sri Achyutananda, 208
Sri Adideva Bachaspati, 222
Sri Adwaita Acharya, 60, 98, 101, 107, 156, 186, 204, 207, 208, 209, 224, 236
Sri Amogh Pundit, 196
Sri Ananada Goswami, 269
Sri Ballavacharya Mishra, 170
Sri Basudeva Sarbabhoum Bhattacharya, 212
Sri Bhadrabati Devi, 133
Sri Billiputtur village, 15
Sri Birchandra, 230
Sri Bishweswar Acharya, 237
Sri Chaitananda, 221
Sri Chaitanya Mahaprabhu, 75
Sri Chaitanyadeva, 55, 142, 200
Sri Chandrasekhar, 275
Sri Chandrasekhar Acharya, 200, 221
Sri Dayamoyee Devi, 222
Sri Debananda Pundit, 216
Sri Debibar Visharad, 236
Sri Dhananjay Pundit, 223
Sri Gadadhar Mishra, 216
Sri Gadadhar Pundit, 52, 154, 159, 160, 161, 194, 207, 221, 224, 249, 278
Sri Gangadas Pundit, 194
Sri Gopal Bhatta of Braja, 247
Sri Gopal Chakraborty, 228
Sri Gopijanaballava, 251
Sri Gouranga Madhuri, 222
Sri Gouranga Mahaprabhu, 28, 49, 52, 56, 63, 71, 79, 96, 115, 124, 127, 157, 170, 194, 198, 201, 221
Sri Gouridas Pundit, 119, 276
Sri Govindagati, 232
Sri Harichand Thakur, 267

Sri Haridas Dasji, 27
Sri Haridas Thakura, 173
Sri Haripriya Devi, 222
Sri Hridaya Chaitanya, 249
Sri Indurekha, 234
Sri Jagadananda Pundit, 194
Sri Jagadish, 96
Sri Jagadish Pundit, 95, 96
Sri Jagannath Mishra, 179, 200, 202
Sri Janhaba Maa, 200
Sri Jib Goswami, 248
Sri Kalidas Mishra, 117
Sri Kamalakar Das, 198
Sri Kanakalata Devi, 240
Sri Kangsari Mishra, 58
Sri Kar Dutta, 132
Sri Kavi Karnapur, 188
Sri Kishore Chakraborty, 233
Sri Krishna, 19
Sri Krishna Mishra, 83, 208
Sri Krishna Mondal, 248
Sri Krishnabalacharitra, 41
Sri Krishnapriya, 232
Sri Krishnapriya Devi, 226
Sri Kumud Chattaraj, 226
Sri Laxmipriya Devi, 173, 175
Sri Lokenath Dass, 209
Sri Lokenath Goswami, 214
Sri Madangopala, 41
Sri Madhab Mishra, 160, 161, 172
Sri Madhabacharya, 237
Sri Mukunda, 194
Sri Mukunda Ojha, 109
Sri Murari, 194
Sri Narahari, 48
Sri Narahari Sarkar, 243
Sri Narayan Sarkar, 71
Sri Nemai Pundit, 124, 125
Sri Nibas Acharya, 128, 224, 225, 228, 230, 232, 233, 245
Sri Nilambar Chakraborty, 179
Sri Nityananda, 224
Sri Nityananda Prabhu, 28, 65, 67, 140, 141, 150, 151, 194, 201, 207, 230, 237, 248, 277
Sri Nivas Acharya, 251
Sri Niyananda Prabhu, 201
Sri Nrisingha Bhaduri, 204
Sri Padmagarva Lahiri, 220
Sri Padmanava Chakraborty, 215
Sri Pundarik Vidyanidhi, 159
Sri Purushottam Deva, 112
Sri Purushottam Gupta, 198
Sri Purushottam Pundit, 220
Sri Radha, 208
Sri Radhaballava Chakrabory, 233
Sri Radhabenode Chakraborty, 233
Sri Radhakrishna, 65
Sri Radhamadhava, 32
Sri Raghab Pundit, 92, 93
Sri Raghunath Chakraborty, 230
Sri Raghunath Shiromani, 212
Sri Ramdas Thakur, 267
Sri Ramkrishna Acharya, 242
Sri Ranganathji, 21
Sri Roop Goswami, 257
Sri Roy Ramananda, 187
Sri Sachi Devi, 182
Sri Sanatan Mishra, 123
Sri Sanatana Goswami, 245
Sri Sarbabhoum, 196
Sri Sarbajaya Devi, 201
Sri Sarbajna, 45
Sri Shailapurna, 25
Sri Shankardeva, 240, 241
Sri Shri Devi, 208
Sri Shyamadas, 204
Sri Sita Devi, 205, 206, 207, 208, 209
Sri Sri Baas, 218
Sri Sri Gopeswar Shiva, 50

Sri Sri Madan Gopal, 50
Sri Sribaas Acharya, 224
Sri SriBaas Pundit, 224
Sri Sribaas Pundit, 182, 186
Sri Suryadas Sarkhel, 119, 278, 280
Sri Swarup Damodar, 187, 221
Sri Uddharan Dutta, 133, 139, 140, 277
Sri Upendra Mishra, 60, 174, 179
Sri Vishnupriya Devi, 129
Sri Vrindaban Bllava, 233
Sri Vrindaban Chakraborty, 233
Sri Vrindabandas, 128
Sribaas Angan, 261
Sribilliputtur village, 21
Srihatta (Sylhet), 175, 200, 211
Srikshetra, 196
Srimad Bhagawata, 19
Srimati Baruni, 274
Srimati Basudhamaa, 237
Srimati Bhadrabati Devi, 278
Srimati Chandrakaladevi, 75
Srimati Chandramukhi, 233
Srimati Chandramukhi Devi, 233
Srimati Ganga Devi, 70, 84
Srimati Hemalata Devi, 251, 252
Srimati Hemlata, 232
Srimati Illamagaru Ballavacharya, 53
Srimati Indumati Devi, 51
Srimati Janhaba Devi, 273
Srimati Kanchana Devi, 244
Srimati Mahalakshmi Devi, 237
Srimati Radharani, 130, 161, 247
Srimati Rebati, 274
Srimati Sadanandi Devi, 198
Srimati Sitadevi, 98
Srimati Stayabhama, 233
Srimati Tulsi Devi, 16
Srimati Vasudha Devi, 273
Sripad Haridas Goswami, 234
Sripati Bandyopadhaya, 65
Sripati Bandyopadhyay, 222
Sripats, 223
Status of women in the society, 147
Subarna Village, 43
Subarnagram, 175
Sudikodutta Nachchier, 17
Sulochana Devi, 218, 219
Sunila or Bhagawati Devi, 216
Suryadas Pundit, 134, 135
Suryadas Sarkhel, 134
Swarnamoyee Devi, 269, 270, 271, 272
Swarup Damodar, 106, 189, 220, 221
Sweet-meat seller, 154
Sylhet, 100, 179, 180
Sylhet district, 60

T

Tamil Language, 260
Tara Devi, 88, 247
Telegu language, 52
Telegu to Kenarij language, 142
Thakur Abhiram Goswami, 152
Thakura Haridas, 163
Tirtharam Kamalakumari, 55
Tirupati temple, 28
Transsexual devotees, 206
Tribeni-Prayag, 52
Tribhuban-Mahadevi, 23
Trilochandas, 48
Tripura Sundari, 236
Tukka Devi's mother, 90
Tular Province, 35
Tulsi Tree, 15
Tulsidevi, 17
Tusi leaves, 274
Twelve Gopals, 152

U

Uddharan Dutta, 139, 275, 281
Udhdaran Dutta of Saptagram, 132
Udupi, 35

Ujjwala Devi, 73
Umapati Dhar, 43
Utkal, 23

V

Vaidik Brahmin, 44
Vairab Singha, 46
Vaishnava, 197, 200
Vaishnava Abhidhan, 240, 262
Vaishnava Balaramdas Madhabi, 67
Vaishnava environment, 232
Vaishnava Janani, 127
Vaishnava Literature, 206, 247
Vaishnava Movement, 48, 114, 115, 208, 240
Vaishnava Poet, 50
Vaishnava women, 85
Vaishnava Yogi, 41
Vaishnavas, 200, 209, 274, 282
Vaishnavas in Braja, 245
Vaishnavi, 167, 266
Vaishnavism, 232, 240, 268
Vaishnavism in Kanchipur, 27
Vaishnavism Movement, 215
Vaishnvism in Assam, 241
Varanasi, 27, 52, 138
Vasudha Devi, 274, 276, 277
Vedabati Devi, 35, 36
Vedanta, 36
Vedas, 36
Vedavyas Acharya, 27
Vedic Brahman, 116
Veer Kumari, 255
Vidyutkanti, 75
Vidyutmmali and Ishan, 211
Vijaya Devi, 116
Vijayanagar, 52
Vikrampore-Panchasar, 174, 175
Village Jajigram, 228
Village Kenduli, 29
Vim Ekadashi, 95
Vishnu Stuti, 41
Vishnu Tirtha, 36
Vishnuchitta, 15, 16, 17
Vishnuchitta Swami, 17, 19
Vishnupriya Devi, 49, 63, 116, 117, 123, 125, 126, 128, 281
Vitadiya, 175
Vrindaban, 245, 257, 262, 282
Vrindaban Lila, 37, 44, 60
Vrindaban-Mathura, 223
Vrindabati Thakurani, 233
Vyas Mishra, 88, 247

W

West Bengal, 33
Western Gate, 149
Wife of Adwait Prabhu, 82

Y

Yaban Administration, 58
Yaban Haridas, 73, 74, 163
Yamuna in Vrindaban, 44
Yamuna River, 19, 152
Yashobanta, 267
Yashobanta Thakur, 267
Yashoda, 16
Yogamaya, 208
Yogamaya Bhagabti, 192
Yogeswar, 200
Yogeswar Pundit, 200

Z

Zaminder Motilal Roy, 270
Zaminder of Chakrashala, 70
Zaminder of Kamsyatpur, 67
Zaminders of Nabadwip, 124